WILLIAM LOUIS POTEAT

Prophet of Progress

W. L. Poteat.

William Louis Poteat

Prophet of Progress

by

Suzanne Cameron Linder

The University of North Carolina Press · Chapel Hill

Copyright © 1966 by
The University of North Carolina Press
Manufactured in the United States of America
Printed by the Seeman Printery, Durham, N.C.
Library of Congress Catalog Card Number 66-19277

To my parents

To my parents

Foreword

About the turn of the century the state of North Carolina began to listen attentively to two remarkable leaders, one political, the other cultural, but both far-sighted and bold to a degree that can hardly be understood fifty years later. Charles Brantley Aycock became governor in 1901, and William Louis Poteat became president of Wake Forest College in 1905. Their achievements have been largely obscured by the astonishing economic development that began about the same time, but it can be plausibly argued that these two did more to modernize North Carolina than textiles, or tobacco, or high-tension electric lines. For between them they prevented the growth of "the closed society," that malignant philosophy that has caused large areas of the South to lag so far behind modern civilization as to be regarded as a wealthy barbarism.

Aycock has come down in history as the Educational Governor because he laid the foundation of the modern public school system. But he was more than that. He was a

politician who staked his political career—and very nearly
lost it—on the proposition that Negroes, too, are people of
North Carolina and must be given their per capita share
of public school funds. Poteat was an intellectual, but he
was more than that—he was an educator who staked his
career, not once, but daily for forty years on the proposition that, in a collision between truth and dogma, truth
must prevail. If North Carolina has been relatively free
from political ruffianism, it owes much of that freedom to
the example of Aycock. If it has been relatively free from
theological obscurantism, it owes even more of that freedom to the work of Poteat. Whether or not North Carolinians realize it, these two freedoms have done more than
all its other accomplishments to win for it the respect, not
unmixed with astonishment, of the outside world.

In the following pages Suzanne Linder has recorded
with sympathy but, as far as I can judge, with rigid adherence to the documented facts, the public phases of
Poteat's Homeric battle for freedom of the mind. Yet there
was one element of his strength that she has perforce
omitted because it does not appear in any written record,
indeed, does not exist except in the memories of the rapidly
diminishing number of those who knew him in the great
days. This was his personal charm.

It was a quality far too elusive to be portrayed in words,
yet it had power to disarm many an opponent who was
impervious to logical argument and to make ardent defen-
ders of some who never fully accepted Poteat's philosophy.
Perhaps it is best approached by negatives. It had no taint
of flattery. It was not even tact, in the ordinary sense, for
the man was outspoken, often blunt. It was not physical
presence, for he was slightly below average height, portly,
and bald, anything but impressive at first glance, and as-
suredly not endowed with a Grecian profile. Even his wit
was largely non-verbal. I have never encountered a greater
master of the eloquent pause; often I heard him, sometimes in the classroom, sometimes on the lecture platform,

build up an argument, layer by layer, swiftly, toward a
patent absurdity, and just as he reached the climax, stop
dead, looking slowly from side to side without a word. In-
variably, after a second and a half, cheers and laughter
swept the hall.

On the positive side, this charm certainly owed somewhat to an intellectual integrity so perfect as to be apparent to the dullest, and somewhat more to a power of
lucid explanation that made him not merely a good, but a
great, teacher. Yet these, after all, were minor contributions to the spell that the man laid upon his associates.
Wit, intelligence, and lucidity contribute to, but do not
constitute, charm. There is a remainder that defies logical
analysis, that is felt but cannot be explained, and therefore
remains forever in the realm of magic.

One constituent of it, though, can be named if never
understood. Poteat respected, and showed that he respected, the personality even of one whose intelligence he
held in slight esteem. This is strong magic, however incomprehensible it may be. It is especially powerful when
it is exerted upon raw youth, hovering on the borderline
between child and man. The uncurried colts who swarmed
each year into the freshman class at Wake Forest were
emphatically not intelligent, but they had wit enough to
know it, and a teacher who pretended to regard them as his
intellectual equals would have incurred their hearty con-
tempt. Poteat never made that mistake. Yet without mini-
mizing the distance between the scholar and the tyro, he
could with a subtlety independent of words imbue the youth
with knowledge that he was at least potentially a man and
that manhood has its dignity not derived from extraneous
circumstance.

Surely, acquisition of this knowledge is the hairline that
separates the boy from the man. Often it is thrust upon
the individual ruthlessly and brutally, so the teacher who
can transmit the knowledge suavely and with dignity exerts

a fascination over the pupil that he will not forget until
death or senility erases all memory. Yet though one spoke
with the tongue of all philosophy, he could not explain this
mystery of personality. Some have called it the highest
degree, the quintessence of tact, but that is questionable.
Tact is deliberate, tact is calculated, but this respect for
humanity *per se* was not studied, it was the way the man
was made. Without doubt Poteat would have ascribed it
to his religion, which distinguishes between mind and soul
and finds the soul undifferentiated in philosopher or college
freshman. It may be so, but one finds many intensely religious people who are utterly devoid of this quality, and
they are anything but charming.

So what it comes to is this: I can attest the existence
of great personal charm in William Louis Poteat, but to
trace its origin or to analyze its constituents baffles me.
Yet the mere attestation has some value as a contribution
toward understanding the man. This account of his long
and magnificent battle for truth against dogma—and not
merely religious, but political, social, and economic dogma
also—presents sufficient evidence of his intelligence, his
energy, his faith, his courage, and his astonishing resource-
fulness in the employment of wit and eloquence. These are
almost enough to account for his profound influence in
shaping the intellectual and cultural development of North
Carolina—almost enough, but not quite. Add, though,
knowledge that the man had a magic power to ensnare the
hearts of men, and especially of the young men and children who were to dominate the state in the next generation, and it becomes easy to understand why this life was
one of the crucial events in the intellectual and cultural
history of the State of North Carolina.

It is the current fashion to describe such a man as "a
charismatic leader." Yet however pompous, the term is
not inaccurate, for *charisma* is the outward manifestation
of an inward grace, and certainly his inward grace assisted

Poteat in his great work of bringing his charges to a firm
conviction that his Lord meant it when He said, ''Know
the truth and the truth shall make you free.''

Gerald W. Johnson
Baltimore, Maryland

Acknowledgments

In working for the master of arts degree at Wake Forest College, I had an opportunity to study the personal papers of William Louis Poteat. These contain records of more than half a century painstakingly preserved by Dr. Poteat during his career at Wake Forest. Getting to know this man through his journals and correspondence, as well as through the comments of those who knew him, has been a most rewarding and enriching experience.

Interpreting progress for his own generation, he evolved a philosophy of life which is pertinent to any age but seems especially relevant in a world that is changing at an ever-increasing rate. Because his skill in communicating his ideas was so much greater than my own, I have attempted to let him speak for himself as often as possible.

I am indebted to Dr. Henry Stroupe, Dr. W. Buck Yearns, and Dr. David Smiley of Wake Forest College for help with my thesis, "William Louis Poteat and the Evolution Controversy," parts of which appeared in the Spring,

1963, issue of *The North Carolina Historical Review,* Volume XL, Number 2.

Dr. Smiley, Dr. Joseph F. Steelman of East Carolina College, and Gerald Johnson read the book manuscript and offered many valuable suggestions.

My deep appreciation goes to Mrs. Helen Poteat Marshall, Mrs. Louie Martin, and other members of the Poteat family for their gracious assistance. I also thank friends of Dr. Poteat who shared their memories of him.

Carlton West and other librarians of Wake Forest College were very helpful as were the librarians at The University of North Carolina at Chapel Hill, Duke University, and the North Carolina Department of Archives and History. J. B. Blaylock of Yanceyville offered valuable aid with Caswell County records. Special thanks go to Peggy Benbow and my parents, Emily and Tom Cameron, for continuous interest, encouragement, and constructive criticism.

Suzanne Cameron Linder
Winston-Salem, North Carolina

Contents

Contents

Illustrations

WILLIAM LOUIS POTEAT

Prophet of Progress

Forest Home

The winter of 1856-57 was severe in its onset even for Caswell County in the Piedmont region of North Carolina. Snow seemed almost to grow upward from the slopes of hills and to pile high in the valleys as it all but obliterated the roads and trails. Tall pine trees drooped under their heavy burdens. Years later story tellers would date their tales from "the big snow of fifty-seven."[1] The blizzard found Julia McNeill Poteat in Kelso, the home of her parents near Kerr's Chapel, where she had gone to await the birth of her first child. On October 20, the healthy boy had arrived and was duly named William Louis Poteat. His proud grandparents would have been delighted for him to stay indefinitely; but, as soon as she was strong enough, Julia seemed determined to return to Forest Home.

Forest Home was the gracious white house that James Poteat had built for her, his bride, only the year before. The plantation home was a symbol of a way of life—the gracious luxury of the old South, fragile ladies, gay and gallant gentlemen, hours of leisure for reading or music or entertaining company. Into this environment William Louis Poteat was to come at a time when the world was fast approaching a crossroads in the realm of ideas and in the harsh realities of war. Many events at this cross-roads would have a far-reaching influence on the nation as a whole and would also have significant bearing on the career of young Poteat. Incidents that occurred when Poteat the child was happily roaming the fields of Forest Home would provide situations that would later demand all the resources of character, personality, and education of Poteat the man.

On the day of Julia's departure from her parents' home, Hosea McNeill, a heavy-set, rather stern-looking gentleman, doubtless surveyed the snowy landscape with concern. The weather was anything but suitable for his daughter and her tiny baby. Nevertheless, in a four-horse sleigh, bundled in feather quilts and toasted by a foot-warmer filled with hot coals, Julia and the baby began the sixteen-mile trek to the Poteat plantation. Two outriders went ahead to locate the roadbed beneath the deep snow. The driver clicked to the team and they were off. Snorting and prancing in the cold, the horses pulled eagerly. Slowly the miles went by until something, perhaps a darting rabbit, scared the horses. The sleigh suddenly overturned, and both mother and baby rolled out into a drift. Nature gave young William an unexpected and very chilly first immersion, an ironic beginning for one who would later light fires of controversy in the Baptist denomination. The incident, however, proved no more than passing excitement, for the tousled pair were soon reinstated. By afternoon they had reached the borders of the Poteat plantation.

As the sleigh rounded a curve in the road, Julia could see smoke making patterns in the chill air above the chimneys at either end of the two-story white house situated on a knoll among the trees. The beautiful double front doors, opening out on the graceful portico, seemed to welcome her return. She must have been very proud of her Forest Home.[2]

Julia could also have been proud of the heritage her child would enjoy. The Poteat name was a respected one in prosperous Caswell. It was of Huguenot origin, and although William Louis' grandfather spelled it "Poteet," it probably began as "Petite." The Caswell County Poteats allegedly descended from Gerard Petite of La Rochelle.[3] Hosea McNeill, William's maternal grandfather, was a relative of artist James A. McNeill Whistler, while his grandmother, Isabella Graves McNeill, was a descendant of Thomas Graves, Captain of the *Mary and Margaret*, who reputedly brought the second group of settlers to Virginia in 1608.[4] Calvin Graves, a relative, served in the North Carolina legislature from 1840 to 1848 and cast the deciding vote to appropriate two million dollars for the building of the North Carolina Railroad to link the mountains with the seaboard. The vote killed him politically, but historians have given him credit for opening the western section of North Carolina. Still another prominent relative, Solomon Lea, was the grandson of the pioneer James Lea for whom Leasburg was named. Solomon Lea was a Methodist minister of good education. He started a school for girls, which flourished in Caswell before the Civil War and was later moved to Greensboro to become Greensboro College.[5]

Thus William Louis Poteat came from a distinguished family that had produced both community and state leaders. Later he was to become a leader in educational, political, and religious circles. In all of his work, his heritage of leadership and his gracious manner, perhaps his most important legacy from Forest Home, were constant assets. Various experiences on the plantation provided an additional influence on his mature years. For instance, as he took the leadership of the Commission on Interracial Co-operation, surely he must have remembered his earliest friend, Nat.

Nat was the son of a slave woman who died at his birth. In recollection Poteat confided to his journal. "He was admitted to the superb abundance of the same white fountain from which I drew my infant nourishment,—my turn then Nat's. With that start we grew up all the way together. Papa gave him to me. He was mine and in a very real sense I was his."[6] Besides Nat there were many other children at Forest Home. A new brother or sister seemed to appear on the scene unannounced every two years. Why Dr. Roan fixed that interval for delivery, the boy never heard discussed. When he was about two years old, William Louis was lifted up to see his baby sister, Ida Isabella. Next came Edwin McNeill, and finally the one he described as "the last and sweetest," Emma Lindsay.[7]

William Louis seldom played with his brothers and sisters, for Ida had her dolls and playthings in the house, while Ed was too young to follow all his wanderings. Therefore Nat was his constant companion. Wherever Louis went, Nat was sure to go, and when Nat led into the yard or garden or grove, Louis trailed faithfully after. They sopped the fried chicken or ham gravy together from the same skillet. When they were old enough, they drove the big brindled ox called "Rock" down across the ravine for three laps on the hill beyond. On one such expedition Louis decided to match his strength against old Rock's. Any boy who could drive an ox must surely be very strong. He set his back against the front of the cart axle, dug his bare heels into the forest mold, and gave the word, "Get up, Rock!" Rock got up, but Louis got down. One of his knees bent backward instead of forward, and it took several weeks to nurse it back into proper habits. The little boy learned to measure his strength more carefully, but he never lost the courage to fight against seemingly insuperable odds.[8]

The nickname, "Loulie," gave no indication of the

bravery of the boy who answered to it, but tradition made the name permanent in family circles. He was actually named William for William Jackson Moore, husband of his mother's next older sister Mary, and Louis for Louis Mason, eldest son of the pastor of the Yanceyville Baptist Church, whose chief distinction was a certain grand manner of carriage and dress. Julia McNeill Poteat intended to call her son Louis, but perhaps because of his own lingual liquidness, the name was soon softened to Loulie. Seventy years later—despite five honorary degrees, hundreds of students who called him "Dr. Billy," and numerous other distinctions—to friends of his youth, he remained Loulie Poteat of Forest Home, and to his family, "Bud [brother] Loulie."[9]

Loulie's name was a familiar one to the slaves at Forest Home, but there were probably too many of them for a little boy to know personally. In 1860 James Poteat owned more than eighty Negroes. He needed a large group to work the two thousand acres of gently rolling, fertile land in northwest Caswell County, but, of course, all of the slaves were not field hands. In fact, there were only thirty-one between the ages of fifteen and thirty-eight, fifteen of whom were women. Although he employed an overseer, Loulie's father remained concerned for the bodily comfort as well as for the religious well-being of his Negroes. "Marse Jim" was imperious but kind. He commanded instant and unquestioning obedience from those under his direction. He was known generally as "Captain Poteat," for he had been a militia officer.[10]

The Captain was a good businessman. In 1860, Forest Home lands produced eighteen hundred bushels of wheat, four thousand bushels of corn, two bales of cotton, forty thousand pounds of tobacco, and smaller amounts of other products. Tobacco was the main money crop. "Marse Jim" once made $5,000 from a crop of tobacco grown on 375 acres. This was probably some of the first bright-leaf tobacco ever produced, for on a nearby farm, in 1852, Eli and Abisha Slade discovered that heat from a charcoal fire in the tobacco barn imparted finer texture and color to the leaves than natural drying. They passed the information along to their neighbors, and Captain Poteat was probably one who profited from it.[11]

James Poteat was an established planter when he courted Miss Julia McNeill at Kerr's Chapel. A widower with five children, he was still considered something of a sport. In smart clothes, driving a spanking two-horse team, he cut a fine figure. At a time when mustaches were the rule, he wore no beard except a tuft in front of each ear. The tufts were always in neat vertical curls, as was the middle top hair, roached in a curl running fore and aft. When Loulie was promoted from the cradle to the trundle bed, his delight was to awaken when "Uncle" Jerry lit the fires in the morning to watch his father shave. Each morning, winter or summer, after his shave James Poteat went across the back yard to a two-story, three-compart- ment bathhouse for his shower. It stood on a slope behind the brick smokehouse at the edge of the grove. Ruffin, a house slave, drew two buckets of water from the well, mounted the big steps to the second story, and poured the fresh cold water into a box with gimlet holes in the bottom while his master stood on the slatted floor some fifteen feet below to receive it. After the bath, the Captain passed across the central compartment to the slatted floor at the other side where the Negro dried him. In winter, some- times Loulie saw his side curls stiff with ice.[12]

But even in winter the brick kitchen across the yard from the house was always warm. The mouth of its big fireplace would take in a six-foot log. The flagstone hearth reached four feet into the room. Sometimes the cooks pulled red hot coals onto the flags and set pots among them. They cooked biscuits in a covered pan with coals beneath and on the lid. There was a big blue chair in the kitchen. The arms and rungs of the ladder-back were all round, lathe-turned, and it had a splint bottom. One day as

Loulie was watching the cooks at work, perhaps his request for a butter-sugar biscuit was denied or it was raining outside. At any rate he seemed a bit impatient as he tipped the big chair against the wall and sang a tune. Suddenly the chair overturned and Loulie landed among the coals on the hearth. The cooks quickly rescued him and treated his burns with molasses. As he grew older, he forgot what the moment's problem had been, but he carried a deep scar on the instep of his right foot for the rest of his life to remind him of the virtue in having patience.

Many happier legacies followed him to manhood. One was a love of the out-of-doors, which having developed early in the rolling hills of Piedmont Carolina was later to find fulfillment in Poteat's biological studies. In June he liked to watch the cutting of the wheat—a half dozen muscular Negroes "singing to their swinging cradles, the strongest man in front, the others following each other a little behind his fellow and a swath's breadth to the right of him, all pushing together a sort of stairway across the field of gold."[13]

Ben was the foreman who drove the four-horse team at harvest time. He was a big, silent Negro, who knew how to win forever the bounding ambitious heart of a little boy. One day as Loulie stood by watching, he scooped him up and set him on the saddle mule, allowing him to drive a load of wheat as big as a house from the field in front of Forest Home to the stacks for threshing. A peripatetic thresher stopped at two places on the plantation. There were many men and horses and much shouting through clouds of dust, a most exciting situation for a young boy atop a mule.[14]

After the threshing, the hands took the wheat to the plantation mill a half-mile to the north of the house. A big stone dam impounded the waters of Rattlesnake Creek for a half-mile toward Yanceyville. An overshot wheel operated the grist mill. On the first floor were the corn hopper and grindstones out of which the warm meal poured through a spout into the deep trough below. Loulie liked to watch the dusty miller catching the stream in his hand and testing its quality as he rubbed it between thumb and fingers. Although the wheat grindstones were on nearly the same level as the corn, spouts and belts carried the flour aloft to the revolving bolting machine whose graded silk meshes separated the ground wheat into first-grade flour, seconds, shorts, and bran. Just inside the door of the mill was a large box stove, curiously divided at the waist. In winter when the cooks sent Loulie and Nat to the mill for a sack of flour or meal, they often waited by the stove. The boys' delight was to toast and eat large kernels of corn.[15]

Another favorite winter pastime was skating on the pond. Young Louis, however, did not escape the inevitable calamities that seem to befall all skaters. He reported that once the skates whisked his feet from under his center of gravity so quickly and so far that the back of his head was the first to strike the ice, "when all the expanse of the sunlit sky blazed with stars."[16]

The surface of the pond was sometimes frozen four inches thick, insuring the plantation a supply of ice to last through the summer months. The icehouse was underneath the carriage-house about sixty yards from the back west end of the house. In winter the slaves hewed the ice out of the pond and stored it in the cool underground room to be ready for Captain Poteat's mint juleps or Mrs. Julia's refreshing summer desserts.

During the spring and summer, Louis liked to fish in the Forest Home mill pond. His favorite spots were along the peninsula on the northern side. He and Nat skinned slender poplar saplings, attached cork, sinker, and "fishin' worms" and caught plenty of suckers, perch, and catfish. Later Captain Poteat stocked the pond with silver perch, a beautiful fish, sporty to catch. For it, the boys used a live minnow for bait, a long line, and a small cork with a feather. Louis later recalled, "The sudden gentle veering of that cork straight this way or that, its increasing speed, and its sloping disappearance made an electric thrill in nerve trunks and endings which trampings of years in the same pathways can never efface."[17]

Across the creek from the grist mill was the saw mill. It was first operated by an overshot wheel but later came into the dignity of being driven by a turbine. Louis loved to swim in the clear, cool pool just under the wheel of the grist mill. For excitement he chose the deep race of the saw mill. He learned to dive deep and crawl under the big sill that spanned the race at its depths. At the time it was only a boyish adventure; in his maturity he realized the possible dangers involved. In spite of learning to evaluate danger more realistically, he never lost his love of excitement.

After a cooling swim, it was fun to chase hares through the woods with George and Hill Williamson, boys from Melrose, a neighboring plantation. When they had run as far as they could and had developed a tremendous thirst, they found "maypops" and opened them gratefully for the acid of the seeds. Even the harsh crimson, sour spikes of sumac berries tasted good to the hungry, thirsty boys. Sometimes, with a certain sense of illicit pleasure, they chewed rabbit tobacco and perhaps imitated the town elders who leaned against the façade of the courthouse and spat tobacco with a deadly aim at a nearby mud puddle.

Another adventure was "helping" drive the big bays, Bill and Pete, when the family went out in the carriage. "Uncle" Jerry was the family hostler and carriage driver. He was short and thick like Santa Claus, his straight hair and full beard indicating a drop or two of Caucasian blood. As the oldest boy, Louis was allowed to sit on the box with the driver. Sometimes they took long trips to Danville or to Richmond where the Captain had a warehouse for his tobacco, but such trips were unusual; the family spent most of the time on the plantation. There was always something interesting at Forest Home for a young boy to do.

Louis liked to watch "Uncle" Isaac, the blacksmith, as he hammered out nails on his anvil. His shop was under the hackberry tree on the slope below Loulie's uncle Tom Poteat's place. Under "Uncle" Isaac's capable hammer, "horse-shoes, plow points, and hoes grew into shape, sizzled a moment in the tempering tub, and leaped to the shop floor with a benevolent warning to bare feet."[18]

"Uncle" Morris was the carpenter and cooper. Louis' delight was to follow him to the deep woods and watch him rive the red oak blocks into shingles with froe and hand maul, clamp them one by one on the draw-frame, shape the butts to a uniform thickness with a magical drawing knife, change ends, and peel off the fresh-smelling, curled shavings down to a thin edge. "Uncle" Morris also made barrels and tierces for tobacco, binding the staves together with white oak hoops tied with an interlocking notch. As an old man, Louis could still hear the music of his driving the hoops on, two taps of his hickory driving stick against the hoop to one of his mallet as he walked around the tightening tierce.

Another sound that Louis would always remember was the zooming of the big cotton and wool spinning wheel. The pitch of the zooming varied with the speed of the wheel. Slaves carded cotton by hand to remove the lint from the seeds, for Captain Poteat raised only a limited amount of cotton. He also planted flax for making linen. To break the dried stems of the flax, the slaves used a homemade flax hackle with stationary wooden blades between which the blades of a movable frame fell. Then they whipped a wisp of flax over the end of an upright board to free the fiber of the entangled bits of stem and spun the fibers into thread on the little flax wheel.

"Aunt" Chanie was the weaver. Her husband, "Uncle" Ephraim, was the shoemaker. One of her daughters, Mira, was Louis' nurse; the other, Sallie, was the housemaid. One day as Louis played on the long back porch, he noticed a stir in the sitting room. There was a great pile of stiffish cloth about the color of graham bread. ''Aunt'' Chanie, Mira, and Sallie were moving to and fro about it under his mother's direction. She was planning and cutting out men's and women's garments. As he remembered the busy picture in later years, Louis always wondered which, after all, was the greatest slave in the group? Julia planned the clothing for the entire plantation community. She also acted as doctor and nurse. Sometimes she would take Louis with her and let him wait outside as she went into a cabin to tend a sick slave.[19]

Food for the plantation was another responsibility of its mistress. For her, one of the major events of the winter months was the supervising of the women's work at hog-killing time. The Forest Home slaughter sometimes included more than fifty porkers at a time. There was a pen at the mill and others here and there on the plantation. One extra large one was on the north slope of the ravine in the grove behind the house. Below it near the branch a great fire of cordwood heated water to scald the hogs in order to loosen the hair. Preparations such as collecting wood and planting the scalding hogshead obliquely in the earth were made the day before. On the appointed day, all hands were up early as were Julia Poteat and the house women. They carried tubs, big pots to boil the lard out of the fat, and a sausage grinder ready for tenderloin.

The activities at the pen attracted Louis and Nat. The fire was already glowing through the tree trunks as they went down. They watched the men enter the pen, catch a hog by the hind leg, throw him on his back and while one man sat astride him and pulled down his forelegs, the other, carrying the knife, grasped the muzzle cautiously, pressed it to the ground and finished the process with two strokes of the keen blade at the throat, one transverse, the second longitudinal. The men declined to tackle one vicious old tusker and dispatched him with a rifle. After the hogs were scalded and scraped with a hoe to remove the hair, they were strung up by the hind feet on a long dressing pole. As the men dressed the hogs, the women's work began, preparing sausage, liver pudding, "chittlings," spare ribs, and hams for curing. In recollection, Louis commented, "The regimen would have shaken the resolution of Moses."[20]

The hams went to the brick smokehouse. In the unplastered room, open to the rafters, with no floor, the slaves hung hams, shoulders, and middlings high up on the beams and ignited small heaps of oak and hickory chips on the dirt floor. Sometimes Louis and Nat helped put more chips on the fire. After curing the hams, the men transferred them to the plastered smokehouse room that had shelves for storage. Here they were ready for use when company came to Forest Home.

Not the least of Julia Poteat's duties was acting as hostess to the many friends and relatives who came in a never-ending stream. Throughout the year, the Poteats seemed to keep open house. Neighbors like the Williamsons, the Womacks, the Graveses, the Leas, and the Robertsons often visited. Never a preacher passed without turning in to refresh himself at "Sister Poteat's" hospitable board.

Perhaps the most colorful clergyman was Elias Dodson. With a red face, a long nose, and a floppy wig the color of brick dust, he was a formidable figure. He arose before daylight, and often the household awakened to the rhythm of his sepulchral voice reading the Bible. He once preached at the Yanceyville Baptist Church on "Without the Shedding of Blood There Is No Remission," Edwin Poteat recalled, "I do not remember anything he said, but I do remember that I put my head down behind the pew and wept like a child. I incline to think that that sermon put a tinge of red in my thinking from that day to this."

James Poteat liked to tell the story of taking Mr. Dodson to a preaching appointment at Beulah Church in

Caswell County. When they came to County-Line Creek and found it overflowing, they decided to cross in a dugout log boat. About half-way across, it suddenly toppled over and Mr. Dodson's precious wig went floating downstream. They got across somehow and the miller of nearby Lea's Mill fitted them out in his own clothes and sent them up the hill to the church.

Elias Dodson was really human after all, and the Poteat children soon found they had a friend. He would take them outside on clear nights and explain the firmament of stars. Nevertheless there was still a sense of foreboding, and it is doubtful if the Poteats ever thought of Judgment Day without remembering their friend, Elias Dodson. With exposure in childhood to such a redoubtable character, it is no wonder that in later years even the staid conservatives of the Southern Baptist Convention could not intimidate William Louis Poteat when he fought for freedom of teaching.

Although few of the Forest Home guests were as impressive as the bewigged Baptist cleric, the house was regularly filled, the ladies using the east room upstairs, the gentlemen, the west. In the dining room there was usually one of the gigantic homegrown hams or a stuffed gobbler at Captain Poteat's end of the table. His carving was excellent and seemed to supply both stimulation and opportunity for his contagious geniality. "Uncle" Jerry, Sallie, and Mira served. Everyone seemed to say, " 'It is good to be here; let us camp forever and a day.' It certainly was an eternity for the waiting children."[21] Doubtless it was also a major undertaking for the hostess.

Still, Julia Poteat found time to be a very loving mother. She enjoyed activities with her children. In the fall, with Louis, Ida, Ed, and Linnie, she climbed the hill at the west side of the grove and hunted for nuts beneath the red-gold screen of hickory leaves. There were two scaly bark hickories in the bottom. The nuts with shells thin enough to crack between the teeth were special treasures.

At least once a year the Poteats made a trip with their cousins to the chinquapin orchard, sometimes on foot, sometimes on the wagon. Instead of using the usual sharp-pointed tweezers to get the nuts out of the spiny burrs, Louis showed his scientific and creative ability by inventing another instrument. He detached a hollow tin dipper handle and sloped the small end to a point easily inserted in the split of the opening burr. The nut fell uninjured into the cavity of the handle. Just beyond the grove a steep slope heavily clothed with yellow broom sedge challenged the children to another kind of sport. They stretched flat on the ground at the top of the hill, turned loose, and rolled with accelerating speed to the bottom.[22]

Autumn was a time for playful mischief, but when the pond froze over and the snow began to fall, the children turned to more exciting contemplations. Christmas was coming and Forest Home would ring with the merriment of even more visitors than usual—uncles, aunts, cousins, friends, and most important—Old St. Nick himself! On Christmas Eve four lank, expectant stockings cast eerie shadows in the flickering firelight of the upstairs bedroom. The curved canopy of the four-poster could almost be the outline of a sleigh—and who could distinguish the soft click of sleet on the roof from the tiny feet of the reindeer? The excitement grew as Julia recited the nursery favorite beginning, "Twas the night before Christmas..." and soon the "little old driver so lively and quick" seemed almost real enough to step into the room.

One Christmas Eve, young Louis did a bit of growing up. Too excited to sleep, he watched the empty stockings as he lay in the trundle bed and dreamed of the morning's surprises. Suddenly, there was a bigger surprise than he had anticipated. His mother was "helping" Santa. Louis lay very still and pretended he had not seen, for despite a little disappointment, it was most exciting to see the presents ahead of time.

During a later Christmas season when he was about eight or ten years old, Louis caused more excitement and consternation than all the presents put together. It was the evening of a lovely holiday party at Forest Home. Relatives and friends came from miles around. The ladies put their fur trimmed coats and bonnets in the upstairs bedroom, smoothed their skirts, and exclaimed over the latest gossip. The men lit their pipes and promptly headed for the bowl of frothy, rich eggnog. On such a gala occasion, who could deny a little boy a sip of the brew? Louis had one cup, then another, and another. As he sat in front of the fire with the other boys, the hubbub of the gaiety seemed to be fading away. Sensing what was happening, one of the older boys handed Louis his half-filled cup. As Louis drank the last drop, the fuzzy room began to sway. The boys laughed with glee as Louis stumbled to his feet and wove his way across the room. His mother quickly rescued him and determined from that day on not to serve anything intoxicating. Poteat later confided, "The individual clinking green mint-juleps, one a day in summer for Papa, were the exception which proved the rule of total abstinence."[23]

Perhaps Julia's attitude influenced her son in future years when he became president of the Anti-Saloon League and later the United Dry Forces of North Carolina. Her emphasis on the value of education also had a profound influence on Louis. Julia had studied at Oxford Seminary for young ladies at Oxford, North Carolina, and was quite capable of teaching her children, but in order to have time for her other plantation duties, she placed the schoolroom in the charge of governesses.

Louis learned to read without assistance before learning his letters. He described this accomplishment as "the foundation of the greatest delight and blessing of my life." To assist him in his learning, Cousin Mat Mebane, a distant relative, came from Mebaneville to be governess for the "green shoots of the family tree."[24] She had a funny, fat, floppy cushion on the tip of her right forefinger which fascinated her charges. Cousin Mat was frail and nervous. The boys laughed at her consternation when a wasp was too attentive and intimate, but they became concerned when she keeled over in a faint. Despite her sensibilities, Cousin Mat was pleasant and kind, a good teacher, and in a real emergency she could do her share. When the dry-house outside the back-yard gate caught fire, she showed strength beyond her muscles. It may have been her nervous excitement that made her stronger than she actually was. She helped carry a huge tub of water that sat under the house gutter out to the fire. The tub was one end of a barrel sawed in the middle.

Miss Margaret Ann Page of the neighborhood succeeded Cousin Mat. With experience and intelligence, she showed the primness, solemnity, and straight back of the professional teacher. When on duty in the big room upstairs, she sometimes permitted her charges to study on the roof of the back porch, which ran the length of the house. Cousin Minnie Turner of Locust Hill joined the Poteat children for a period during Miss "Marg'et-ann's" reign. The children learned the fundamentals of reading, writing, and arithmetic. When their governess withdrew, they went to the village school taught by Miss Lizzie Lowndes. Miss Lowndes taught Latin, but she used the English pronunciation.[25]

These early teachers were probably pleased with the intelligent Poteat children. At least one of these ladies must have possessed that rare, important quality, the ability to stimulate not only a desire for accuracy but also creativity. Ida, Edwin, and Louis all became prominent educators. Ed became president of Furman University, Louis was president of Wake Forest College, and Ida was chairman of the Art Department at Meredith College. Meningitis claimed Linnie's life while she was still in her teens, or perhaps she might also have made an important contribution. Although the teachers doubtless aided in the development of their charges, Julia Poteat played a particularly important part. The Christian ideals and the appreciation of culture that the children learned from their mother would be passed on to thousands of others, in the classroom as well as from the pulpit.

The boys may have received their talent for delivering stirring sermons from their father. Captain Poteat and his wife kept a plantation school on Sunday in the little chapel the Captain had built for slaves. Some of the white neighbors came to the Poteat Sunday School. The Captain supplied the preaching but offered instruction in reading as well as religion. James Poteat was active in the Baptist church at Yanceyville. He was moderator of the Beulah Baptist Association for several years and he frequently attended Baptist State Conventions. Thus even as a child, Louis probably heard many discussions of Baptist business.[26]

Most discussions, however, would eventually have led to the outstanding topic of that day, the war. Louis was only three years old when hostilities began. His older half-brother, John M. Poteat, left the University of North Carolina in the middle of his sophomore year to become a cadet at the North Carolina Institute at Charlotte. When war broke out, John became a lieutenant in the First Regiment of North Carolina Volunteers, and he later served in the Thirty-third North Carolina Regiment. Both of his commanders mentioned him complimentarily in reports. Another half-brother, Lindsay, was wounded in a heroic stand at Reams's Station. The brothers returned home, but both died soon after as a result of war wounds.[27]

After the war, hard times came to Forest Home. As did many wealthy southerners, the Poteats found themselves land poor. James Poteat owned large tracts of land, but with no slaves, ready cash was hard to accumulate. Preston, a half-brother only nine years older than

Louis, got a job in a dry goods store in Yanceyville. The town was busier than usual as carpetbaggers and freedmen enjoyed their new status.

The Reconstruction period proved more difficult in Caswell County than in most areas of North Carolina. Albion W. Tourgée, one of the state's leading carpetbaggers, organized a Union League. The Negro leaguers drilled every night to the beating of drums. Tourgée made many speeches telling the former slaves that the government had sent him and he would see that they each got forty acres of land. The square of Yanceyville resounded with the laughter and boasts of the freedmen who came to hear the magic promises of Tourgée. How strange the scene must have seemed to Louis Poteat just entering his teens. How suddenly his world must have changed.

The degree of change became even greater when the Ku Klux Klan became active in the area. Members of the Klan murdered John W. Stevens, a justice of the peace suspected of killing his own mother, and on July 8, 1870, Governor William W. Holden proclaimed Caswell County in a state of insurrection. Holden sent George W. Kirk, a former colonel in the United States Army, with more than six hundred men to subdue the Klan. Kirk and many of the troops occupied the Caswell County courthouse, and the so-called "Kirk-Holden War" began. The undisciplined troops terrorized the town. They plundered and robbed and felt no qualms about undressing to bathe in full sight of the populace. It became unsafe for women to appear on the streets even when escorted.

In August of 1870, North Carolinians elected the legislature that was later to impeach Governor Holden. His power waning, Holden on November 10 declared the insurrection at an end. The troops withdrew, and conditions in Caswell County improved rapidly.[28]

When order was restored to Yanceyville, the Poteat family moved to town and opened a hotel across the square from the courthouse. Since James Poteat was nearing seventy, much responsibility fell on Julia. Louis later called her a "better man" than his father. The move to town must have been hard on her, but she of course had help from her sons.

Louis left his boyhood with the plantation. The beautiful, sheltered world of Forest Home was gone, but its influence would remain with him in his gracious manner, in his ideas and ideals in later life. He left Forest Home, but Forest Home never left him. The Reconstruction years also left their mark upon Louis. At a very impressionable period in his life forces beyond his control destroyed the cultured society he knew and in its place left a world of fear and violence, hate and corruption. The brutal deeds of Kirk's soldiers as well as the vicious attacks of the Klan undoubtedly weighed heavily on Louis' sensitive mind. In later years, he often recalled his boyhood years at Forest Home or his life as a student at Wake Forest, but there is no record whatever of what happened to him during this period of social upheaval. He seemed to blot it out of conscious memory. For the rest of his life he hated violence. He did not even want to read about it in the newspapers. He determined, perhaps unconsciously, to work for peace at every opportunity. He possibly began to understand the ideas he voiced later in his books, *The Way of Victory* and *The New Peace*, that true peace and true victory must come to each man from within.[29]

The various influences of his boyhood years worked together to mold his personality and temper his character so that in manhood he would be prepared to meet the challenges offered by intellectual and technical progress. As the boy watched his family and friends adapt to the tremendous changes wrought by the Civil War and Reconstruction, he learned valuable lessons that would help him later to lead others in accepting new ideas.

All the while, the forces that would produce controversy were at work in various parts of the world. In the summer of 1868 while the Klan and the carpetbaggers horrified the residents of Yanceyville and Louis Poteat fished in the Forest Home pond, Othniel C. Marsh of Yale University left the Union Pacific train for a short wait at a Nebraska station and found the first of the fossils that gave him a complete developmental history of the horse and enabled him to publish the conclusive documentation of the theory of evolution. At the same time the corruption of the Radical Republican rule, coming on the heels of an expensive war, drained the wealth of the South and left the region poor for generations to come—too poor, in fact, to afford adequate educational opportunities. The difficulty of receiving an education affected the churches of the region also. The Episcopal and Presbyterian denominations required a seminary degree for ordination, but other denominations often asked nothing more than a call from God. Ministers without training and educational background sometimes found it difficult to accept the findings of scientists such as Professor Marsh. It was just such difficulty that would challenge William Louis Poteat in his mature years. He took the first step toward meeting this challenge in 1872 as he left Yanceyville to go to Wake Forest College.

Time for Decisions

The resolution to continue his studies at college was a
very important one for Louis, since this move initiated
a period in his life during which he was to make decisions
that would set the pattern for his future. With his
parents' advice, he realized that further education would
open doors for him later. Wake Forest College was the
natural choice, for James Poteat was a trustee and had
supported the school even in its darkest days in the struggle to reopen after the war.

Thus, in September of 1872, the Poteat household was
moving at a faster pace than usual. Louis was preparing
to leave. He had studied diligently so that he could begin
college work without first entering the preparatory department, which Wake Forest and many other schools at
that time found necessary to maintain because few of
their students had the advantage of attending a good
academy. Since Louis had worked hard, he felt confident
of being admitted to the college.

As the time drew near for his departure, Julia helped
him pack, and together they tried to think of all the things
he might need for the next nine months, because the only
holidays, December 25 and 26, gave scarcely time enough
for the long trip to Caswell County. It must have been
difficult for Julia to send her oldest boy away for so long
a time. He had not yet turned sixteen that early fall day
when he set out into a man's world. Julia found the Bible
she had been saving, wrote a message in the front to remind Louis of the value of the scriptures, and kissed him
good-by.

At the start, the trip was something of an adventure.
Perhaps Louis had been to Wake Forest before, for his
half-brother, Preston, had studied there several years
earlier. But this trip was different. Louis traveled with
a Caswell gentleman who was taking his own son to college.
The journey was a long one in a wagon loaded with the
boys' heavy trunks. It took the better part of a day. As
Louis got farther and farther away from home, his excitement and anticipation diminished considerably. When
he finally reached Wake Forest, he begged to go back with
the gentleman who had brought him.[1]

This unknown friend could not have realized the significance of his insisting that Louis stay at school. With
no further education, he could never have become the beloved president of Wake Forest. If the timid boy from
Yanceyville could have guessed his destiny, how different
his own first impressions might have been. Undoubtedly
the old brick building, sparsely furnished, with benches
for seats, with few draperies or woman's soft touches,
looked like a cold, bleak place in which to live. Summer
was barely over, and it must have seemed to Louis a very
long time until the next summer when he could go home
again.

Nevertheless, he stayed and threw himself wholeheartedly into his work. He was very impressed when his
Latin teacher, Professor Charles E. Taylor, addressed him

for the first time as "Mr. Poteat." Taylor was an excellent professor, and Louis did well in Latin, Greek, and mathematics. He read Livy, Cicero, Horace, Xenophon; he thrilled to Homer, puzzled over Plato. His mathematics included algebra, geometry, trigonometry, calculus, and land surveying.

In addition to their regular classwork, the young men of Wake Forest spent long hours preparing debates and orations for their literary societies. The Euzelians and Philomathesians each had a "hall" in the main building where they met on Friday nights and Saturday mornings. On Friday, October 11, 1872, W. Louis Poteat became a member of the Euzelian Society. Along with other unanimously elected new members, he entered the hall and was introduced to the society. F. R. Underwood, an upperclassman, made a "very beautiful, impressive and instructive speech on the subject 'Excellence the Reward of Labor,'" and undoubtedly the green freshmen revered his words of instruction. The next morning Louis found himself required to apply the wisdom of his not quite sixteen years to the preparation of the affirmative side of a debate on the question, "Is the existence of political parties beneficial to a state?"

That query was about as close to the subject of politics as the debaters ever ventured, possibly because the trustees had expressed disapproval of students' attending political gatherings of any kind, but more probably because of the scarcity of communication with the political currents of the day and the fact that conservative white southerners stood largely united on political questions in the early 1870's. The topics of debate ranged from "Was the Noachian deluge universal?" and "Is the pen mightier than the sword?" to "Was Lady Jane Grey justly executed?" and "Is early marriage advisable?"[2]

Poteat later recalled, "The literary society was the main feature of Wake Forest in those days. We would sit up there in the Euzelian Society until one o'clock in the morning debating questions, and that was in the winter time when we had no fire. The hall was so beautiful that we did not want to smoke it up. We would wrap our feet in overcoats."[3]

The literary societies maintained strict discipline. The long hours of speeches and debates must have grown tiresome at times, but any member who talked, laughed, slept, left the room for more than fifteen minutes, or wrote something not pertaining to the subject had to pay a fine. Practically every member entered the ranks of the delinquent at one time or another. Young Mr. Poteat was no exception when one spring morning the irresistible urge to laugh cost him the sum of twenty-five cents.[4]

In the Euzelian Society hall, Poteat and his colleagues learned parliamentary procedure, the rules of debate, and many intangible lessons that would help them in later years. The young debaters learned to think on their feet and to speak with force and dignity. Each member had to deliver a "dissertation" from time to time while the other members criticized. This offered opportunity for constructive work and continuous improvement on the part of the speaker. The societies also maintained libraries and bought additional books whenever funds permitted. In the spring of his freshman year, Poteat served as librarian and became even more closely associated with the "delight" of his life.[5]

Louis did well his freshman year. No doubt his parents were proud of him and wanted him to continue his studies. Unfortunately he became ill and could not return to college in the fall of 1873. Many of his classmates also failed to return that year. The Panic of 1873 made ready cash even scarcer. Tuition of $35.00 a semester, plus almost that much for room and board seemed like a great deal of money. For the school years 1872-73, there were 106 young men enrolled at Wake Forest, while the next year only 70 attended, and the enrollment did not reach 100

again until 1878. Nearly all who came remained only one
or two years.[6]

Consequently it was somewhat unusual for Louis to
return after a year at home, but his parents were determined that he should have an education. Just after
the Civil War, the *Biblical Recorder*, the newspaper of
North Carolina Baptists, had declared that education was
a defense against moral and intellectual absorption by the
conquerors, an offset to subjugation. James Poteat realized that the material heritage he had planned to leave
his sons was depleted. The total value of his estate decreased from $145,000 in 1860 to $26,000 in 1870. The loss
of slaves accounted for a large portion of this depletion,
but the devaluation of property values by $31,000 was also
significant.[7] Captain Poteat realized that his sons could
not make a living from the land as he had done. He believed that in order to be successful and to make a contribution in the new era they would need an education. This
belief showed his foresight, for many Baptists in 1872
did not feel the need for higher education. A student complained in the *Biblical Recorder*, "... the Baptists of North
Carolina, with a few honorable exceptions, do not want,
and are not going to have an education."[8]

But Louis Poteat was to be one of those exceptions.
He returned to college in the fall of 1874. To his studies
of Latin, Greek, and mathematics, he added English expression, and later he studied physics, logic, German,
political economy, chemistry, and English language and
literature. Senior Greek and Latin included studies of
Greek and Roman history. Poteat's grades were all admirable, but some were very exceptional: an average of
not less than ninety-five in all senior subjects; one hundred
in English expression, physics, and logic; and grades of
ninety-nine and one hundred for two semesters of senior
Greek.[9]

Louis also became a leader in the Euzelian Society. He
served as recording secretary, corresponding secretary,

and president of that organization.[10]   One of the highest
honors at Wake Forest was being chosen debater or orator
at the celebration of the founding of the literary societies.
The Friday nearest February 14 was Anniversary Day.
In the afternoon one junior and one senior from each society engaged in a debate, one member from each society
being on each team so that rivalry between the societies in
public would be kept to a minimum.   Poteat represented
the Euzelians in his junior year when the query was, "Is
the career of Oliver Cromwell more to be condemned than
admired?"   The societies had chosen anniversary debaters
and orators the previous May, so Louis had enjoyed ample
time to prepare his remarks.

The debates reflected months of careful preparation.
In interest and intensity they contributed greatly to the
celebration and spoke well for the college.   Anniversary
Day was one of the highlights of Wake Forest social life.
The many visitors who came from Raleigh often included
members of the legislature, the state supreme court, and
even the governor.   The afternoon's debate excited great
interest, but the evening's orations, often somewhat dull,
were respectfully tolerated in anticipation of what was to
follow.   After the orations the society halls on the fourth
floor of the college building became the setting for gay
receptions.   The debaters and orators received with pride
the congratulations of the dignitaries and with bashful
blushes the feminine smiles.

The splendid halls took on an entirely new aura on such
auspicious occasions.   Gentlemen punctuated sentences
with taps of their canes, while the Wake Forest ladies kept
their eyes open for the latest styles from the state capital.
The society's best debater sometimes seemed to get a frog
in his throat when a pretty lady posed a query.   Some
couples found the climb to the fourth floor too long for one
trip and halted for a rest on the dark third floor, which
soon got the name of "courting alley."   The revelry lasted
until midnight when the whistle of the locomotive, more

insistent than a worried mother, called the young ladies of
Raleigh home again.[11]

Poteat must have done well in the public debate, for
in May the Euzelians chose him to be their senior orator
at the next year's anniversary. This was a challenging
opportunity to further develop his public speaking ability.
He also gained valuable experience at the "Senior Speak-
ings" held in October and April. All seniors with a few
exceptions gave short talks on either humorous or serious
topics. With only six in the graduating class, ten-minute
speeches did not seem too long, and the "Senior Speak-
ings" were rivaled as social occasions only by anniversa-
ries and commencements.

The seniors also spoke at commencement. Poteat
found that he had double duty, for as the senior with the
highest average, he gave the salutatory address in Latin.
Edgar E. Folk, who was to receive the Master's degree,
delivered the valedictory. The other graduates in 1877
were James W. Denmark, who led in the establishment
of the Wake Forest Student's Aid Fund and later helped
found the *Progressive Farmer*; Charles W. Scarborough,
later a minister and leader in the Chowan Association;
James Redden Jones and Erastus B. Jones, who also became Baptist ministers.[12]

As a student at Wake Forest College, William Louis
Poteat learned mental discipline from his classical studies
and mathematics. He developed an appreciation of both
ancient and contemporary literature, learned something of
leadership, and gained valuable practice in the art of public
speaking, which was to aid him in becoming perhaps the
most outstanding lecturer in the state in later years.

When he left the college in the summer of 1877, he could
not have realized how soon he was to return. He decided
to read law in Caswell and began to study his Blackstone
with determination. But for a young man full of idealism
and imagination, with a passionate love of nature and

poetry, law could not offer sufficient inspiration—or more
practically for a young student, sufficient remuneration.

In the summer of 1878, when Dr. Charles E. Taylor
asked him to return to Wake Forest as a tutor of languages, Poteat was glad to accept the year's salary of
$400. He recalled, "It sounded like a welcome bird in
the hand. It was attractive." He worked hard, teaching
five hours every day for five days a week. Still he had
leisure time to stray off into the woods and lie down on a
sunny broomstraw hillside; to read a New York newspaper,
a book of poems, a selection in Latin; or to call upon some
young lady.[13]

The leisure that he managed to find gave the tutor
time to meditate upon the meaning and purpose of his life.
On January 1, 1879, he confided something of his dissatis-
factions and his dreams to his journal in a poem for the
new year. He compared the past year to a messenger travel-
ing "To that dread bar where faith gains high reward"
and lamented the fact that the year so pure and white
became soiled and torn. He wished the year could return
so that he might change its cargo:

> In all the jumbled plunder of my life
> The eager eye of memory no thing
> Of beauty finds,—and turns to weep.
> My heart still yearns for spotless innocence,
> The smiles of gratitude, and joy that comes
> Of duty done—The past cannot be changed;
> The coming year may realize these hopes.
> Be thou my help, O God![14]

Poteat did not dream idly; he worked hard for the perfection that he so admired. In addition to his teaching he
continued to read and study on his own. He recorded in
his journal those quotations he particularly appreciated
from Goethe, Horace, Edward Gibbon, Shakespeare,
Milton, Coleridge, and Tennyson. He especially enjoyed
George Eliot's works.

Emma P. Poteat

"Bud Loulie" posed for this portrait in Richmond, Virginia, in the late 1860's

Forest Home Plantation, Caswell County, North Carolina

Wake Forest College Faculty, 1903. Standing, left to right: George W. Paschal, J. B. Carlyle, C. C. Crittenden, Charles E. Brewer, J. L. Lake, W. L. Poteat, J. H. Gorrell, Walter Sikes. Seated, left to right: W. R. Cullom, Needham Y. Gulley, J. F. Lanneau, President Charles E. Taylor, William B. Royall, Luther R. Mills, Benjamin Sledd

The Lea Laboratory, Wake Forest College

In the spring of 1879, George Eliot's idealistic conception of romantic love had a special meaning for the young tutor. On March 14, he eulogized a flower "whose happy bower would scarce be bright without it" and a shining star "From heaven afar whose shimmer pales her sisters."[15] He later confided that the unnamed lady had "hair almost golden, and eyes honest blue."[16] Could the lowly tutor have aspired to the favor of Miss Emma Purefoy? The only child of Addison Purefoy was the belle of Wake Forest, and the Purefoys were an old and respected family. James S. Purefoy, brother of Addison Purefoy, was perhaps the most influential man on the college board of trustees. Lovely Miss Emma, adored by her parents and admired from afar by Wake Forest young men, was one of the most beautiful and accomplished young ladies in the community.

But the romantic scholar was destined to be disappointed; the warm springtime hopes turned cold with the frost by November. He mused, "I have seen a fair rose; In its beauty it blows, But a hand waves me back when I near it."[17] As Poteat's friend and colleague, Needham Y. Gulley, planned to wed another fair lady in December, the disappointment must have grown more acute. In a poem called "Solitude" in his journal, Poteat insisted:

> I am tired of living this life without love
>> With its cold, dull routine of duty;
> I am lonely, and long for one word just to prove
>> That on earth there is yet light and beauty.
> I am lonely; and oh! how my heavy heart aches
>> For the sweetness of sympathy deep,
> For the smile that responds to the joy that it wakes,
>> And the soft liquid eye when I weep.

But even in loneliness, he found some consolation in his second love, literature. For encouragement, he copied Longfellow's assertion, "But noble souls, through dust and heat, Rise from disaster and defeat the stronger."[18]

He occupied his time in writing the first of many
articles for the *Biblical Recorder*. His subject, appropriate to the season, was "Christmas." He noted that the
celebration began about the fourth century and traced its
history to his own era. He commented, "With us Christmas sometimes seems to be the feast of Bacchus rather
than of Christ. Yet it brings much innocent amusement;
old and young conspire to increase the sum of happiness;
and domestic joys bubble up from a fresh fountain, which
flows all the year." Poteat closed his article with the hope
that "the generous will remember the desolate homes
which even Christmas cannot brighten, and the hearts that
ache more sorely in the surrounding gladness in which
they cannot participate."[19]

Nevertheless, the happy carols at church and the gay
holiday parties in town could not fail to cheer even the
aching heart of a romantic young man of twenty-three.

Soon after Christmas came Anniversary Day in February, conveniently close to St. Valentine's Day, a wonderful
time for reconciliation. In 1880 the anniversary was
especially gay. A brass band from Raleigh added to the
hubbub of the huge crowd. Edwin Poteat, Louis' brother,
had the honor of introducing the Euzelian Society's orator
of the evening. After the speeches, Ed invited the audience
to socialize in the literary halls where he suggested that
they could "talk airy nothings or substantial some-
things."[20]

It would be difficult to say under which category the
elder Poteat's conversation would have fitted. Did he and
Miss Emma Purefoy discover "courting alley" on the
way to the reception? Perhaps they did, for by February
20, Louis was happy again, and his poetic muse induced
him to rejoice:

> See when great Sirius shoots from azure deeps
> His lambent light, and in the room of day
> A-dying rules bright monarch of the stars!

O, not so beautiful as the light
That, soft, through azure portals that I love,
Forth from a deep, clear soul beams liquidly!
My footsteps turn, and straight upon me gleams
Old Jupiter's huge lamp. Ah! hide thee quick
Behind those clouds that skirt the couch of day.
For thou art pale; I heed thee not!—a smile
More radiant, dispels the gloom which thou
Couldst never penetrate. O'er gentle slopes
Beyond the woodland, streams a brilliant blaze
By which ambitious youth, with silent toil,
Plods eagerly the path to glory. No!
Not glory, but a holier thing for me
My being brightens, fixes, elevates:
My love's my inspiration; all my joy,
That Fancy finds her dreams realities.[21]

For someone so in love, certainly the next step was quite plain. The *Biblical Recorder*, which offered advice to Baptists on practically every subject from corsets, liniments, and fertilizer to politics and Judgment Day, also spoke out on the matter of proposals. There seemed no pat formula, but the *Recorder* recounted that Daniel Webster took the plunge while holding a skein of thread or wool for his lady love and remarking, "Gracie, we have been untying knots. Let us see if we can't tie one which will not untie for a lifetime." The method of a certain Scotchman seemed grim even to the staid Baptist newspaper. The lad took his lass to the family graveyard and said, "Mary, my folks lie there. Would you like to lie there, Mary?"[22]

These examples were amusing, but they held no appeal for the romantic tutor. His "star" and his "rose" was too lovely and fragile for any but the most delicate approach. In his wanderings about the woods and fields, Louis had no doubt discovered a little resort at the edge of the village known as Rock Spring, for the dense little

thicket near it was the spot where many aspiring young
orators went to blend their eloquence with the melody of
the birds before venturing to speak in the societies. There
on a beautiful, warm spring day in 1880, perhaps Louis
was the professor described by the student magazine who,
"catching inspiration from the soft, musical tune of a little
current rippling by, and the many little songsters all
around ... whispered in the ear of his destined, those first
words which laid the foundation for matrimony."[23]   In
such a lovely setting, Emma Purefoy must have agreed.

Unfortunately, however, matrimony also required economic foundations, and contemplating the future, young
Poteat soon felt the need for a raise in salary. Following
the commencement of 1880, the *Biblical Recorder* reported,
"Wake Forest College has just closed the most prosperous
session of its history. . . ."[24] The trustees were thus amen-
able to financial suggestions. President Thomas Henderson Pritchard urged them to improve the department of
physical science, which included biology, chemistry, and
physics. One improvement was the appointment of Poteat
as an assistant professor of science at a salary of $600 a
year.[25]

After encouragement from both Miss Emma and the
trustees, it must have been difficult to leave Wake Forest
for the summer in Yanceyville. But the days soon passed,
and in August he confided to his journal:

> I have wandered away full long, love,
>   And my heart's grown aweary with sighing;
> But I now change the key of my song, love,
>   For southward, Oh! southward I'm flying,
> To my home in the light of your smile, love,
>   For I pine as who watch for the day,
> As a flower that's hid for awhile, love,
>   From its sun-god wilteth away.

Upon his return to Wake Forest, much work in preparation for his classes awaited Professor Poteat. The fact

that he had never studied natural history, as biology was then called, did not seem a handicap to the trustees. In those days an educated man was supposed to be able to teach almost anything. Certainly, however, the young professor had to do a great deal of studying on his own. With many busy hours of reading science and many pleasant evenings at the Purefoys, the year passed quickly. In the early summer, Louis took several steps that were to have tremendous influence on his future life—steps down the aisle to meet Miss Emma Purefoy. They were married on June 24, 1881.

With his marriage, Poteat began a very happy period in his life. On October 20, 1881, his twenty-fifth birthday, he exclaimed in his journal: "One quarter of a century! Whether a large part or a small part of the remaining three quarters shall be completed, is wholly unknown to me; but, quite certainly, only a part." Emma's present for the occasion was Geikie's *Life and Words of Christ*. Louis commented, "May that Life which was the light of men, be the light of my own, long or short."[26]

With this inspiration, Poteat faced the future. He had already set the pattern of his future life. He had developed the pattern of continuous reading, study, and meditation that was later to prove a valuable asset to his leadership. In choosing to teach at Wake Forest College, he began the work of education that he would later lead as a member of governmental education committees, president of the North Carolina Teachers' Assembly, denominational adviser, and president of the college. The decision to change from teaching languages to natural history was most important, because this forced the young man to search for a personal reconciliation of science and religion and so prepared him to lead others in this direction.

Poteat's life in his second quarter of a century was to be very full. It was during this time that his three children were to be born. He was to have a stimulating job with leisure time for continued reading and study. He was to travel widely and develop prestige as an outstanding lecturer. On his twenty-fifth birthday, he was an obscure assistant professor just getting started. By his fiftieth year, he was to become a mature scholar, president of Wake Forest, a leader in educational and religious circles, and a well-known lecturer. The years following his twenty-fifth birthday were years of work and service, but they were also years of preparation for a greater contribution in a position of leadership.

···◈ıı III ıı◈···

Experiment in Courage

When Poteat began teaching science, one of the first things he had to accomplish was the reconciliation in his own mind of science and religion. He explained that he was called to teach the most revolutionary of the sciences in the period when the biological revolution was taking shape in England. He said, "I had to make some adjustments for my own comfort, don't you see? I was learning that what I knew in biology was in direct conflict with what I had been taught in the field of religion."[1] This conflict brought about a critical period in Poteat's personal history which corresponded to a critical period in the history of society, for at that time many other people were puzzling over the same problem.

The theory of evolution, or the belief that man descended from a lower species, seemed directly contradictory to the account of creation in Genesis. In addition, it took from man the exalted position as the crown of nature and the image of God and relegated him to common ancestry with bestial creatures. To people with little scientific background, the very idea seemed humiliating and impossible. It was not surprising that even educated religious people had trouble in accepting evolution. Could ministers conscientiously deny the very scriptures they had been ordained to proclaim?

The three major denominations in the South soon made clear their position. In 1878, the Methodists removed Alexander Winchell from the faculty of Vanderbilt University because he did not believe that the creation of Adam was the origin of man. Soon after, the trustees asked Dr. Crawford H. Toy to resign from the faculty of the Southern Baptist Theological Seminary because he doubted the literal authenticity of certain parts of the Bible. The *Biblical Recorder* had been especially critical of Dr. Toy and concerning his resignation stated, "We heartily approved the action of the Trustees, regarded it as a necessity. . . ."[2] Dr. James Woodrow, Perkins Professor at the Columbia (South Carolina) Theological Seminary was the object of Presbyterian concern. Woodrow believed that the theory of the evolution of man did not contradict the Bible. He said, "I have reiterated over and over again in every form my belief that the Scriptures do not teach God's *mode* of creation; that they teach the fact, but not the method. . . ." Nevertheless, this position was unacceptable to the Presbyterian General Assembly, and in 1886 that body recommended that Woodrow be dismissed from the seminary.[3]

With such examples in the news, Poteat undoubtedly realized that taking an even mildly liberal position in a small college controlled by Southern Baptists was indeed an experiment in courage. Evolution was a highly explosive subject. The *Biblical Recorder* admitted that the theory of the survival of the fittest might contain some truth, but declared that the species definitely could not be related.[4] The Euzelian Society ventured to debate the plausibility of the evolution theory on November 23, 1883,

but the next morning Euzelians passed a motion to strike
the query from the record books. A similar question, "Did
man spring from a monkey?" met the same fate.[5]

When the subject was frowned upon by the Baptist
press and was taboo in the literary society, certainly it was
not readily acceptable in the classroom. Poteat must have
felt much pressure to avoid the issue. Perhaps he was
thinking of this pressure when he wrote in his journal,
"Cicero (De Nat. Deorum 1 · 22) represents Cotta an
orator and magistrate as saying that it would be allowable
in a private conference to hold views which it would be
difficult to advocate in a public assembly." However,
Poteat also recorded two quotations from Emerson:
"Every true man is a cause, a country, and an age," and
"To be great is to be misunderstood."[6] The temptation
to stay on the safe side and follow Cotta's advice must
have been heavy, but William Louis Poteat was no hypo-
crite, and he chose to follow Emerson's philosophy with
the possibility of being misunderstood.

To gain knowledge of the problem, he read widely. In
addition to some theology, he studied Darwin, Herbert
Spencer, Lyell's *Geology*, and Joseph Le Conte's *Evolution*. Henry Drummond's *Natural Law in the Spiritual
World* helped him towards reconciliation. Drummond
traced natural laws as explained by science into the spiritual world. For instance, he compared the New Testament
doctrine of the new birth to the scientific doctrine of bio-
genesis or the development of living organisms. Of Drummond's book, Poteat said, "The unbelieving scientist must
now surrender or keep silent. There is no book on this
vexed question better worth reading."[7]

After much reading and study, Poteat found his personal key to the problem. He later recalled that when he
learned that biology was in direct conflict with what others
had taught him in the field of religion, he made the most
important discovery of his career. He said, "I found that
religion was one thing and intellectual effort to account for

it was another thing. I came to distinguish between the religious experience and theology." After that he was at peace. "I was at peace," he explained, "because I did not have to accept what Mr. Smith told me. I could think as well as he could.... I could then think what I had to think and still retain my attachment to Christ and His program in the world."[8] With this conviction, he was not afraid to express his ideas about science.

Poteat expressed many of his ideas in the *Wake Forest Student*, a college monthly that he had helped to establish in 1882. He served as alumni editor and conducted a department known as "Science Notes." Under this heading Poteat reported interesting bits of information. In 1883, he noted that Pasteur was to send a scientific expedition to Egypt "for investigating whether the cholera be not due to the development of a microscopic animal in the human body." Poteat also described Edison's ideas on the future of electricity. He predicted that it might even compete with gas for lighting houses, be used for driving the sewing machine, or to fan people in summer! Other topics of interest were "Porcupine Quills," "Spider Life Wonders," and the predominance of German influence in the scientific world.[9]

The alumni editor also ventured to discuss the subject of evolution, although he was very careful of what he said and most of his comments were quoted from others. He noted that a writer in the *Smithsonian Report* for 1880 stated, "The doctrine of evolution is now not only recognized by all scientific workers in biology, but it is postulated as the starting point for investigations in the affinities of various types...." Poteat balanced this statement with a quotation of Asa Gray, "Science offers no hindrance to our belief that God made heaven and earth." In another issue of the magazine, Poteat reported an article from *The Eclectic* about the relation of Darwinism to other branches of science. Poteat said that Robert S. Ball, Astronomer Royal of Ireland, tried to explain how the first life started by an arrangement of atoms. Poteat then asked, "But if they do exist, and if their mere arrangement does produce such wonderful results, pray what is it that so arranges them?" He asserted, "The great question still haunts us like a ghost, and it will take many a silver bullet like this to lay it low." Of Darwin himself, Poteat said, "He was most patient, painstaking, and truth-loving." As an illustration, the professor noted, "We find that this work is the outcome of *twenty-seven* years of thought and labor. During this long period only a very few of his most intimate friends knew that he had left the beaten paths of science."[10]

Poteat's "Science Notes" undoubtedly helped to arouse interest in the science curriculum. Perhaps his comments made scientific subjects more familiar and thus not so fearful to many readers who did not study biology or chemistry. The "Science Notes," however, were but a minor part of the magazine.

The *Wake Forest Student* greatly stimulated literary productions of both the students and the faculty. Contributors wrote on almost every conceivable topic from Wake Forest news to international events, including education, art, literature, athletics, politics, industry, and society. Subscription to the magazine was $2.00 a year, but individual copies were available at 25c a copy at book stores in Raleigh and Asheville. Newspapers mentioned the publication favorably. *The Fayetteville Observer* noted, "It is without doubt the handsomest college magazine yet published in the State," while the *Wilmington Star* praised, "It is the best college magazine in the South that comes under our eye." The *National Free School Advocate* of Washington, D.C., called it a "very creditable magazine" and recommended subscription in order to "get an idea of the ambitions and hopes of young blood in the South."[11]

The editorship of such a publication was a valuable experience. Professor Poteat had very exacting standards of writing. It was not unusual for him to spend twenty minutes searching for an appropriate word or concise expression, but once he set it down, he was satisfied that it was the best way to express his idea and he seldom changed it. Notwithstanding, according to Poteat, beautiful expression was not the most important thing. As he told a Wake Forest student editor, "The most important thing about writing is having something to say." The alumni editor warned young writers against striving for rhythmical order of words at the expense of forcible and clear expression of ideas. He believed this style of writing could be attributed to a choice of abstract subjects about which the young writer knew little. "Having little or nothing to say," Poteat asserted, "he sets himself to the ornamentation of that little or nothing in order that it may pass for something." This did not mean that everything published in the magazine had to be of an intellectual nature. Poteat allowed the young men to comment freely on campus activities. One writer bemoaned the fact that there were only twenty young ladies in the community and two hundred boys. He said, "Wake Forest would indeed be a paradise were there a hundred more 'angels' here.... One-tenth of a girl for each boy! Some poor fellows don't get that much." On another occasion a writer reprimanded his fellow students for rude and ungentlemanly behavior. "It is next to impossible for a lady to pass through the campus, by the college, or among certain streets, without being greeted with such cries as, 'heads out,' 'angels in the campus!' and other words of the kind." When a dozen heads leaned out the windows, "How then must a timid, refined, modest lady feel?"[12]

The *Student* was a readable and popular magazine. The editors learned much from working with Professor Poteat. Many of them later became professional journalists. Josiah W. Bailey and George W. Paschal subsequently edited the *Biblical Recorder*, although Bailey was probably better known as a United States senator and

Paschal as an historian. A. L. Goodrich edited the *Baptist Record* of Luling, Texas, and J. O. Atkinson, the *Christian Sun* of Richmond, Virginia. Others were editors on the staffs of daily newspapers: R. F. Beasley and R. W. Haywood edited the Greensboro *Telegram*; F. A. Smethurst worked on *The News and Observer* staff, while Gerald W. Johnson wrote editorials for the *Greensboro Daily News* and the *Baltimore Evening Sun*, and is now known as a biographer. Thomas Dixon became an outstanding fiction writer, and John Charles McNeill, a favorite southern poet. The achievements of these writers spoke well for the journalistic training they received at Wake Forest, even though other factors were naturally important in their success.[13]

The college trustees soon recognized Poteat's excellent work with the student magazine and in the classroom. At their meeting in June, 1882, President Thomas H. Pritchard recommended that Professor Poteat merited a larger salary. Pritchard said, "He is a very accurate scholar, a careful, painstaking and enthusiastic teacher, and one of the most valuable members of the faculty." Pritchard further pointed out that Poteat taught four regular classes, acted as keeper of the rolls, and served as alumni editor of the college magazine. Pritchard admonished, "For such arduous and responsible labors, I submit he has been inadequately paid." The trustees therefore raised his salary to $800 a year. This was indicative of great esteem, because money was scarce. In 1882 the bursar paid a total of $8,214.07 to the faculty members; but over a period of several years, arrears in salaries had amounted to more than $5000. In this situation the young professor must have been especially deserving to warrant a raise in salary.[14]

When Pritchard resigned as president in 1882, the trustees faced the problem of finding someone for that position. They chose Amzi Clarence Dixon, an alumnus of Wake Forest and an outstanding North Carolina minister

who was at that time serving the Baptist church at Chapel
Hill. He declined the offer from Wake Forest, so the
trustees requested that Professor William B. Royal, chairman of the faculty, act as president until they could find
someone for the position.[15] Poteat was possibly disappointed at Dixon's refusal, but he could not have realized
how important this refusal would become. Dixon became
one of the nation's leading fundamentalists, ardently opposed to the teaching of evolution. If he had become
president of Wake Forest, Poteat might have lost his
position; certainly, he could not as readily have become a
leader for freedom of teaching. Thus, the meeting of the
trustees in 1882 proved influential in the years to come.
Since Dixon refused the presidency and Poteat received
a raise in salary, the Wake Forest trustees were able to
keep one of their most prominent professors.

An important contributing factor to Poteat's teaching
ability was his interest in the subject. He defined natural
history as "the scientific description of the earth and its
animated inhabitants, there being no other term which
recognizes the essential relations existing among all the
sciences of observation." Zoology, botany, physiology,
and geology were branches of natural history; they com-
prised the study of man and his environment. Like a great
epic with man himself as the hero, natural history was full
of human interest. Although it combined mental and
moral improvement, Poteat said that the study was nevertheless "an inexhaustible source of amusement."[16]

Professor Poteat worked hard to prepare himself
properly so that his classes would be interesting. In addition to private reading and study, he visited other schools
to get ideas about appropriate methods. In the summer
of 1883, Poteat toured New England and the Middle At-
lantic States and visited Yale, Harvard, and Brown uni-
versities. He attended a course of lectures at Martha's
Vineyard Summer Institute. According to the *Wake
Forest Student*, "The recreation was much needed after

the arduous labors of last session, and he returned looking much better.'' The *Student* also reported, ''His department is greatly helped by the accession of a fine microscope purchased this summer in the North.'' Obviously Poteat was already moving away from the old didactic method of teaching natural history solely by lectures and proceeding toward the new laboratory approach. A visit to Johns Hopkins University in 1887 increased his esteem for the laboratory. He was especially impressed with the fact that at Johns Hopkins scholars were not only spreading knowledge but were producing it as well.[17] He attempted to do the same thing at Wake Forest and later received credit for being one of the first to introduce the laboratory method of teaching science in the South.

Poteat realized that a laboratory needed specimens for students to examine and so worked to improve the college natural history museum. Through the *Biblical Recorder*, Poteat requested interested Baptists to send minerals, fossils, petrified wood, or ''any object of nature that is peculiar or has an interesting history.'' The college magazine asked that students collect specimens during summer vacation. Poteat was able to exchange some duplicates with the United States National Museum, and he obtained a series of fossils from a company in New York. In addition, he collected many specimens personally, both in the woods and ponds surrounding Wake Forest and on the North Carolina coast. His wife, Emma, studied taxidermy and preserved numerous examples of bird and animal life.[18]

Members of the faculty sometimes aided Poteat. One of the bachelor professors, while on his accustomed evening stroll, captured two little snakes. He put them in an envelope, sealed it precisely, and laid it away carefully in the breast pocket of his coat. At the faculty meeting that night, he presented the envelope and its supposed contents to Poteat—who wondered why his colleague should hand him an empty envelope. Then, with a look of unutterable horror on his face, the helpful bachelor retired quickly to an adjoining room where his friends assisted in the search for the reptiles. They located one, but the other must have made good its escape. The professor surely hoped so![19]

Of course, the natural history museum was necessarily limited in its acquisition of larger zoology specimens. A highlight of the course was, therefore, a class visit to the circus when it came to town. The professor probably found some difficulty in inducing his students to concentrate on the zoological specimens with other forms of wildlife around—in grass skirts or harem costumes.

Poteat's botany field trips offered no such distractions, but sometimes the students conducted private expeditions. The college magazine reported that once when Poteat asked a student, "Do you recognize this specimen of fern, sir?" the unabashed gentleman replied hopefully, "Yes, sir, Miss —— and myself have examined every variety of fern within a radius of two miles."[20]

Nevertheless, most of the time the young gentlemen took their work seriously. Of the study of botany, the *Wake Forest Student* said, "The fruit of the field makes the face of man to shine, and walk where he will, the plant world rejoices his heart with green, white, crimson and gold." In an even more spiritual tone, the writer continued, "And in more senses than one grass blade and pine point toward the sky. A nobler and more beautiful science than botany cannot be named."[21]

But Poteat found excitement in the field of zoology also. As he watched a microscopic bit of living matter divide, he wondered why the tiny creature should halve itself. Was its size too great for self-support? Or in a more philosophical vein Poteat inquired, "Is there a germinal 'struggle for the life of others,' a surrender of one personality that there may be two personalities?" Perhaps there was no loss at all, but rather multiplication; no death, but immortality. "But what ambitions can stir and part the molecules of this speck of slime? How can the charms of altruism and the martyr crown shine fair to

The biologist at work in his laboratory

A rail fence enclosed the Wake Forest College campus in the late 1880's. Wait Hall, Wingate Memorial Hall, and the Heck-William library building appear in the background.

Fearing smoke damage in the beautifully appointed Euzalian Society Hall, the students preferred to be uncomfortable during the winter months.

an atom of protoplasm and win its whole stock in trade of energy?'' The process was inscrutable, yet there it was, advancing before the human eye. ''The mystery of life—it meets us in the lowliest forms which life takes, no less than in the highest, the human mind, which owns itself baffled.''

When a professor taught science in this way, it became not merely a learning experience but an inspiration. Rufus Weaver, a young minister who had studied with Poteat, said that he was able to hold the attention of thinking people in his congregation because of the methods of thought that he had learned in Poteat's classes. Weaver recounted that Poteat had strengthened his freedom from tradition, his enthusiasm in making investigations, and his abiding faith in God's revelation of Himself through nature. Weaver told his former teacher, ''During that period of doubt which comes to every thinking man as he faces the apparent contradictions of science and the Bible, I leaned upon your faith more than you knew. For the blessings of a larger life I thank you.''[22]

This tribute from Rufus Weaver showed that even early in his career Poteat had begun to perform a singular service for the people of the South. Through Weaver and many young ministers like him, Poteat's special message of interpretation went out to hundreds, even thousands, of people. When the time came that those who feared science challenged the professor and with him the right of freedom of teaching, there were many ready to stand by Poteat and the right to learn the truth.

In addition to his teaching, Poteat also lectured publicly and wrote articles on the question of science and religion as well as on other topics. He often spoke in the college chapel. When his subject was ''Genesis in the Light of Modern Knowledge,'' he pointed out that the contest was not between science and the Bible but between science and man's interpretation of the Bible. He explained that the order of creation described in Genesis was the same as

that described by the findings of geologists.[23]   At the
1884 commencement of Kinston College, Poteat spoke on
"The Groundless Quarrel" between science and religion.
He asserted that the history of the race was the history of
the struggle after truth and every revolution in the discovery of truth was necessarily a break with established
authority.   However, because both religion and science
have bases in truth, there must be fundamental harmony.
Of Darwin, called "the monkey man," Poteat stated, "I
repudiate that caricature of one of the most learned, patient, candid seekers after truth in all the history of
scientific research."   This statement did not seem quite so
bold, however, when Poteat qualified it by saying, "This
tribute to the man, however, means no sympathy with his
account of the origin of different kinds of animals and
plants."[24]

At that time Poteat evidently believed in development
from lower to higher forms, but not in the common origin
of the species. His own ideas were still in the process of
taking shape, and when he discussed the science-religion
controversy, he usually dealt with fundamentals and gen-
eralities rather than with details.

In the spring of 1888, Poteat discussed the controversial problem in the *Biblical Recorder*.   He said that
interpreters of the Bible were mistaken in not realizing
that God had made in natural forms and processes another
record equally authoritative.   Scientists were also mistaken in trying to apply physical laws to the spiritual
world.   Nevertheless, science broadened the conception of
God by discovering the ever-broadening universe governed
by natural laws.   Science could continue to help religion
by overcoming superstition among savage peoples, thus
preparing the way for Christianity.[25]

This conception of the work of science was evidently
acceptable to North Carolina Baptists as no objectors appeared.   Therefore, when Poteat decided to study at the
University of Berlin in the summer of 1888, the Wake

Forest administration agreed, despite the fact that Berlin was becoming noted for liberal tendencies. The university was also noted for excellence in the field of science, and Poteat wanted to learn about the laboratory method employed there.

Accompanied by his wife and his brother Edwin, Poteat left for Europe, carrying with him a letter of introduction to the university. Dr. Charles E. Taylor, president of Wake Forest, had written, "It gives me great pleasure, in behalf of the faculty of the College, to commend him to all whom he may meet as an accomplished scientist and as a gentleman of the highest character."[26]

Poteat presented his credentials and studied for a short time at the Zoological Institute of the University of Berlin. He was particularly interested in methods of preparing slides and assembled notes as to what chemicals produced certain desired effects. The slides that he prepared during his stay in Berlin were useful throughout his teaching career.[27]

Because Poteat's Christian faith was strong, tempered by years of serious personal questioning, the materialistic philosophy prevalent among many Berlin professors could not influence him to any appreciable extent. On July 3, he enjoyed an experiment in which an established authority, Professor Emil Heinrich Du Bois–Reymond exhibited the effect of an electric current upon a nerve fiber. He spoke a word in German into the telephone, whereupon the muscle began to contract. Du Bois–Reymond remarked, "Gentlemen, the muscle understands what I say." Much as Poteat respected the professor's scientific ability and enjoyed his graphic experiment, he had no use (as he later stated) for Du Bois–Reymond's materialistic philosophy.[28]

One feature of Poteat's Berlin study probably did affect his ideas. The Zoological Institute exhibited large collections of bones and fossils for the purpose of tracing the derivation and evolution of domesticated animals. Possibly this collection helped to convince Poteat that Dar-

win was correct in assuming a common origin of various
species. When he returned home, he possessed a personal
experience upon which to base his own opinions.[29]

At that time American scholars with German training
were greatly in demand. Poteat received an offer of a
position on the faculty of Yale, and he probably received
other promising offers. As a professor in a large university he would have had a chance for fame, intellectual
companionship, and an opportunity to extend the bounda-
ries of his knowledge by working in the best equipped lab-
oratories. However, he decided to return to Wake Forest
College, a small school that had scarcely recovered from
the ravages of the Civil War. No one knew its need better
than he. The offer from Yale was tempting, but Poteat
did not accept it because he was the kind of man for whom
the greatest need had a most powerful appeal.

Of course, another deciding factor was that he had
established a home in Wake Forest. His family and friends
were nearby, and it would have been difficult to leave such
a pleasant southern community. Poteat's trip to Europe
was both enlightening and enjoyable, but both he and
Emma were undoubtedly glad to return home to their little
son who had arrived in December of 1886. The Poteats
had lost their first child before its birth when lightning
shocked Emma as she sat on the front porch of their home.
Hubert McNeill Poteat arrived later and early showed
signs of being a precocious child. His father thoroughly
enjoyed the boy's antics. The elder Poteat reported to his
own father, "You see we are bringing him up on the same
songs you and Mama used to sing me to sleep with some
thirty or more years ago." Such songs as "I Want to Be
an Angel" and "There Is a Happy Land" seemed to suit
the purpose better than any which had been written since.

The young father further explained that Hubert seemed
to be turning into an interrogation point. " 'Faver, what
dat?' he says many times a day already, and while I want
to encourage that by answering him promptly ... many

times I know I shall have to say, 'Father doesn't know.' "
About five o'clock every afternoon, Hubert arrived at the
laboratory to visit. He liked for his father to look all
around over his head and ask, "Where's my man?" Then
Hubert would pat his chest and laugh as his father punched
him and said, "That's the very fellow I've been looking
for all dis day."

Hubert liked to look at the "baby moles," the "big old
'nake," and the "yizzard" in the laboratory. Then he
wanted to "go see the man workin'." Poteat's class-
rooms were in the Lea Chemical Laboratory, which was
so new in October of 1888 that carpenters were still busy
in parts of the building.[30]

Poteat's three rooms in the new building represented
an improvement over his old quarters, but he still felt
somewhat cramped. In spite of this, he was able to conduct
rewarding experiments that he reported to the Elisha
Mitchell Scientific Society, a state-wide organization centered around the University of North Carolina. In the
society journal, Poteat published an article on the tube-
building spider; in a national journal, *Science*, he published a report on the reproduction of snails.[31]

In recognition of his personal research and his German
study, the Wake Forest trustees conferred the master's
degree on Poteat at the 1889 commencement. Poteat
gained further recognition in 1891 when he became a
member of the American Association for the Advancement
of Science. Still he desired continuous improvement. In
the summer of 1893, he traveled north to study at the
Marine Biological Laboratory at Woods Hole, Massachusetts. There he heard lectures by many prominent scientists and collected specimens for use in the college laboratory.

He particularly enjoyed a trip to Penikese in the Elizabeth Islands about two hours' sail from Woods Hole. The
party of zoology students which he joined was in two
groups, one in a steam launch, the other in a lifeboat towed

by the launch. He chose the boat to get away from the evil
smelling hot steam of the engine. He reported to Emma,
"The water was—I must say it—lovely. As smooth as
glass almost with just enough ripple to give it life." Poteat and two others amused members of the group by
making sketches of them. They had a lunch of sandwiches
at the well-shaded pump of a Mr. Matthews who lived
alone on Penikese, after which Poteat went up to the
highest point to look around and observe the outline of
the island. Then he pulled on his rubber boots and joined
the rest of the party collecting specimens on the beach.
He was pleased to hit upon a method for killing some
delicate specimens in the expanded condition.

From Penikese the party crossed to Cuttyhunk and
spent about an hour there. Although the day was calm,
there was a considerable surf. Poteat enjoyed walking by
the water and fishing out seaweed. The children who were
playing with the waves made him wish for Emma and his
own little ones. Late that night when he wrote to her he
said, "What a joy the photographs of my dear family are
to me. They are in two feet of my eyes and immediately
in front of them. I love you so, my precious wife."[32]

In addition to providing interesting experiences and
intellectual stimulation, the trip to Woods Hole helped
Poteat to bring his knowledge up to date with the latest
findings. Unfortunately some people did not appreciate
his careful study. A Presbyterian friend, recalling James
Woodrow, warned Poteat that biology was a dangerous
department for a professor in a denominational college
"because he has the disadvantage of seeing clearly ten
years in advance what his denomination will recognize only
after the lapse of that time and in the mean time his head
is in jeopardy."[33]

Some Baptists did indeed object to science at Wake
Forest. John S. Hardaway, a Baptist of conservative
sentiments, told Columbus Durham, Secretary of the Baptist State Convention, "The school that teaches Darwinism

ought to be blasted with a curse, for we must judge the tree by its fruit, and the fruit of Darwinism is agnosticism. . . .'' Hardaway accused Wake Forest of being in sympathy with the University of Chicago and not with the Southern Baptist Theological Seminary. He continued, ''I hope that Wake Forest College is not as reports represent. If that is her condition our people should be warned against sending their children there.'' J. A. Stradley, a minister whose son obviously disagreed with him on scientific matters, said of the college, ''My own dear boy was tainted and corrupted there by the skeptical teachings of men who taught there. I have wished a thousand times that he had never seen or heard of Wake Forest College.''[34]

But such outbursts were unusual at that time, and the trustees did not pay much attention to them. Nor did they seriously worry Poteat. He felt that he was doing the best he could. He wrote in his journal, ''I feel that if the boys are not in possession of the method of biological thought it is not my fault.'' He explained, ''I have taken special pains to preserve the judicial attitude on vexed questions, for scientific dogmatism is as offensive as ecclesiastical.'' The students appreciated Poteat's sincere approach. J. L. Kesler, who later taught science at Baylor University, called Poteat ''a teacher whose influence has grown, whose abiding impetus and growing inspiration have increased with the deeper earnestness and larger mystery of life.'' Hubert M. Evans, a teacher at Southwest Virginia Institute in Bristol, told Poteat, ''I learned more from you than I learned from anyone else.... If it had not been for you it would be impossible for me to do the work I am doing here.''[35]

What was the key to Poteat's ability not only to teach but to inspire his students? Perhaps it was the fact that his interests were not narrowed merely to scientific pursuits. He made it a practice to leave his science at the laboratory. To his journal Poteat confided, ''I did a little microscopic work at the Laboratory this morning on an interesting *Rotifer*. I am fond of such work and might achieve some success and reputation in it, but it requires more time than I am willing to give to it." He might work in the evening, but then he explained, "I should be compelled to forego the refreshment and culture of the great books of the world. These I cannot surrender, since myself is more to me than my reputation in science circles."[36]

On another occasion when he found a particularly large amoeba, he could not work with it because he had to leave the laboratory to lead the choir. He commented, "This circumstance has brought up afresh the limitations which the conditions of my life here set to any independent work I might put my hand to." Because he devoted his evening leisure to maintaining intellectual interest and outlook, much of the possible scientific work did not reach completion. "What shall I do?" he asked. "Rail at Fate and grow unhappy? or compromise upon surrender of my ambitions scientific? or trample on domestic, social, and religious obligations?" The answer for Poteat was to "be content to be faithful in all relations according to opportunity, judging the rank of any work, not from the sphere of it, but from the way in which it is done."[37]

Consequently, the scientist made room in his schedule for a broad range of activities, including lectures, church work, family, reading, and social life. Reading was particularly important to Poteat. He thoroughly enjoyed intellectual stimulation, and in literature he found many ideas to share with others in his lectures. He especially enjoyed Robert Browning's work and various commentaries on the Bible. Magazines held little interest except for the pictures. He said, "Periodical current literature I have come to look on as a prime thief of time from whom it is rare that one recovers stolen goods." He felt that it was important to use his time for reading of a more substantial nature, for he wrote, "Nature, like some fair Lady of Shalott, weaves into the web of nerve cell and fibre what she sees passing in the magic mirror of the mind." Yet he also realized, "The culture which develops upon great books is prone to show the taint of bookishness, unless it have also wholesome and numerous contacts with the great world of men."

Social life in Wake Forest was somewhat limited but none the less enjoyable. The Ladies' Aid Society, in order to make money for the cemetery improvements, sponsored several social functions. Sometimes the entertainment consisted of tableaux, recitations, and music; but for a change the ladies had a Dickens party with everyone costumed as a favorite character from *Pickwick Papers, David Copperfield,* or one of the other novels. Musicales and Literary Society meetings also brightened the social scene. Poteat thoroughly enjoyed the literary meetings. Once a discussion of Wordsworth became so heated that Poteat said he felt like getting a gun after Professor Benjamin Sledd of the college English Department. Sledd was a very good friend, however, and the two professors usually agreed.[38]

The Poteats often entertained. In the summer of 1896, they invited all the young people of the community to a lawn party. Poteat reported, "Young men and maidens of '96 actually played 'King William,' 'It Rains and It Hails,' and 'Drop the Handkerchief.' I wish there were more things in the simple life of the old days that we could not get beyond."[39]

The Poteats also frequently entertained individual guests. Thomas Dixon, the noted orator and journalist was a welcome visitor who especially enjoyed coming during quail season. Poteat kept a fine bird dog, and when Dixon arrived, he was ready to offer his guest an exciting hunt. Dixon, whom Poteat declared was "as quick to cut down a partridge as to utter his winged words," lectured to the student body when he visited Wake Forest. When President Taylor had to be away from the college to solicit funds, Poteat took over the president's duties. Thus, he sometimes introduced guest lecturers. On one occasion

when Dixon was to speak, Poteat's sense of humor would
not let him pass up a golden opportunity. He announced,
"We are to have a lecture, I understand, *on* 'Fools' by
one—by one who only knows them only by observation."[40]

Most of the occasions on which Poteat spoke in public
were much more serious. A student of the Bible, he often
spoke at the Wake Forest prayer meeting, or at churches
and schools in neighboring towns. His fame as an excellent speaker spread, and each year the invitations to
lecture steadily increased. Once in a while it was necessary
for him to be away from Wake Forest for several days.
As he prepared to attend the North Carolina Teachers'
Assembly meeting at Asheville, Hubert asked why he could
not go along. On being told he was too little, he replied,
"Father, I would go with *you* to New South Wales!"[41]

Poteat found the Asheville meeting pleasant. He remarked that he "enjoyed intensely the beautiful view from
the porch of the Battery Park Hotel." One whole afternoon he watched the shifting mists and clouds on the
mountains with Browning unread on his lap except for a
page or two. He heard from Emma, who missed him on
their fifteenth wedding anniversary. She wrote, "I almost
cried this morning when no word came from you. . . . I
wonder if you know how much I love you! more than I ever
did, right now, and so it shall be as the days go by." His
letters to her were no less tender.[42]

After the close of the assembly, Professor Charles E.
Brewer, a Wake Forest colleague, and Poteat started west
for a little outing in the mountains. Crossing the Balsams
beyond Waynesville made them feel that they had not
really seen mountains about Asheville. They left the railroad at Sylva and reached "The Glen," home of Thomas
Cox, in the Cullowhee valley at about nine that night. Cox
shared their interest in education as he was closely associated with the founding of Western Carolina College
and at one time served as a trustee of the University of
the South.

The next day they climbed Cullowhee Mountain, stopping for a sight of the Cullowhee Falls and, beyond, Tuckasegee Falls. One of the horses refused to pull the buggy because of a sore neck, so they got saddles at Glenville and had a glorious ride through the oaks, chestnuts, hemlocks, and rhododendrons. When they reached Highlands that evening at nine-thirty, their legs and feet were quite wet from contact with the dewy leaves. The view from the top of Satulah Mountain next morning was extensive. It took in the whole circle of a wide horizon with Chimney Top, gigantic Whiteside, Short Off, Yellow Mountain, Rabun Bald, and the lowlands of Georgia and South Carolina beyond. "Here is elemental Nature!" Poteat exclaimed, standing for a time in tears with his hat off. The next morning he took the train at Sylva and reached Wake Forest the following day.

In August he returned to Asheville, this time to speak at the Southern Biblical Assembly, a religious convention that attracted some of the outstanding scholars, educators, and church leaders of the nation. On the west-bound train, Poteat had interesting conversations on theology and politics with his fellow passengers. The free silver issue was foremost on the political scene, and the gentlemen agreed that the agitation was a symptom of a deep-lying discontent.

In Asheville, Poteat lodged with Dr. George W. Purefoy, one of Emma's relatives. Emma wrote, "To say we miss you is not saying anything! I seem not to *live* here when you are gone." He missed his family too but was very busy as secretary of the conference. The biology professor thoroughly enjoyed a talk by John C. Kilgo, President of Trinity College. Poteat said, "Several times the audience were laughing a happy laugh for the wit and vitality of his manner. No polish; all force."[43]

The conference also afforded opportunity for social pursuits. One afternoon Poteat had tea in the elegant parlor of a gentleman in the cotton textile business. He recalled, "The host could talk about nothing, apparently, but free silver. His wife complained about his being in a rut so deep that he couldn't see out." Another day Poteat went with the Purefoys and some friends to "Gold View" about five miles from town, "the finest view to be had in and around Asheville." As the group walked down, Poteat noticed that two lustrous-eyed children stood by the road and offered handfuls of common flowers for sale. He said, "Those great brown wistful eyes needed only to shine on me to command me."

On the evenings of August 11 and 12, he was present at two society events in Asheville. One was a "flower party" given by the Gudgers, a prominent western North Carolina family. The other was a "hen tea"—no "roosters" admitted. This was at the home of George Mebane, a cousin, where Poteat went to tea, arriving before the ladies had finished. Mebane joined with his guest in laughing at the absurdity of certain social regulations. On these two occasions the Wake Forest professor was interested in observing two new methods of handshaking "approved in advanced society." One was with the elbow at the side and the hand at the level of the ear, while the other was with the forearm against the waist and the palm turned up, the four fingers being hooked in the fingers of the other party. Poteat was reminded of a quotation he had read about the "end of the age" society, puzzling itself in the effort to discover new sensations.

In addition to pleasure in social activities, Poteat was also happy with the reception of his lecture "The Thirty Silent Years of Christ." The size of his audience was the largest that had gathered for the evening lectures, and a number of people acknowledged that they had benefited by hearing it. He was a forceful speaker, and the content of his lectures was both interesting and thought provoking. It was not surprising that he received many requests for his services. Although he often complied, he more often refused these invitations and stayed at home to enjoy his family.[44]

In 1896, nine-year-old Hubert had two little sisters, Louie, who was seven, and Helen, a baby. Louie was convinced that she had a part in bringing the baby, for after visiting the Otho Holdings who had a new child, Louie told her mother that she would like to have one in her family too. Emma told her that maybe God might send one if she would write him a letter and ask for a baby. When Louie inquired how the letter could be sent, her mother suggested that she might say it in her prayer. After supper Louie took a tablet to her father and dictated, "My dear God, I want a baby when it gets a little warmer. You send that baby whenever you think it's best to send it." And about a month later a baby sister arrived, an Easter gift on Easter Sunday.

Helen was a special delight to her father. Because Emma was ill for weeks after her birth, he often took care of her. She was pretty from babyhood, with a clear pink complexion and very bright eyes. When she was about six months old, her nurse, Julia, would take her to meet her father as he came home at noon for dinner. When she heard him clap his hands, she would look up, throw out her hands, and smile. By the time he reached her, her mouth was stretched to its widest limits. Later, as a toddler, Helen sometimes went to the college with him and quietly played around his feet as he lectured to his class.

Louie often went to the college too. She was a good little housekeeper and helped in the laboratory by washing test tubes. She was a friendly child, less exacting than her brother and not as afraid of shadows or thunderstorms. She liked to gallop on horseback and to work in the garden, but she came to her father in tears when a little tree toad died. Although she did very good work in school, Louie was not fond of books. She would rather visit her girl friends or go with her father in the buggy when he went away to lecture or to Raleigh on business. Sometimes on the way home she would crawl sleepily into his lap while he read, for old Daisy knew the way.

Hubert liked to read with his father. He was intensely interested in literature from Homer through Sir Walter Scott to Jack London. He memorized easily and learned long poems. Religion was a serious matter with Hubert; at a very young age he thought seriously about what it meant to be a Christian. Encouraged by Emma's apt teaching, he also showed quite early a remarkable talent for music.[45]

The family enjoyed singing together. Emma would play the piano and sing with Hubert and his father from the "Song Folio" book of ballads. By the time they had reached the "Torpedo and the Whale," Louie was fast asleep on the long-haired black rug. Then, when the others tired of singing, Hubert would play. With almost perfect pitch, he improvised easily and composed tunes of his own. When he was only ten years old, he began playing the hymns for the morning chapel services at the college.[46]

Perhaps seeing Hubert at the college at so tender an age made Poteat reflect upon his rapidly accumulating years. That autumn on his birthday, Poteat asserted, "I cannot realize that I am forty."

"Father, just think!" said Louie incredulously at the dinner table, "Forty years ago you were a little baby like Helen."

For Julia Poteat those years had passed quickly. Mrs. Poteat was in Oxford, North Carolina, with her daughter Ida, who taught art at a girls' school there. Unable to be present on her son's birthday, she wrote, "Are you too old to be called my boy? No, you are my boy just as dear and precious to me *now* as you were forty years ago, when I first felt the thrill of motherhood ... and wondered if I should live to see you a man with whiskers on that fine soft face."

Apart from his mother's word and his rapidly thinning crown, Poteat could find no evidence to support the high figure of his age—"whether of the work I have been able to do in the world, or the degree of culture which I may have achieved, or yet any small pains and weaknesses of body and spirit which are the advance guard of decrepitude." His fortieth birthday semed to make him feel dissatisfied with his personal contribution. "Let me be up and at it from now on!" he said. "Procrastination, with many a month of mine in thy bag, put no foot henceforth on my demesne upon pain of death." He further invoked, "God and all good influences support me in the concentration of time and energy upon the service of man and the enrichment of my nature to that end. Forty years old!"[47]

Poteat had won success in his occupation. With courage to stand irrevocably for the truth as he saw it, he was a distinguished teacher and a scientist of some reputation in North Carolina. He had a fine family and a beautiful home. Many men would have been ready to relax and to enjoy the fruits of previous labors. Many would have been satisfied to be successful in only one field of endeavor. But to Poteat, his scientific achievements were only a part of his life; he felt that there was still other work for him to do.

Scientific Philosopher

Certainly, all would not have agreed with Poteat's modest estimate of himself. Already he had begun the work of interpreting progress, which was to be his major contribution. People in the late nineteenth century sought an interpretation of the tremendous changes that were rapidly taking place. The self-confident, agricultural America, concerned with domestic problems and conforming to the political, moral, and economic principles of the seventeenth and eighteenth centuries, was giving way to a new order faced with international expansion, amoral big business, and the declining importance of the individual.

Americans were acclimated to change, but in the early nineteenth century this change took place within an economic and social framework reasonably stable. Traditional ideas about ethics involved in property and in the institutions of school, church, family, and state were never seriously challenged, but with the decline of individual proprietorships and the growth of impersonal corporations, individual ethics in business no longer seemed quite so important. Politics reflected the impersonal note with the growth of political machines, and in many cases the "boss" replaced the statesman. Crime and violence, the keynotes of yellow journalism, served to emphasize the ethical confusion.

Other blows to the moral system came from scientific and philosophical circles. There had been no philosophical preparation for the effort to adjust to the new world of science. American philosophy was at a low ebb in this period, for transcendentalism had lost prestige while William James's pragmatism was still to come. The neat, orderly universe of the Enlightenment, a universe governed by specific laws, was disintegrating under the blows of Darwinian evolution, the new physics, and the new biology. Evolution was a blow to man as it relegated him to common ancestry with the lower animals. Biologists merely emphasized the kinship by their discovery of protoplasm, a common element in all animal flesh.

Not only did evolutionists seem to dethrone man, but they substituted for his neat, orderly universe a world in constant flux; its beginnings incomprehensible and its end unimaginable. The evolutionary process seemed to reduce man to a passive role, to rob him of authority to determine the destiny of his world. Herbert Spencer explained that society had evolved from simple to complex, from savage to civilized, and ultimately would reach perfection if left alone. If monopolies forced small companies out of business, if machines caused unemployment and starvation, it was merely the survival of the fittest, and society would benefit in the long run. William Graham Sumner, Spencer's American apostle, was aware that society must pay a price for the removal of all restraints on individual power and greed, but he was convinced that in the long run it was less exorbitant than the price that society paid for coddling the weak. Some people found reassurance and justification for cutthroat competition in this philosophy, but for others the evolutionary view reduced the whole of human striving to insignificance. For them the new universe was illimitable, impersonal, amoral, and incomprehensible.[1]

To make matters worse, American optimism had to face the economic depression of the 1890's. The price of cotton fell to 5¢ a pound in 1895, and other farm products were also low. The population increased while money circulation tightened, and farmers produced surplus goods for which there was no market. The old frontier with good, cheap farmland was rapidly passing, but new immigrants arrived in hoards to compete for profits.

No wonder that men should feel disillusionment—no wonder that they should question the meaning of change. But average men could follow the scientists and philosophers only so far. They felt that the order of life was different, but it remained for interpreters to explain the nature of the change. Poteat, as a scientist, an educator, and a sincere Christian, was ready to offer his ideas. In an address to the young ladies of Chowan Institute, Poteat explained that the progress of the physical sciences had been marvelous. He pointed out that closer observations of matter might have brought about materialism. "Who can wonder," he asked, "... when nearly all her secrets, and the wonderful properties of matter are dazzling the minds of countless eager inquirers ... that the atmosphere of the scientific world is heavy with its leaden negations?" But Poteat could not accept these negations. He declared that man was both physical and spiritual. In the world of ideas, man could find dignity. Poteat admitted that "pushing, practical Americans" might think the world of ideas dreamy and unsubstantial, out of harmony with the period. "For every age, an adjective," he asserted. "Our own is materialistic, not only in the tendency of its philosophy, but also in the motives of its everyday living." Poteat struck out at this problem of his day. He showed that ideas and ideals were more important than battles, governments, meetings, or speeches because ideas could stimulate all these. "An exalted ideal is the pledge of an exalted destiny." Poteat believed that the excellence and perpetuity of social institutions, as well as the beauties and blessings of individual lives, depended upon the health of human sentiments—veneration for the holy and noble, patriotism, hope, love. He warned, "There is sham in commerce, in politics, in literature, in art, in religion. Greedy ambition has all but devoured patriotism.... I call upon you to build the dikes against this tide of destruction."

One attempt to rectify the ethical problems partially brought about by the discoveries of science involved an effort to find a physiological basis for morality—thereby making science strengthen rather than destroy high standards of behavior. In 1895, the Reverend Mr. Walter Rauschenbusch, a leading proponent of the social gospel, invited Poteat to lecture at the Baptist Congress meeting in Providence, Rhode Island. Poteat's topic was to be "The Physiological Basis of Morality."[2]

The Wake Forest science professor was well qualified as a teacher of physiology and biology as well as an outstanding religious speaker. Nevertheless, on such a new topic, he felt it necessary to do much reading and soul-searching. The work on his paper prompted him to work out his own "tentative theory of man's relation to God in sin and redemption." Poteat based some of his ideas on Dr. A. H. Strong's articles on "Ethical Monism," but he could not agree with Strong entirely. Monism, the idea that reality is a unitary, organic whole, appealed to him. He believed that Christ, the personification of God, was the source of man's personality, and although man had moral freedom to sin and thus to rupture the spiritual bond with God, he could never destroy the natural bond. Poteat said that Jesus represented the age-long suffering of God. He endured the cross for the purpose of self-revelation. "Innocence became sin for our benefit (not in our place)."

He continued, "It was the revelation of God in Jesus' life and death that wrought the redemption of man. In the vision (faith) of God the conquest of sin is effected and the spiritual bond is re-established."[3]

In this concept of the atonement for sins through Christ, Poteat differed from the accepted Baptist theology that held the suffering of Christ was a vicarious act, that Christ suffered in the place of men. Poteat, however, believed in the moral influence of Christ's suffering—"for our benefit (not in our place)." In other words, man could comprehend God's love through the cross, and thus gain courage to overcome sin and re-establish the spiritual bond with God. This idea of Poteat's, evidently formed while he was studying the physiological basis of morality, was to serve as the tiny spark that was to light a roaring fire of criticism against him in the 1920's. But in 1865, the idea lay tucked away in his mind, confided to his journal along with other ideas for his paper.

In connection with his conception of monism, the spiritual, moral, and physical were "merely the different aspects of the one law reflecting the special characteristics of the several spheres of its operation." He said that the universe was one in law and the universal law seemed to be the law of righteousness. "In its most general terms, it is the law of the self-realization of the parts of the organism in subordination to the whole."[4] Therefore physical and moral law were complementary in the development of man, and morality could conceivably have a physiological basis.

To get additional ideas, Poteat read Charles Darwin's *The Descent of Man*, "What Mind Is" from Mercier's *Sanity and Insanity*, Miller's *Christian Doctrine of Sin*, and various selections from Herbert Spencer.[5] In preparing his lecture, Poteat sometimes worked outdoors. On October 19, 1895, "Two and a half hours of the mid-day were passed at the foot of a great pine in a quiet wood. They were delightful hours." He was writing an explanation of the emergence of scientific ethics under the stimulus of new knowledge of nature. He said, "My white Gordon setter, Rob Roy, was with me. As he lay now here, now there, not far from me, he served me for company without its usual distraction."

After much reading and study Poteat remarked, "The preparation of that paper ... for the Baptist Congress has led me into a field almost entirely new to me, and whether I enlighten the Congress or not, I feel that I have added somewhat to my own little intellectual domain."[6]

Poteat delivered his lecture at the Central Baptist Church in Providence on November 14. He remarked that because of the progress of science, the world had changed. Thus it was inevitable that the foundations of morality should be freshly examined. He said that if a system of morals were to guide the life of the new era, it "must not only take account of its special problems and its contributions of fact having an ethical import, but it must authenticate itself by falling into alignment with the drift of knowledge in nonethical spheres." In other words, a system of morals must expand and adjust to apply to problems that did not exist previously. Such a moral system must remain in tune with intellectual developments in order to ring true.

Poteat traced the development of ethics from the Greek sophists to Darwin, who held that morals had a physical basis and evolved from the lower animals. He explained that the Neo-Christian theory accepted the derivation of man's body from lower series and that moral nature had its root in the same organic series. However, whereas physical theory held that the moral nature was mere sensation or ancestral experience, the Neo-Christian theory insisted that these were merely the vehicle for morality. "God's hand is on the physiological process, and as with his energy and nourishing it rises into higher planes, he can put into it more and more spiritual significance."[7]

The Wake Forest professor was pleased with the warm

commendation that his lecture received. He enjoyed the hospitality of Dr. H. M. Bixby, Pastor of the Granston Street Church in Providence. A special treat was visiting with his brother Edwin, who was then serving a church in New Haven, Connecticut. Ed, always full of fun, tried to persuade Louis to shave his heavy mustache. Of the handlebar variety, it was very dark and thick. It nicely balanced his shock of black hair and heavy brows. Louis had grown somewhat tired of the mustache, but he hesitated to shave it off because it amounted almost to the loss of his personal identity. Finally, when Ed bribed him with the promise of a nine-dollar Bible, Louis took the plunge. "As the process of *clearing* advanced," he said, "I recalled Gray's line 'How bowed the woods beneath their sturdy stroke?' "

Determined that the whiskers would remain shaved, Ed jokingly told his brother, "Send me a certificate signed by the members of your household, that your upper lip has been regularly shaved.... In the absence of a notary public convenient to you, this certificate will answer my purpose."

On his way home, Poteat met acquaintances who had difficulty in recognizing him, and once in Wake Forest, he said, "My changed aspect was the occasion of not a little merriment and some regret among my friends."[8]

Poteat held another surprise in store for some people at Wake Forest. He had expressed extremely liberal views in his lecture at the Baptist Congress, and when he repeated the speech at the college, there was some reaction. It came from the Reverend Mr. W. R. Gwaltney, the Wake Forest Baptist minister. "There was one thing I did not understand," he declared. "You said the Neo-Christian theory accepted the view that man's body was descended from the lower animals; but you didn't say whether you believed it, and I thought I would ask you if you did."

"I do," Poteat boldly replied.

"What! that man came from the monkey and the tadpole!"

"You must go further back than that," rejoined Poteat, "from the amoeba."

As Gwaltney turned away, he said, laughing, "No monkey or tadpole is my great grandfather."

And the science professor silently thought to himself, "As if the fancied discredit of a given parentage could disprove the fact of it."[9]

In spite of the minister's disbelief, Poteat felt that Wake Forest had succeeded in keeping pace with the times. The very fact that he could discuss the doctrine of evolution as applied to man's body and the derivative theory of the moral nature in a Southern Baptist denominational college was in itself an accomplishment. Poteat admitted that even he would not have ventured to express such ideas ten years previously.[10] His gentle, intelligent leadership had borne fruit. For many years in the student magazine, in the *Biblical Recorder*, in the classroom, and in the Sunday school, Poteat had worked to broaden the acceptance of scientific truth, and he was beginning to see the results of his labors. Others recognized his exceptional work, and from this time on, his life became more and more filled with service to others. His declaration to "be up and at it" on his fortieth birthday proved prophetic. In 1896, he served as president of the North Carolina Teachers' Assembly, an organization for all white teachers in the state. He commented, "I felt no desire for the responsibilities or the distinction of the position, but the heartiness and unanimity of the choice was pleasing to me."[11]

The next year the state Board of Education asked him to serve on the Board of Examiners, which at that time was setting the requirements for teachers' certificates and making up qualifying examinations. Poteat insisted on the addition of physical geography, elementary physics, and elementary botany to the list of subjects for the examination for "life certificates," and he prepared articles on a proposed course of study for teachers in botany and physiology.[12]

As a member of the board of trustees, he also helped to form the curriculum of the Baptist Female University (later Meredith College) just getting started in Raleigh in the 1890's. Mary Lynch Johnson, in her history of the college, stated, "William Louis Poteat ... did more than any other one person in putting the curriculum of the Baptist Female University on a sound basis."[13]

The energetic professor also took an active part in church activities. Notes in preparation for teaching a Sunday school class in his home church show careful preparation and sincere study of the Bible.[14] He also was a faithful member of the choir and an occasional speaker at the Wednesday night prayer meeting. Poteat sometimes spoke at other churches, educational institutions, and Sunday school Chautauquas. He soon became one of the state's favorite lecturers. Many agreed with the *Wake Forest Student* that "Professor Poteat has the rare gift of combining the qualities of a thorough scholar with those of an able and interesting public speaker."[15]

In May of 1898, Poteat addressed the American Baptist Education Society meeting at Norfolk, Virginia, on the topic "Christian Education and Civic Righteousness." Poteat disagreed with the idea that there should be two codes of righteousness, one for the individual and another for the corporation or state. He believed that righteousness was absolute and uncompromising and that the ideals applying at home should also apply to society in general. Great progress in the rights of the individual and in altruism had been made, but some areas, such as the spoils system, party machines, and lobbies, needed much improvement. The speaker insisted that society must turn to Christianity for the further amelioration of evils. "The Gospel was put into the drama of human history as the controlling factor in its destinies, and if Jesus cannot save the world, it is time to inquire whether he can save the individual," he stated. But the method of Christianity was not legislation, not an ecclesiastical state. Poteat explained, "Briefly stated, the method of Jesus is social regeneration by an inward spiritual ministry, civic righteousness through the leaven of individual righteousness." Thus, it was the duty of the Christian college to prepare leaders to fit men for the service of the state.

The lecture was very well received. One acquaintance told the speaker, "The Missouri delegates to the Southern Baptist Convention report that your address at Norfolk was THE speech of the meeting—the only one that was fairly entitled to be called 'great.' "[16] Many other people read Poteat's ideas on "Christian Education and Civic Righteousness in the *Baptist Argus* of Kentucky and in the *Biblical Recorder*.

Poteat, however, did more than simply talk about civic duties. He tried to serve when the opportunity arose. In 1881 Governor Daniel G. Fowle asked Poteat to represent North Carolina at a Quarantine Conference at Montgomery, Alabama, in the hope that he could bring back some helpful ideas for the prevention of epidemics.

Other governors also called upon the science professor. Charles B. Aycock sometimes visited in the Poteat home. When he was to come to dinner one day, Emma told baby Helen she must be on her best behavior. Helen, who was just learning about royalty, asked, "Moder does de Gov'nor wear a crown?" At the dinner table, Emma reported the incident to the governor who said, "I don't wear a crown, little girl, but sometimes my head rests as uneasy as if I did."

In September of 1901, Governor Aycock requested that Poteat join the North Carolina delegation to attend the funeral of President William McKinley, who died of a wound inflicted by an assassin's bullet. The Wake Forest professor saw many distinguished men in Washington, including the new president, Theodore Roosevelt. Poteat felt that the funeral service in the rotunda of the Capitol

was unfitting in many respects because there was a great
crush of people but seats for only eight hundred, and the
addresses were inaudible to the North Carolinians. "The
thought of the complexity of civilized life was not long out
of mind at any period of the day," he said, "a complexity
which confers upon the evil minded a proportionate power
to do widespread mischief. The only hope of society is to
change the evil mind."[17]

As head of two organizations for the improvement of
men's minds, Poteat did what he could. In 1902, he was
president of the North Carolina Academy of Science, and
in 1903, he became president of the State Literary and
Historical Association. He also contributed to the general
store of knowledge by publishing some of his ideas in a
book, *Laboratory and Pulpit: The Relation of Biology to
the Preacher and His Message.* Poteat adapted to book
form the Gay Lectures that he delivered at the Southern
Baptist Theological Seminary at Louisville, Kentucky, in
1900. He had attempted to interpret progress for the
ministerial students, and as his purpose in publishing the
book he explained, "We are in a period of transition, more
distinctly so, perhaps, in our conservative South than in
some other quarters; and it is of this transition that I
purpose to speak. Now, all transitions are perilous." He
compared the change to a crab breaking its shell to build
a new one. "Our old habits of body, mind, spirit are at
once our comfort and our safety. To break their protecting
shell for a new one is not only painful, it exposes us the
while to thronging perils." Yet the repeated passage from
a limited to a larger life was one of the conditions of life
itself. "We must grow to live."[18]

Poteat summarized the changes taking place in biology
and declared that adaptation to scientific progress would
lend strength to Christianity. But he clarified his position
by stating, "Christianity is absolute, our apprehension
of it is progressive." From Poteat's point of view the
conception of God had been purified and ennobled by the

revelations of science. "The existence of God being given," he said, "the testimony of science is three-fold: God is one, God is near, God is great." He advised the student ministers to cultivate three characteristics of the scientific spirit: sympathy with nature, reverence for truth, and acceptance of the law of cause and effect. "There is no infidelity so deep or so dangerous," he said, "as the fear lest the truth be bad." Rather than fearing scientific truth, ministers should learn to understand it so that they could give help to others who had doubts.[19]

The *Biblical Recorder* described the book as "a clear, frank statement of the aim, results, and attitude of modern science from one in whom the ageless realities of religion abide in so deep degree" and suggested that the book would win recognition not only in North Carolina but "wherever men are thinking." Further praise came from the *Baptist Argus*: "There is charm of style, originality of thinking as well as grasp and reach that hold you. There is also ripeness of culture and wealth of reading."

According to the *Baptist Commonwealth* of Philadelphia, the book contained two errors. First, Poteat seemed to magnify the bearing of biological learning on the business of the preacher, and second, he minimized the openness of the preacher's mind to scientific light. The paper admitted that Poteat's portrayal of the pulpit's aversion to science was perhaps fair in respect to some portions of the South even though it was not applicable in Philadelphia. Nevertheless, the criticism concluded with the suggestion that "every preacher at least ought to read the book. He cannot well fail to be roused and refreshed by it."[20]

Others also thought that Poteat had a message for ministers. In 1905, he delivered the Brooks Lectures on science and religion at Hamilton Theological Seminary at Hamilton, New York. Later Poteat published these lectures as *The New Peace*. One reviewer commented, "The author is a scientist, possessed with a charming literary style, able to clothe what might be considered a dry and uninteresting discussion with the beauty of poetic fervor, of spiritual taste and of vital personal power."[21]

Poteat's abilities won public recognition in June of 1905 when Baylor University of Texas awarded him the honorary degree, Doctor of Laws. The *Biblical Recorder* declared, "Our pride is the finer because we know the honor is so well deserved, and that it comes from an institution whose recognition is so much desired." Earlier, the Baptist paper had called Poteat an ideal teacher, stating, "His scholarship lies not only in his department, Biology, but in Letters, Education, and Religion. He is perhaps the best rounded man in the State, and his life is as full and as high as any life that we know of."[22]

Recognition of Poteat's varied abilities soon brought him an opportunity to serve in a position of active leadership. In June, 1905, representatives of Mercer University in Macon, Georgia, asked him to accept the presidency of that institution. Poteat hesitated to accept because he enjoyed his work at Wake Forest and had established his home there.[23]

In the summer of 1905, Poteat was on his way to Europe to speak at the Baptist World Congress meeting in London. More than three thousand Baptists from twenty-eight countries attended the conference. He made a short talk and opened the discussion on the topic, "The Relation of Baptists to Social Questions," repeating many of the ideas that he had expressed in his lecture on "Christian Education and Civic Righteousness." The idea that individuals must become good before society as a whole can improve was his major theme. It was indeed an honor to have the opportunity to speak at the World Congress, and Poteat had left Wake Forest in anticipation of the challenge of such an opportunity, but he was to return home to an even greater challenge.

During Poteat's absence, Dr. Charles E. Taylor, President of Wake Forest, resigned because of increasing deafness. As the Wake Forest trustees realized that Mercer University desired the services of William Louis Poteat, they hurriedly cabled a request that he take over the leadership of Wake Forest. The choice was not difficult for Poteat. He replied through the *Biblical Recorder* that he approached the responsibility with some trepidation, but he would depend on the advice and help of the faculty and of Dr. Taylor. He continued, "With these supports, and in hope of our Master, whom I serve in the cause of education, I devote myself wholeheartedly to my new work."[24]

The *News and Observer* expressed the confidence many North Carolinians felt in Poteat by saying, "His noble character, genuine piety, great ability, and growing reputation in the State and out of it made him peculiarly suitable and qualified for the place."[25]

Poteat assumed the duties of president when the fall term began, but his official inauguration occurred on December 7. Forty-nine years old, he had the energy of youth but the dignity and wisdom that only experience can give. He was a man who knew what he wanted and went after it by making himself useful. He was indeed "up and at it" as he had determined to be. Because his dignity was natural and uncultivated he was approachable; students were in and out of his office constantly. *The News and Observer* commented, "In this student intercourse one saw the executive and felt the man. The two qualities merged in a personality as distinct as it is indescribable."[26]

Poteat was a dynamic man. His tremendous energy, which played almost visibly in the muscles of his round thick body, was half concealed by his admirable poise. Confidence in his ability to accomplish considerable work enabled him to take his time without worrying. Entirely frank but without the time or the inclination for self-exploitation, he was impervious to any temptation to pose.

The academic costume seemed superficial to Poteat, and he refused to allow its use at his inauguration. He said, "It's clerical in its origin. What the college of today

should seek to do is to multiply the points of its contact
with modern conditions and modern needs, not to emphasize its aloofness."[27] As president of Wake Forest he carried out this aim by becoming a leader not only in education but in the social, economic, religious, and, to some
extent, the political activities of the state.

Poteat's inauguration was a fitting recognition of his
accomplishments and an expression of promise for the
future. Wingate Memorial Building, scene of the cere-
mony, was an old-looking place but well kept, with soft,
dull colors, a look of simplicity, and proud self-conscious-
ness. Portraits of former college leaders lined the walls.
One observer commented, "Still looking down upon their
work, these old faces seemed to admonish and yet to glow
with pride. And under their eyes the room settled itself in
contentment and in confidence."[28]

The inauguration began with the processional march
from Tannhäuser with Hubert Poteat at the organ. As
the dignitaries slowly moved toward the front, the line
came to a halt. William Louis Poteat stepped to the side
of the aisle and kissed his mother. He spoke no word, but
in this eloquent gesture paid his personal tribute to Julia
McNeill Poteat. Her son Edwin was serving as president
of Furman University in Greenville, South Carolina, and
when Louis took over the leadership of Wake Forest, surely Julia must have been fully satisfied with the results of
her long years of love and labor. An observer that day
declared, "Swallowed as she was in the audience, Mrs.
Poteat was the center of the inauguration to those who,
passing the immaterial, knew where to look for the deeper
causes of the day."[29]

The new college president spoke on "The Christian
College in the Modern World." He explained that he
loved teaching and did not seek the duties of administration, but he took heart from the confidence of the trustees.
"Another reflection gives me heart for this new position,"
he said, "... I recall in your presence the hope, realized to-

day, of a father long passed into the skies. If he is pleased, I am content."

Poteat said that the purpose of the Christian college was to equip men for service to society. He explained that Latin syntax, mathematics, and other subjects were not essentially Christian but could become so if taught in a Christian manner. "The function of the teacher is the total forming of the human being, the bringing of the child into lively and harmonious relation with his whole environment, physical, intellectual, and spiritual." To Poteat, character was the teacher's crowning achievement; it was the responsibility of the Christian college to train men for leadership in religion, in culture, and in politics. "So will the Christian college link itself in a new place to the purpose of God in the redemption of society," Poteat said in conclusion.[30]

In his work as college president, he recognized the opportunity not only to aid society in the interpretation of progress but also, through his influence on the lives of future leaders, to help shape the progress of the South. During his term as president of Wake Forest, he was to do just that.

Contributions to Culture

The honor of being inaugurated president of a college would seem to many people the crowning point of a career; certainly the responsibilities and duties of a college president would provide full-time employment for most men. But for Poteat, the opposite seemed true. His new position not only increased his influence but also aided in broadening his field of interests and affording him many more opportunities to serve.

His work at Wake Forest and in the state of North Carolina, from the time he became president of the college in 1905 until the evolution controversy demanded the major portion of his time in the 1920's, could be summarized in one word—culture. According to his own comprehensive definition of the term, this was indeed a large contribution, for to Poteat culture included "what biology would call health, what psychology would call sanity, what ethics would call sympathy, and what religion would call holiness." He often included the subject of culture in his lectures, especially to young people. He said, "It is the sum of the elements of the higher life, and nothing else is to be compared with it for building up a complete human life, for beauty, for service, and for efficiency."[1] These were not empty words because the Wake Forest president was active in many areas of social and cultural concern. He was interested in Baptist activities in the local church, as well as in state and regional organizations. He became a leader in several social service organizations that promoted such things as prison reform, regulation of child labor, better treatment of the insane, and co-operation between the races. North Carolinians often sought Poteat's leadership because of his personal ability and because of his position as president of Wake Forest.

On the other hand, Poteat's acceptance of the Wake Forest presidency also increased his vulnerability to criticism, especially from conservative Baptists. Some who did not understand his scientific ideas feared that his leadership might cause Baptist boys to stray from the folds of orthodoxy. Although active opposition to Poteat personally did not materialize until the 1920's when the fundamentalist movement reached its height, the movement had already begun to grow at the turn of the century.

In the late 1880's, the Serial Science Society had prepared the way by issuing monthly tracts using "Natural Facts in Vindication of Bible Truth."[2] Bible conferences held at Niagara Falls, New York, had strengthened the religious conservatism of many people. Following the turn of the century, new figures and new associations carried on the controversy. In 1902, George McCready Price produced a work rejecting evolution and declaring the deluge to be the cause of geological formations. Price was an outstanding fundamentalist, but his qualifications as a geologist left much to be desired. Poteat told an associate, "Forgive me if I warn you against a book by a man named Price, upon whom the opponents of the doctrine of evolu-

tion appear to rely with implicit confidence. It is called
the *New Geology*, but I think a better name for it would be
Catastrophism Redivivus."[3]

Few fundamentalists went so far as Price in attempting to discredit evolution, but many were nevertheless active. In 1902 arch-conservatives founded the Bible League
of North America "to meet and counteract the *Current
Destructive teachings* concerning the truthfulness, integrity, and inspiration of the Bible as the word of God." In
like manner, the Moody Bible Institute and the Bible Institute of Los Angeles stood squarely for the old faith
against the new. Expositions on the subject extended beyond theological circles, for in 1909 *Cosmopolitan*, in an
article entitled "Blasting at the Rock of Ages," gave proof
of alarm at the trend in religious thinking.[4]

There is evidence that some industrialists encouraged
fundamentalism. It is true that fundamentalists tended to
oppose progressive ideas in politics and economics as well
as in theology. George M. Price declared, "When Christ
himself was here, though surrounded by crying abuses,
oppression, and tyranny, he attempted no civil reforms;
nor has he left his church any commission to purify the
governments of earth."[5] Kirsopp Lake, a Harvard theo-
logian, believed that large financial interests would support the fundamentalists because they favored maintaining
the *status quo* in politics and economics as well as in
theology.[6]

Confirmation of the fact that some industrialists opposed evolution appeared in the *Manufacturers' Record*
in 1923. An editorial writer stated that when people acted
on the assumption that there was neither divine purpose in
the universe nor divine laws that must be followed, life
became merely a brutal struggle for existence. The writer
continued, "Evolution has well-nigh wrecked every land
that has adopted it."[7]

There is some indication that big business interests
helped to finance the fundamentalist movement. Milton

and Lyman Stewart, California oil millionaires, in 1910 donated money for the publication of ten small pamphlets known as *The Fundamentals*. These pamphlets were to be sent, insofar as possible, free of charge to every pastor, evangelist, missionary, theological student, Sunday school superintendent, and Y.M.C.A. and Y.W.C.A. secretary in the English-speaking world. The Stewarts gained the support of many able exponents of orthodoxy from the United States, Canada, England, Ireland, and Germany, including George F. Wright and Melvin G. Kyle, archaeologists and founders of the Bible League of North America; lawyer Philip Mauro; James M. Gray, dean of Moody Bible Institute; Edgar Young Mullins of the Southern Baptist Convention; and Amzi Clarence Dixon who had refused the presidency of Wake Forest in 1882.

The ideas upon which most fundamentalists agreed were expressed in the pamphlets sponsored by the Stewart brothers. Many essays in *The Fundamentals* condemned higher criticism and Darwinism, but the primary importance of the work as a whole lay in its doctrinal exposition. The series proclaimed the "Five Points" that were to become the *sine qua non* of fundamentalism: the infallibility of the Bible, Christ's virgin birth, His substitutionary atonement, the resurrection, and the second coming. The conservatives' creed was thereby reduced to clear essentials. These pamphlets were influential in the formative stages of the fundamentalist movement. Later opponents were to use ideas expressed in these pamphlets in attempts to discredit Poteat.[8]

The college president's position was in jeopardy partly because he continued to teach a class in biology even after assuming administrative duties. He had never attempted to hide the fact that he taught evolution, as his published articles indicate. In 1893 he had written an article for the journal *Science* on "The Effect on the College Curriculum of the Introduction of the Natural Sciences." The battle for recognition of the natural sciences in colleges had been

won, he said, but the teaching of science should extend to
the public schools and academies as well. Poteat noted
that in North Carolina only Trinity, Guilford, and Wake
Forest required science credits for entrance, and he suggested that other institutions do the same. Realizing that
there was some religious opposition to evolution, Poteat
said that the adverse reaction was melting away as the
limitations and real bearing of scientific inquiry became
known.[9] Again, in an article for the *Popular Science
Monthly* in 1901, he had expressed without public opposition his belief in evolution. He advanced the thesis that
evolution was not original with Darwin or even with the
nineteenth century. Poteat cited passages from *De Rerum
Natura* to show that Lucretius accepted evolution.[10] Finally, Poteat's book, *Laboratory and Pulpit*, left no doubt
about his position.

In the first decade of the twentieth century, the fact
that Poteat could express his ideas on evolution without
stirring up a flood of criticism from the conservatives perhaps indicated that they were not yet ready to take decisive
action. In addition, other factors that tended to offset any
opposition were his exemplary Christian life and his contributions to the social progress of North Carolina. Poteat was one of the first southerners to recognize the difficult social problems of the twentieth-century South and
to make an attempt to do something about them. Here
again, his role was that of interpreting progress by bringing others into contact with certain humanitarian efforts
that were taking shape at the time and that would have
come within the scope of Poteat's definition of culture.

As a college president, he came naturally to leadership
in the field of education. At Wake Forest he sought to
implement his ideas of what a good education should in-
clude. Although academic studies were very important,
Poteat placed more value on the less formal part of the
learning process. To the graduating class of 1908 he said,
"The main question about you now is, not what you know,

but how you feel.'' Even though the young men might forget certain facts they had learned, the cultural influence
of their college years would remain with them. ''You
will not lose the outlook on life which you have acquired
here, your inspirations, or your moral and spiritual al-
liances, and these be the great things, the determining
things in life,'' Poteat said.[11] To aid the students in their
cultural development, he shared his love of great literature.
Having acted as curator of the college library from 1886
to 1901, he had a large part in expanding that collection.
A friend commented, ''It is safe to say that there was not
a year from 1879 to 1938 in which he did not make gifts of
books; to these were added after his death in accord with
his desire more than seven hundred volumes.''[12]

Certainly there was not a year during that period when
he did not contribute to the growth and development of
the college in other ways as well. Under the president's
leadership, the number of students more than doubled,
and the college endowment increased from little more than
$200,000 to nearly $3,000,000. The value of the physical
plant also more than doubled with the addition of Gore
Athletic Field, Hunter Hall, the Lea Laboratory Extension, Bostwick Hall, a heating plant, professors' houses,
and the acquisition of some additional land. Poteat also
attempted to raise the academic standards of the college.
Beginning in 1906, the administration cited definite entrance requirements, a minimum of fourteen units with
twelve units prescribed. However, it was still possible for
students to enter with some deficiencies to be made up at
the college.[13]

The president made an active contribution to the religious life of the college and the town. Probably no other
person ever attended as many services of the Wake Forest
Baptist Church as did William Louis Poteat. Unless he
was out of town or too ill to come, he was at all the preaching services, prayer meetings, and special services. For
nearly all the years of his career at Wake Forest, he taught

Sunday school classes that were interesting and responsive. In many other services he also had a part, and he frequently led the singing or made the announcements.

The Poteat family naturally came into leadership in the song services. Emma sang a rich alto in the choir, while her husband contributed a strong baritone. Often he stood at the front of the church by the little reed organ and led the congregation in singing old Baptist hymns. His favorite was "The Crowning Day Is Coming." He also belonged to a quartet whose services were in demand all over the state. Professor Darius Eatman of the Education Department, who had studied music, sang second tenor; Professor James L. Lake sang the first tenor; Poteat, the first bass; while Charles E. Brewer of Wake Forest supplied the second bass. Hubert Poteat acted as church organist after 1900, a decided honor for a boy of fourteen. Later he also directed the choir. While Hubert was in New York working for a doctorate in classics at Columbia University, he served as assistant organist for the university, as member of the choir of the Brick Presbyterian Church, and later as bass soloist in the Church of the Intercession. Louie took over the organ and the choir leadership at home for a time during her brother's absence from 1908 to 1912.[14]

Dr. Poteat emphasized the importance of the chapel services at the college, where he often spoke and constantly presented an example to the students and faculty by his own attendance. Being present at chapel was compulsory for students, but the faculty members sometimes failed to make an appearance. In 1910, the *Wake Forest Student* commented on the situation under the heading "Faculty Discipline Department." Stating the premise, "What is sauce for the goose is sauce for the gander," the magazine proceeded to reprimand errant faculty members for their absences. Student monitors supplied attendance statistics for the preceeding month, noting that several professors had been absent as many as twelve times. The magazine continued, "As everybody who has ever heard Dr. Poteat make a speech in chapel knows, this is a Christian college, and therefore it behooves everyone connected with it to be most punctual in attendance upon religious exercises." The presumptuous young editors then facetiously demanded that all faculty members report to the publications office to account for their absences.[15]

While the spiritual development of the students was tremendously important, Poteat realized that physical development was also necessary. During his administration, the college developed a strong athletic program. In 1895, the trustees had discontinued football because of the large number of injuries. At that time, before the days of shoulder pads and other protective equipment, it was indeed a rough sport. Nevertheless, when high schools started teams and Wake Forest began losing prospective students who wanted to play, the trustees had a change of heart and reinstated intercollegiate football in 1908. After 1904, the college had a full-time director of athletics, J. Richard Crozier, who introduced intercollegiate basketball in the state. The Wake Forest tennis team was perhaps the most successful athletic group on campus. In 1907 E. B. Earnshaw and Hubert Poteat captured the southern intercollegiate tennis championship for doubles, and Hubert became the singles champion.

Wake Forest also had a baseball team coached by Crozier, but the annual faculty-senior game was the highlight of the season. In 1910 there were nearly two hundred spectators to see the seniors win seventeen to eight. The *Student* reported, "With plenty of runs and hard batting, not to speak of numberless errors, the game was full of interest from beginning to end." Professor J. Henry Highsmith did a fine job on the mound, while Dr. Charles E. Brewer held first base for the faculty. "Dr. Poteat, who started out playing right field, could not locate the sphere while at bat, and was retired to the bench, giving place to Dr. Paschal."[16]

How Poteat found time to participate in such college activities while carrying out his duties as biology professor, president, churchman, author, and lecturer was amazing to all. He was constantly called upon to address churches, schools, Baptist associations, and various other organizations. During a one-month period in the fall of 1913, he spoke to the Mt. Zion, Roanoke, South Fork, Raleigh, and Robeson Baptist associations. He addressed delegates to a Y.M.C.A. conference Sunday morning, October 6, at the Memorial Methodist Church in Durham and spoke in the same city again that evening at the First Baptist Church. Another Y.M.C.A. engagement took him to Knoxville, Tennessee.[17]

Of course, Poteat was often called upon to speak at Wake Forest. Perhaps the only person on campus who could rival his popularity as a lecturer was "Dr." Tom Jeffries. Son of slave parents, Tom had worked as a tenant farmer and day laborer until he came to work at Wake Forest in 1884. For the next forty-three years, until his death, he was an institution at the college. Of medium size, strong and wiry, no amount of work seemed to tire him. He could keep in mind instructions for a month or a season, would do everything at the appointed hour and ring the bell at the proper minute. Of unusual intelligence, he was obliging but never obsequious or servile. No one ever thought him other than a beloved, respected friend with a keen sense of humor. At any college function when speeches were included, "Dr." Tom, dressed up in his cutaway, was almost sure to be on the program. He was a master of homespun philosophy and delighted in using long words, whose pronunciation he had picked up from his academic compatriots. Sometimes, however, he failed to grasp the meaning of the words, with hilarious results. At a watermelon cutting during one summer school session, "Dr." Tom was telling some young lady guests from Meredith and Saint Mary's about the fine qualities of Wake Forest boys. "I jus' wan to admin' de young ladies here dat any of you dat gets a Wake Fores' boy sho' will get a prolific enterprise,'' he declared.

Tom's wit was quick, and the college boys could tease him at their own risk. One fall as Tom was burning some grass, an uninitiated freshman remarked, ''It is almost as black as you are, Tom.''

''Yassir, yassir, and next spring it's be mos as green as you is,'' the ''Doctor'' replied.

Tom Jeffries was a respected member of the community. He owned his own home for the last twenty-five years of his life and owed no man. By frugal planning he managed to educate his children. Tom said that he did his ''mostest to gain frien's stid of foes by tendin' to my own business.'' He said he trusted in the Lord and ''used all my exertions to make people like me so dat when dey leaves and meets me later on, dey looks as if dey is glad to see me and greets me as if I was the President of Wake Fores' College.''[18]

Certainly Poteat accorded Tom this kind of respect, for the college president, without prejudice, was sincerely concerned for the happiness and well-being of his fellow man. His first concern was for the development of the college over which he presided, but he was also interested in the social and cultural development of the state in which he lived. In the decade from 1910 to 1920, North Carolinians began to realize more keenly the desperate need for social reform within the state, and Poteat naturally became a leader in this reform—though, of course, he could not have succeeded alone.

Seeds of concern had been planted in the early 1900's by Edwin A. Alderman, Charles B. Aycock, and Charles D. McIver in the statewide crusade for better education. In 1913, interested citizens led by Clarence Poe (editor of the *Progressive Farmer*), Louis B. McBrayer (director of the eastern North Carolina tubercular sanitorium), James Yadkin Joyner (superintendent of public instruction), the Reverend M. L. Kesler (director of the Thomasville Orphanage), and others formed the North Carolina Conference for Social Service to study and to improve the social, civic, and economic conditions in the state. The aim of the organization as stated in the constitution was "To have the population of the State the best equipped of any in the Union, and to insure here and now an environment of physical, mental, and moral healthfulness that will prevent human waste and make for the fullest development of every individual within our borders...." The methods of the organization would be to investigate conditions, to awaken the people through meetings, addresses, and public documents, and to secure the remedies through influence on organized bodies of citizens such as religious denominations and the legislature. At the first meeting in Raleigh on February 11 and 12, 1913, there were four or five hundred people present. Clarence Poe presided, and William Louis Poteat spoke on "The Correlation of Social Forces." He discussed the roles of the home, school, press, and institutions of religion and government is social progress. The *Biblical Recorder* reported, "It was a most adequate and appropriate address, introducing and covering the spirit and purposes of the Conference."

The Baptist newspaper regarded this meeting as one of the most significant ever held in North Carolina. "It means that some of the alertest minds in the commonwealth are going to study intelligently its social conditions; that many of our best citizens are going to project their personal influence and enlist others in the work of social betterment...." With public opinion aroused and directed to neglected but needed reforms, surely the necessary legislation could be secured. "These workers are the heralds of a better day," declared the *Recorder*.[19]

The Baptist denomination in North Carolina also promoted awareness of social problems. Dr. Poteat was chairman of a committee to investigate social conditions which reported to the Baptist State Convention meeting at Goldsboro in December, 1912. The committee report stated the theme of Poteat's ideas on social problems—that progress of society must be achieved through the betterment of individuals. The report went on to explain that the local church was responsible for the regeneration of the men and women about it and thus for the regeneration of society. Poteat later stated more graphically his own belief when he said, "The church must protest against traffic in all racial poisons, against commercialized vice, against the layer of filth spread over all life by an irresponsible section of the press... against the ignorance and inhumanity of much prison discipline...."[20]

In 1909 the superintendent of the state prison reported that the chain gang policy of the state was "as defective and as full of possibilities for wrongdoing, cruelty and inhumanity as was the old convict-lease system."[21] Four years later Poteat headed a committee of the Board of Missions of the Baptist State Convention on destitution in prisons. This committee urged that local pastors visit prisons and county homes, bring spiritual comfort to the inmates, and try to promote better treatment for them.[22]

The sentiment for social betterment grew in North Carolina. The most outstanding citizens of the state supported the Conference for Social Service. Of the 1914 meeting, Governor Locke Craig stated, "I doubt whether any meeting has been held in North Carolina with such a comprehensive and constructive program for the general upbuilding of the state and its people." He urged every patriotic North Carolinian to attend the conference. The second session met in Raleigh on February 13, 14, and 15, 1914, with the theme, "North Carolina Forward for Human Betterment and a Richer Civilization." Poteat spoke to the group on "The Church and Social Service."[23]

In 1915 child labor legislation was an outstanding political topic. Poteat took a leading part in promoting reform by speaking in Raleigh on February 3, 1915, before a Joint Committee on Manufactures of the Senate and House. Poteat tried to smooth out the differences between

the representatives of the manufacturers and the re-
formers. He suggested prohibition of factory labor for
children under fourteen, an eight-hour limit for those under
eighteen, and no night or hazardous employment. The
proposal was not successful at that time, but when Poteat
became president of the North Carolina Conference for
Social Service in 1919, he and others went back to the legislature and continued fighting for the next decade until
they were finally successful.[24]

The conference was influential in promoting progress
in many areas of social concern. However, other forces
were also at work. One of the most outstanding reform
organizations was the North Carolina Society for Mental
Hygiene. Founded December 4, 1913, at Raleigh, the aims
of the organization were the conservation of mental health
and the attempt to raise standards of care for those suffering from mental disease or those in danger of developing
nervous or mental disorders. W. A. Erwin was the first
president of the society, while Poteat served on the board
of directors along with W. P. Few, who was president of
Trinity College, Bishop John C. Kilgo, Senator Furnifold
M. Simmons, and others. During its first year, the society
distributed pamphlets and leaflets such as ''Principles of
Mental Hygiene Applied to the Management of Children
Predisposed to Nervousness,'' and ''Hospital Treatment
or Almshouse Care or Confinement in Jail for the Mentally
Sick.''[25]

Early in 1915 *The News and Observer* declared, ''Mental hygiene is to become a live issue in North Carolina and
the North Carolina Society is pressing the subject to the
front....'' On January 9 the society met in the House of
Representatives with quite a number of the legislators
present to hear Dr. William A. White, Superintendent of
the Government Hospital for Insane at Washington, D.C.,
and Dr. W. L. Poteat. White spoke on the need for better
equipment and hospitals while Poteat concentrated on the
public attitude towards insanity. Poteat firmly believed

that all the legislation in the world would do no good unless the public attitude was fair and just. "And do not many among us ..." he said, "still regard the epileptic and insane with a degree of suspicious awe akin to the medieval atittude?" Recalling the horror of committing the victim of some brain disorder to the neglect of the common jail, he asked, "And how are we to account for the public indifference reflected in the inadequate provision for the care of the insane, except on the view that we are in need of several more degrees of enlightenment and humanity?"[26]

Poteat and other members of the society worked hard to bring about such enlightenment. In 1916 the organization began an active campaign in eastern North Carolina under the direction of A. S. Pendleton, fieldworker for the society. At the 1917 meeting Dr. Pendleton reported that he had visited nineteen counties and contacted approximately 6,800 people. He found that those he had spoken to seemed interested in the problem. At the same meeting W. A. Erwin resigned and Poteat was unanimously elected president of the group. Poteat said, "In spite of considerations which I think I might make impressive, I find myself unable to decline the service with which you honor me." He did claim one qualification for the office—"the earnest wish to serve the State in preserving to her all her children in the fullness of their powers, in fighting whatever tends to destroy or mar them." He further declared that he would "save her from the shame of neglecting them, or of caring for them on a policy which is either ignorant or niggardly."

Poteat delivered his presidential address, "The Nature and Prevalence of Insanity and Its Treatment by Diversional Therapy," at a meeting held in the House of Representatives and open to the public. He pointed out that statistics showed that insanity was increasing and that some cases which could be cured if treated in time became hopeless because of lack of proper care. "It is at once horrible and shameful," he said, "that North Carolinians with crippled minds lie in common jails under the care of

ignorant and sometimes brutal men, awaiting a jury's decision on their obscure condition, deepening in the mean-
time the defects and diminishing the chance of recovery.''
He lamented the fact that many were turned away at hospitals, and those who gained admittance were usually past
help. Constructively, Poteat suggested provision for diversional therapy at the state hospital, such as a machine
shop and a garden for the use of the patients. ''With the
greatest deference,'' he said, ''I beg to suggest to the
General Assembly that, in furnishing forth our Lady of
the Commonwealth, the first concern should be to provide a
warm dress and good low heeled shoes. Ribbons and gold
slippers can wait.''[27]

Most suggestions of the Mental Hygiene Society were
readily acceptable to North Carolinians. One policy, however, did meet with some opposition. Poteat believed that
a low level of mentality was the chief cause of delinquency
and that heredity often determined the level of intelligence.
He pointed out that people with a low mental capacity
usually reproduced at an alarming rate. He stated, ''The
formal processes of education will do little in themselves
to arrest the decline which appears to be the possible fate
of the most complex and highly developed civilization in all
of history.'' Poteat felt that a social emergency might
arise if people with hereditary degeneracy were allowed to
reproduce. He included the feebleminded, the insane, the
epileptic, the inebriate, the congenitally defective of any
type, and the victim of chronic contagious disease. Speaking as an evolutionist, Poteat said, ''Civilization ... is
saving these individuals. Under barbaric conditions they
would be eliminated by the law of natural selection. It is
right to save them, but it is perilous to allow them parent-
hood.'' The Wake Forest president emphasized the need
of race improvement through restrictive mating to eliminate the obviously unfit. ''We standardize everything
from colleges to motor cars ...'' he declared, ''but there
appears to have been but little improvement of the human

stock within the historic period." He visualized a standard man who would "be well born, well conditioned, but also born from above." Thus, spiritual regeneration was definitely a part of his ideal. In many other instances he emphasized this point, insisting that mere legislation could not make a good society out of bad people and that the road to social improvement lay through the active Christian service of individuals. However, he did feel that some physical improvement would ensue if the state would deny marriage licenses to unfit persons unless they would agree to sterilization. Public opinion seemed generally in agreement, but there was some opposition. The Raleigh *Times* criticized Poteat's ideas, raising the question of who could decide whether fellow human beings were fit or unfit to reproduce. The paper pointed out that there was some mental disease in the family of Abraham Lincoln, and if ideas such as Poteat's had been strictly enforced, Lincoln might never have lived.[28]

Despite this type of criticism, the North Carolina Society for Mental Hygiene was effective in bringing the state to an awareness of the problems of insanity. Through influence on public opinion, Poteat and others prepared the way for legislative reform. One of the first steps applied to wards of the state. In the county homes where feeble-minded people often resided, it was sometimes impossible to isolate the sexes and likewise impossible to educate them in moral values. This not only presented an immediate problem, but frequently children born in county homes became wards of the state like their parents and contributed to establishing a cycle of degeneracy at public expense. Therefore, in 1919, the Mental Hygiene Society secured the passage of an "act to benefit the moral, mental, or physical conditions of the inmates of penal and charitable institutions." This act was to permit the medical staff of such an institution to perform surgery if the operation would be for the improvement of the mental, moral, or physical condition of the inmate. The governor and the secretary of the State Board of Health had to grant authorization for such operations. Later, in order to obtain a marriage license, a man had to certify freedom from venereal disease, tuberculosis, and insanity, while women were tested for tuberculosis and insanity. These reforms were not as comprehensive as Poteat would have recommended, but they showed a growing public consciousness of the problems of mental hygiene and a step in the direction of progress.[29]

Another area of reform in which Poteat played an important part concerned railroad rates. Both before and after 1900, there was strong anti-railroad sentiment in North Carolina and other states. People accused the railroads of excessive rates, poor service, dodging taxes, stock watering, pooling, discrimination through rebates, and even influencing judges. The North Carolina railroads suffered because of competition from Virginia lines that enjoyed a lower rate scale as set by the Interstate Commerce Commission. The Virginia rate was lower because many Virginia railroads had to compete with waterways. Another advantage of the Virginia companies was increased business because of an east-west trunk line connecting western areas with the port of Norfolk. However, there was tremendous pressure from commercial and industrial interests to secure rate reduction in North Carolina. In 1907, at the insistence of Governor Robert B. Glenn, the General Assembly reduced by law the intrastate passenger rate to 2.25¢ per mile. The Southern Railroad defied the regulatory statute on grounds that the rate reductions would deprive the company of its property without due process of law. Railroad representatives declared that interstate commerce was impaired because the rates affected interstate business. After 1907 the courts upheld the defiance of the railroads; nevertheless, the railroads agreed to a compromise rate of 2.5¢.[30]

At its special session in 1913, the General Assembly passed another act fixing freight rates within the state.

In spite of his pressing duties, Dr. Poteat found time to read

Julia McNeill Poteat with her sons, William Louis who was President
of Wake Forest College and Edwin McNeill who was President of
Furman University

The act provided that if any of the common carriers affected by the act should find the rates unreasonable or confiscatory, they could report to a special commission appointed by the governor to investigate the situation. Governor Locke Craig appointed Michael H. Justice, William L. Poteat, and A. A. Thompson to serve on the special freight rates commission. The *Wake Forest Student* reported Poteat's appointment and quoted *The News and Observer* as calling Dr. Poteat one of the foremost scholars and thinkers of the generation. ''He is broad, comprehensive and patriotic.... He is of that type of college man who is now President of the United States, who has convinced the world that he is not out of place.''[31]

The freight rates work proved very time-consuming even though the commission did not attempt to fix rates on lines under seventy-five miles in length. Having announced that its policy would be to welcome light from any quarter, the commission received testimony in great detail from the principal public carriers, from boards of trade, from various industrial associations, and from individuals. The commission held the first two hearings in Raleigh from January 12 to January 22, and from April 7 to April 14, 1914. From July 7 to July 16, the commission heard testimony in Asheville. The executive sessions of the committee began on July 20, and the final report was complete by August 13. Included in the report was a detailed schedule of rates that seemed acceptable to the majority of those concerned. The work of the commission did not solve all the railroad problems of the state, but it was one step in the direction of fair practices by both the railroads and the manufacturers.[32]

Another problem of concern to North Carolinians was prohibition of alcoholic beverages. The Democratic leaders, after 1900, allied the state government with churches, temperance societies, and women's organizations in a fight against liquor as a social evil related to the problems of race relations, rural life, universal education, industrial ef-

ficiency, morality, and law enforcement. The Anti-Saloon
League, in which Poteat was active, was a leading force in
bringing prohibition to North Carolina in 1909. After that,
however, the problem of alcohol persisted because there
was nothing to stop importation of liquor from other states.
In 1915 Poteat served on a committee of the Baptist State
Convention appointed to encourage passage of an act to
make it illegal to deliver or receive alcoholic beverages at
any point in the state. Poteat wrote articles for the *Biblical Recorder* and *The News and Observer* urging passage
of such a law. He also pointed out that the Baptist State
Convention represented 250,000 citizens. Surely this had
some influence on the General Assembly which did pass a
law forbidding importation of liquor in quantities of more
than one quart.[33]

The Anti-Saloon League remained active, and Poteat
often spoke at annual conventions. With the possibility of
national prohibition increasingly evident, the convention
of 1917 was an outstanding meeting. William Jennings
Bryan, former secretary of state and candidate for president, came to Raleigh to address the gathering. Despite
the cold and sleet, the First Baptist Church was full and
many were standing. Bryan advocated women's suffrage,
the initiative, and the referendum, but he told his audience
that prohibition was the paramount political question of
the day. The people became so enthusiastic as his speech
progressed that they began clapping in the church. After
severe reprimands from the pastor and Bryan, they resorted to a hearty chorus of "Amens." Poteat also addressed the 1917 convention. He expressed encouragement
with the victories of prohibitionists but declared, "We are
looking ahead.... We shall not be content until the part-
nership of the government with the mother of poverty and
crime is dissolved for good and all."[34]

From 1919 to 1923, Poteat served as president of the
North Carolina Anti-Saloon League. Even though the
eighteenth amendment prohibiting alcohol was in effect,

there was still work to do in securing enforcement of the laws. Poteat remained active in the organization throughout the 1920's, but his most effective leadership came in the 1930's pending the repeal of the eighteenth amendment. During the time he was president of the Anti-Saloon League, prohibition problems were not as demanding as problems that involved the war effort and the beginning of the evolution controversy.

World War I demanded the full attention and energies of the American people. Although Poteat had earlier expressed strong opposition to war, he did his best to contribute to the war effort. In 1914 he had aided in the movement to send help to Belgium, which had been invaded by the Germans; and after the United States entered the war in April of 1917, he spoke at Liberty Loan rallies and other patriotic gatherings.[35]

Wake Forest College continued to function despite the fact that many students left school to join the armed forces. In September of 1917, only 361 students enrolled, about 200 fewer than the administration would normally have expected. Finances were strained because many students who returned were ministerial candidates who did not pay tuition. President Woodrow Wilson advised the young men to stay in school to equip themselves better for future service, and he set up the Student Army Training Corps to aid them in doing so. Some Baptists objected to military training at Wake Forest, but Poteat declared, "I cannot fancy a book of doom big enough to record the guilt of the men who precipitated this atrocious war. But American participation for the defense of her national ideals and the ordered life of the world is as righteous as it is splendid." Many of the college trustees felt that military training had no place in a denominational college in peacetime, but they finally accepted the program for the duration of the war. Strident bugle calls replaced the mellow tones of the college bell while students hiked, dug trenches, and took their turns on the kitchen police. A faculty member could

no longer muse and dream as he walked along campus
paths for he met a student salute at every turn. Nevertheless, assurance that they would receive salaries was sufficient compensation for the inconveniences imposed by the
military. The government paid the tuition and living ex-
penses of all students enrolled in the S.A.T.C., and in September of 1918, Wake Forest had a greater number of first
year students than ever before. There might have been even
more except for the influenza epidemic that raged through
the country at that time. After about seven weeks of
classes, the war ended and with it military training at the
college. The trustees had never really liked the idea, and
when the government no longer supplied tuition money,
they withdrew support of military training.[36]

In an effort to meet the problems involved with the cutting down of war industries and the return to a civilian
economy, Poteat served on the North Carolina Reconstruction Commission. Created by the General Assembly
of 1919, this commission was principally an advisory
body, which contributed such suggestions as hard work,
economy, faith in fellow citizens, and the use of wood
for fuel to combat the coal shortage. The group also
recommended government aid in transporting fertilizer to
farmers and suspension of immigration for five years to
give the country time to "put its house in order."[37]

One of the foremost problems arising from the war
could not be solved by mere suggestions. Racial tension,
which had greatly diminished during the war years, burst
out again, and many Negro soldiers who had fought for
their country in Europe were ready to fight for a fair
chance at home. There were race riots in some cities with
casualties on both sides. Poteat was ready to join forces
with other leaders to seek progress for the Negro. As the
occasion arose for him to become a leader in this area, perhaps his mind returned to Forest Home plantation and
his boyhood friend, Nat. The Negro boy had taken full
advantage of the educational opportunities offered him by

the Poteats, and by 1908 he had a good job with the national government in Washington. He did not forget his benefactors and wrote a moving poem in memory of James Poteat called "The Black Sheep." He explained that every family must have a "black sheep" and James Poteat worried about his children.

> But trouble filled that father's heart which would
>   not roll away,
> For of the thought was he possessed that one
>   *must* go astray.
> In every home, it mattered not how much might
>   parents weep,
> That home could not remove the blot of raising
>   one black sheep.
>
> So presently that good old man began to rumi-
>   nate
> As how 'twere best that he should plan to miss
>   so sad a fate.
> At length within his anxious mind that thought
>   began to creep
> That he adopt, if he could find, somewhere a
>   real black sheep.
>
> A colored youth dwelt on the place, an orphan,
>   tho' supplied
> With aunts and uncles, who, with grace, would
>   for his wants provide.
> The good man said—this urchin he would in
>   in his household keep
> And rear him tenderly to be the family's black
>   sheep.

Nat said that the influence of the Poteat family proved his greatest boon and that James Poteat had no cause to worry about a black sheep who would bring disgrace, "For he had reared one black of face but white his deeds would

show." As for himself, he still felt a part of the family
for he said:

> The Black sheep's hand has penned these lines
>   that he may doubly prove
> Unto that flock and other minds how deep is
>   set his love.
> The storm of racial hate may rise and waves
>   of distrust sweep the deck
> Unsevered are the ties that bind this flock of
>   sheep.[38]

This relationship in his background surely must have
influenced William Louis Poteat to take a leading role in
the first attempts for interracial co-operation. Poteat was
unusual in this, for Southern Baptists, with a few exceptions, accepted and defended the racial caste system. In
general, the Southern Baptist press seemed satisfied with
the racial *status quo*. However, following World War I,
Poteat and others realized a need for improvement and
took appropriate action.[39]

Early in 1919, Dr. Will Winton Alexander, a Y.M.C.A.
leader, along with John J. Eagen and M. Ashby Jones,
decided to do something constructive to avoid bloodshed
and to increase understanding. Dr. Alexander secured
$75,000 from the War Work Council of the Y.M.C.A. to
start a co-operative movement and people from all sections of the country were invited to meet in Atlanta,
Georgia. The group formed the Commission on Interracial Co-operation and issued a statement declaring, "We,
a group of Christians ... irrespective of race or class distinctions ... would call the people of our own beloved
community to *a calm consideration of our situation before
extremists are allowed to create a condition where reason
is impossible. ...*" At the request of the commission, the
Rt. Rev. Mr. Theodore D. Bratton, Bishop of Mississippi,
Dr. W. L. Poteat, and Dr. R. E. Blackwell, president of
Randolph-Macon College, issued invitations to representa-

tive clergymen of the Protestant denominations in the South to attend a conference on interracial co-operation at Blue Ridge, North Carolina, in August of 1920.[40]

The Commission on Interracial Co-operation was the first organization of its kind founded and maintained principally by southerners. It was, consequently, a conservative group. The members assembled at Blue Ridge issued a statement declaring absolute loyalty to the "best traditions and convictions of the South, and especially to the principle of racial integrity." They also affirmed that "the real responsibility for the salvation of inter-racial problems in the South rests directly upon the hearts and consciences of the Christian forces of our land." Because they realized that members of the Negro race often suffered grave injustices, they offered some constructive suggestions for improvement. The best method seemed to be local organizations made up of the recognized church leaders of both races which could establish communications and promote understanding. The commission further recommended that interested persons, through the pulpit, the religious press, denominational literature, and in every possible way, should oppose mob violence and lynching. Ministers and laymen were advised to keep in touch with the administration of justice in local courts and to form legal aid societies to assist accused Negroes in getting fair trials.[41]

The commission had its national headquarters in Atlanta with branches in Oakdale, Tennessee, in Louisville, Kentucky, and in Richmond, Virginia. The organization had no creed, no final goals. Its philosophy was not to solve the race question but to take the next step toward justice and goodwill through informative techniques and personal contacts.[42]

Poteat was chairman of the North Carolina Interracial Committee. Under his leadership members of both races met together to try to improve conditions in the state. Realizing the need for a fair allocation of tax provisions for

Negro schools, the committee pledged a willingness to co-operate through local and county boards of education in securing better education for Negroes. Poteat appointed a special committee to follow the progress of establishing a training school for delinquent Negro boys. The women's section of the organization recommended that the Board of Charities and Public Welfare form a Bureau of Social Work that would employ Negro women to work with women and girls of their own race.[43]

In North Carolina, the organization was mainly advisory, but even though tangible examples of activity were limited, it served a very useful purpose in promoting communication and in laying a foundation for racial understanding in North Carolina which in the future would be equaled by few other southern states. Poteat's contribution lay in using his influence and speaking ability against prejudice and in favor of co-operation, and he spoke often on the subject of race relations in various parts of the South. He also served as a member of the Commission on the Church and Race Relations of the Federal Council of the Churches of Christ in America.[44]

The New York Times cited Poteat as representative of "the Christian pity of eminent Southern churchmen for the lowly man and brother, helpless in the white man's land." The newspaper further commended the Commission on Interracial Co-operation for helping to prevent race riots, aiding the Negro population with parks and schools, and generally improving the social conditions of Negroes. The commission worked so intelligently and efficiently, said the *Times*, that what people in 1919 discussed as an impending social crisis passed quietly from the forefront of the national consciousness. As proof of progress, the paper compared the eighty-three lynchings in 1919 with only ten in 1929.[45]

The trend toward understanding continued until the Great Depression upset economic and social progress. At that time Poteat was again ready to step forward to leadership, and then he no longer had the heavy criticism of the anti-evolutionists to combat as he had in the early 1920's. From the time he became president of Wake Forest in 1905 until about 1920, Poteat took an active part in the social awakening taking place in North Carolina. Through service as state president of the Conference for Social Service, the Society for Mental Hygiene, the Anti-Saloon League, the Commission on Interracial Co-operation, and through activity on various social service committees of the Baptist denomination, Poteat had a formative influence on the most outstanding forces for social progress of his day. Certainly if culture was as he described it—health, sanity, sympathy, and holiness—he also made an outstanding contribution to the culture of his society. His interest in promoting culture continued throughout his life, but his participation in the various organizations of social progress necessarily diminished as it became imperative for him to turn his full energies to the support of freedom of teaching in North Carolina.

The Teacher and His Tormentors

In the years following World War I, severe disillusionment spread throughout the South. Before the war southern denominations had become increasingly identified with social causes, and their endorsements of the war to end war followed logically from previous reform commitments. But idealistic hopes remained unfulfilled as wars and rumors of wars continued in Europe, and at home the Harding scandals and big-time gangsterism shocked the nation.[1]

In 1920, for the first time, the national population was more urban than rural. The growing complexity of life caused a decrease in the amount of time people gave to religious pursuits. The coming of the automobile and the motion picture left the church less able to influence young people. Also there was a decline of strict parental discipline as more and more mothers left the home to enter business or industry. New recreational agencies took from the home some of its traditional features. Failure of strict religious codes to adjust to modern conditions produced a more individualistic type of morality, and practices that were once unacceptable were incorporated into daily life. Frankness in discussion of questions once unmentionable, freedom in social relations between sexes, shorter skirts, jazz music, and new dance steps caused conservatives to fear for the younger generation. With extension of the suffrage and greater freedom in occupations brought about by wartime necessity, the American woman was trying to clarify her new position.[2]

Problems of adjusting the role of the church and the ideas of established morality to new factors in society, as well as the increased rapidity of technological development, contributed to a sense of instability and insecurity. Scientific progress and Biblical higher criticism presented problems of intellectual and spiritual adjustment. People feared change, and the task of its interpretation in the 1920's provided for William Louis Poteat the greatest challenge of his life. As a scientist and denominational leader, he was especially suited to this interpretation.

The problem of adjustment was far from superficial, for many southerners saw in technology not progress but destruction of a way of life. They saw in higher criticism and the theory of evolution not an increase in the store of human knowledge but destruction of Biblical literalism that was the basis of their faith. Because they could not stem the tide of destruction on intellectual terms, they turned to emotionalism, emphasis on individual salvation, and crusades against liberals. Fundamentalism was not new in the 1920's, but its militant aspect was a product of postwar forces. Opposition was directed primarily against the teaching of evolution.

Many people were surprised at the agitation over the theory of evolution. In an article for the *Biblical Recorder*, Poteat expressed some amazement that a debate had arisen over a question that was settled in professional circles some thirty years previously—to the advantage of

Christianity. Of the agitators, Poteat said, "One wonders
where these excited gentlemen have been? Were they
asleep when the procession passed?"[3] Before World War
I, many important Protestant leaders in the United States
had either accepted Darwinism and modernism or had
turned their endeavors to more productive fields than that
of heresy hunting. Clergymen had thus progressed far
beyond their congregations in their thinking. The proponents of orthodoxy had always defended their faith with
determination, but until 1918 the fundamentalist movement
lacked the strength to become a major issue in American
life. Just after the war, however, with the acceleration of
change, instability, and insecurity, several fresh elements
were enough to precipitate the conflict.

When it was first discussed, evolution had fostered the
conviction that nothing could prevent the human race from
creating, slowly or rapidly, a good society free of evils, but
the catastrophe of the war contradicted the theory that
society was continually improving. Many people rejected
the optimism that evolution had once inspired and turned
instead to one of the five major points of the fundamentalist creed, the second coming. The propaganda of hatred,
useful to inspire the nation to greater wartime efforts,
produced during the ensuing years an unanticipated harvest of bitterness that prepared people for a crusade upon
unacceptable beliefs at home. The war had convinced
people that intolerance was justified when the nation was
fighting foreign enemies. In 1912 and 1913 the religious
conservatives attempted to overcome heretical tendencies
primarily by reasoned argument, but after 1918 some of
them sought forcibly to expel those who did not adhere to
their rigid creeds.[4] Violence in action and language became characteristic of the fundamentalists who welcomed
the opportunity to carry militancy into action. One zeal-
ous gentleman, Charles F. Bluske, challenged Poteat and
three other scientists to meet him in the boxing ring.
Bluske intended to knock out all four in two minutes,

"proving to the Public that Scientists are weak in mind and body."[5]

Before World War I, fundamentalism did not have this militant aspect and it could not be described as an active movement on an extensive scale. There were several fundamentalist organizations, such as the Bible League of North America, but they showed no intention of taking the offensive. In 1916 a small group of clergymen had organized the World's Christian Fundamentals Association in Montrose, Pennsylvania. According to William Bell Riley, one of the leaders of the organization, it was impossible to define fundamentalism to satisfy all interested parties, but in any adequate attempt, three major propositions were necessary. Fundamentalism included the Christian creed, the Christian character, and the Christian commission. Incorporated in the creed were the *"greater Christian doctrines,"* the inspiration of the scriptures, the Trinity, the virgin birth, original sin, atonement through Christ, the resurrection of all for reward or punishment, and the premillenial second coming.[6]

In 1919, at a convention held at the Moody Bible Institute in Chicago, the World's Christian Fundamentals Association did more than simply organize and make a statement of beliefs. The leaders determined to take the offensive, and they prescribed a definite plan of action to combat evolution and the acceptance of liberal theology known as modernism. The spokesmen of the association requested all present to purge their denominations of heretics and, if that proved impossible, to consider forming new churches. Among those who gave life to the movement were William Bell Riley, James M. Gray, dean of Moody Bible Institute, Amzi Clarence Dixon, one of the editors of *The Fundamentals*, and J. Frank Norris, Baptist minister and editor in Fort Worth, Texas, who was later to lead in attempts to oust William Louis Poteat from the presidency of Wake Forest College.

In the early 1900's, as a dynamic young writer, Norris

had created a sensation by his attacks upon gambling, and
he was partly responsible for the Texas race track law of
1910. In 1909 he encountered trouble when his church
burned under suspicious circumstances. In the ensuing
trial he was accused of arson, writing himself threatening
letters, and hiring a detective to shoot at him, all to win
public sympathy. The prosecution, however, could not
advance sufficient evidence to prove a case. Later he shot
a man but was acquitted on grounds of self defense. By
1925 Norris' crusades and tactics in the pulpit had made
his church in Fort Worth the largest Baptist church in the
world. It could boast a congregation of 8,000, a Sunday
school of 7,500, a nonprofessional choir of 600, and an
orchestra of forty instruments.[7]

Norris took the commission of the World's Christian
Fundamentals Association most seriously. Through his
newspaper, the *Searchlight*, he led in the attacks upon the
teaching of evolution. One of the principal objects of criticism was the teaching of William Louis Poteat of Wake
Forest College. Poteat's "heresy" probably came to the
attention of Norris through the efforts of Thomas Theodore Martin, an evangelist, who attacked Poteat in several
articles published in the *Western Recorder* of Louisville,
Kentucky, during February and March, 1920. In pamphlet
form, Martin sent the articles to virtually every Baptist
minister in North Carolina, many of whom looked to Poteat
for leadership. As president of a Baptist college, his influence was widely felt both in the denomination and in the
state as a whole through the graduates of the college. In
addition, Poteat made no attempt to conceal the fact that he
believed in and taught the theory of evolution. Thus, he
became a focal point for attacks by the ardent Fundamentalists. After Martin began the attack on Poteat, agitation against the teaching of evolution rapidly increased.
In the opinion of Nell Battle Lewis, editorialist for *The
News and Observer* of Raleigh, this was the beginning of
the anti-evolution agitation in the South. Later, in 1925,

as George N. Coad traveled over the South gathering information for the New York *World* on attempts to bar evolution from the schools by law, he found that most ministers and editors of the Southeast believed that the movement was actually caused by the agitation of certain Baptist evangelists and editors against Poteat.[8]

Although the underlying fears that produced fertile ground for controversy had much deeper causes, Martin's attack on Poteat was a precipitating factor. It marked the change in the nature of Fundamentalism from a conservative reaction to an organized movement ready to take the offensive. One reason that Poteat was a principal target was that throughout his career as president of Wake Forest he had continued to teach a class in freshman biology. Although many conservatives objected to the fact that the president of a Baptist college openly taught the theory of evolution, opposition from the students themselves never arose. This was significant because most Wake Forest boys at that time were from conservative rural homes. Few had been exposed to a broad variety of ideas, and for many, the viewpoints presented at college produced a rude jolt. This jolt was softened somewhat by the exemplary influence of Poteat's character. One alumnus recalled that as a student he felt that he might not understand evolution, but if Poteat could believe in it and still live the kind of Christian life he did, it must be all right.[9]

Poteat was one of the most distinguished men in North Carolina, but he remained in close touch with the students on the campus over which he presided. He spoke often at chapel services, and the door of his office was always open to the young men. The students respected him not only as a college president but as a friend. Imagine the surprise of the Wake Forest freshmen who heard upperclassmen singing heartily:

> Sure his head is bald and his eyes are blue,
> And he's a Dutchman through and through—

> Has anybody here seen Billy?
> Billy with the red necktie?[10]

There was no doubt that the song referred to the greatly admired "Dr. Billy," but how could it be applied to the august president, noted for his intellectual discussions of both scientific and religious subjects? The rowdy song certainly did not coincide with the descriptions of the man which the freshmen had heard before coming to Wake Forest. This paradox was typical of William Louis Poteat, for his words and actions were often surprising, often unexpected, and usually troubling.

In the classroom, Poteat was polite and even courtly, but his ability to make shattering observations kept his students always on the alert. To a rash and argumentative youth who cried out, "But I have a right to my opinion," Dr. Poteat replied blandly, "No man has any right to an opinion, Mr. Blank, until he has first made himself acquainted with the facts."[11] The teacher could afford to make such a statement because he was careful to survey the facts before drawing conclusions. Even when enemies wrote articles criticizing him, he read the critiques carefully to see if the criticisms were valid.[12]

Poteat was one of the first teachers in the South to use the critical method in the classroom. He instructed his biology students to maintain a spirit of open-mindedness. Dr. Billy said, "The word which best fits the lip of physicist, chemist, biologist, psychologist is *nescio*, I do not know."[13] As was true of most educated biologists, Poteat accepted the theory of evolution and taught it in his classes at Wake Forest. He defined the theory thus: "In most general terms, evolution is the doctrine that the present is the child of the past, whether we think of the physical universe as a whole or any member of it.... In short, the doctrine of descent with modification."[14] Because Poteat believed that evolution was simply God's means of creation, he endeavored to enable his students to see that the

Dr. Poteat with his grandson, Hubert McNeill Poteat, Jr., now a
surgeon in Smithfield, North Carolina

At eighty-one, Dr. Poteat had not lost his love of beauty and
his keen interest in nature

Christian religion and science were not contradictory. To the learned biologist, the invisible world was just as real as the visible. He remarked, "Science stands before the central mysteries of nature quite impotent with its apparatus of clock, footrule and balance. In all departments it has to say 'I do not know' when the crucial question is asked. This bankruptcy of science is the opportunity of faith."[15]

That Poteat was successful in enabling his students to reconcile religion and science is demonstrated by the fact that attacks on his unorthodoxy came not from men he had taught but from those who had merely heard that he taught evolution. Throughout the years of controversy, the Wake Forest alumni stood by Dr. Poteat, declaring that his teaching had not hurt their faith but had strengthened it. Unfortunately, many Fundamentalists could not believe that this was true and they determined to force Poteat's resignation.

The first assault came from Thomas Theodore Martin of Blue Mountain, Mississippi, in the *Western Recorder* articles of 1919 and 1920. Martin, an evangelist of some note, was a white-haired man, small of stature, with a fiery eye, a courteous address, and a profound admiration for Henry L. Mencken, the editor of the *American Mercury.* Martin did not agree with Mencken's point of view, because the New York editor was a severe critic of the Fundamentalists, but the Blue Mountain evangelist did admire Mencken's ability for acrid criticism. It is possible that Martin attempted to imitate the style of the noted journalist.

The evangelist wrote a book concerning the teaching of evolution called *Hell and the High Schools,* which earned for him the nickname of "Hell and the High Schools Martin." He admitted he deserved the designation but declared he would rather be known to the public as "The Blue Mountain Evangelist," for, he explained, "It's more general and the way issues crop up in evangelism these

days, it's poor policy to hitch yourself to something that
may be superceded by a bigger thing tomorrow.'' Heresy
hunting proved to be a lucrative business for Martin. A
contemporary exclaimed, ''Now there's a business, evangelism. . . . Look at old 'Hell and the high schools.' He
just tore through Mississippi and Tennessee with that
slogan about not teaching the young to think they sprang
from monkeys. A good few pennies he got himself, I'm
here to tell you.''[16]

In his *Western Recorder* article of January 22, 1920,
Martin criticized an address made by Poteat at Richmond,
Virginia, in 1900. He particularly objected to Poteat's
interpretation of the doctrine of the atonement. In the
Richmond address, Poteat had stated, ''The work of Jesus
in Reconciliation, therefore, must be concerned with the
change of man's attitude only.'' He explained that the
crucifixion revealed both the irrational and monstrous
character of sin and the love of God, and that this revelation contributed to a change in man's attitude. Thus,
rather than believing in atonement by faith in the vicarious
suffering of Christ, Poteat believed in the moral influence
of the crucifixion.[17] Many Baptists objected to this interpretation of the atonement. In his criticism, Martin quoted
passages from the Richmond address, and then quoted
scripture such as I Corinthians 15:3, ''Christ died for our
sins,'' to repudiate Poteat's position. Martin declared
that it must have been Poteat's noble qualities of personality that caused North Carolina Baptists to retain him as
president of Wake Forest, ''where his teachings can con-
taminate the young men of Wake Forest and especially
the young Baptist preachers who are educated there.''[18]

The *Biblical Recorder* replied that Dr. Poteat had made
a mistake in the Richmond speech but that people should
remember that in 1900 he had not reached the mature
conclusions on the ''great doctrine of the Atonement to
which his subsequent study has led him.'' The Baptist
newspaper quoted a recent speech in which Poteat re-

ferred to "the fundamentals of the Christian faith—the Scriptures as the infallible rule of faith and practice, the deity, atoning work, and lordship of Christ, personal regeneration which makes men new creatures in Christ Jesus." The *Recorder* accused Martin of overreaching himself in his extreme statements and pointed out that there were thousands who knew the Wake Forest president and who believed that he was trusting in the blood of Christ for salvation.

Poteat wrote to Livingston Johnson, editor of the *Biblical Recorder,* thanking him for his support and declaring that he did indeed believe in the New Testament. Poteat said, "The mystery of His compassion and His redemption I do not understand, but to His sacrificial life and atoning death I look for the forgiveness of sin and the life eternal."[19] Johnson published the letter as a testimony of faith. Poteat did not say, however, that he repudiated his stand in the 1900 address. He merely stated his position in terms less objectionable to critics and left it up to others to decide whether he still believed what he had said at Richmond. Poteat wrote to his brother Edwin, then teaching at Shanghai College, that there were pressures on him to adopt some theory of the atonement. He did not feel disposed to do so, for he did not feel that the New Testament had such a theory. He said, "I prefer to leave the matter where Jesus left it,—the birth by the Spirit is like the mystery of the wind."[20]

Adoption of a particular doctrine of the atonement did not prove necessary at that time, because Poteat's letter to Johnson satisfied critics. However, the question of his belief in evolution was not settled, and Martin severely criticized the biologist for his belief in the theory. According to the evangelist, evolution was the cause of World War I. He said that the Germans believed in the survival of the fittest, and since they considered Germany the fittest, they thought they ought to conquer the weaker nations. He asked, "How can President Poteat reconcile such a doctrine with his teachings, of God being the Father of the human race? Would a father fasten such a law on his children whom he loved?" Martin declared that if evolution could be proved as a fact, then Genesis could not be the inspired word of God. He went on to quote statements of twenty-one scientists who denied the theory of evolution. Although the works quoted were outdated,[21] Martin proclaimed "overwhelming evidence from these twenty-one great scientists of the world" against evolution. He said, "The Baptists of North Carolina through the president they have for their great Baptist college are partners with Chicago University in fastening this German-ruining, world crushing, soul-destroying doctrine on the South. . . ."[22] Martin declared that to receive payment for teaching Baptist doctrine and to teach something contrary to that doctrine was to receive money under false pretenses. To Dr. Poteat, however, there was no contradiction between science and religion, and in his classes he emphasized that fact. Nevertheless, Martin stated, "More than once . . . have I seen bitter tears over the wrecked faith of boys from teachings that emanated from Wake Forest, and often have I heard of others."[23] This was a strong statement on a subject of great importance to North Carolina Baptists, but the *Biblical Recorder's* support reassured them, and no opposition materialized at that time.

In the early 1920's, however, Baptists all over the South were becoming vividly conscious of their ownership and control of denominational colleges through publicity for the "Seventy-five Million Campaign." The objective of the Southern Baptist Convention was to raise $75,000,000 for support of Baptist colleges in the South. This interest in education provided fertile ground for heresy hunts among science professors. Sentiment in favor of direct attacks on professors did not, however, take form immediately. In North Carolina, after the debate produced by Martin's articles subsided, the *Biblical Recorder* was relatively free from the evolution issue until March of 1922, when an article by Dr. Poteat entitled "Was Paul an Evolutionist?" appeared. Having quoted Acts 17:26, "All nations He has created from a common origin, to dwell all over the earth, fixing their allotted periods and the boundaries of their abodes," Dr. Poteat explained that "fixing their allotted periods" might mean periods of emergence of species into distinctness or periods of dominance and survival into distinct races, whereas the "boundaries of their abodes" might refer to the Darwinian idea that divergence is in direct relation to the degree of isolation.[24] Although such ideas were farfetched, they were no more so than the ideas of the conservatives who tried to disprove the theory of evolution by quoting passages from the Bible.

Several of the Fundamentalists objected to Poteat's calling Paul an evolutionist. In the *Biblical Recorder,* W. J. Berryman, moderator of the Chowan Baptist Association, wrote a caustic rebuttal to Poteat's article. He said that evolution left no place for God, destroyed the very first words of the Bible, and made the whole of it a fable. Berryman asked, "Did Paul believe that he descended from a monkey? Of course he didn't." Another article signed by "A Puzzled Old Man" remarked, "I note that in almost every letter that Paul wrote, he begins by stating that he was called to be an apostle by the Will of God, but he does not say one word about being a theistic evolutionist or even a simple evolutionist." J. J. Taylor, a minister from Leaksville, wrote a more scholarly article on the subject. He declared that the word evolution was not known in Paul's day. "There is not at hand any evidence that the word was in use before the eighteenth century, and its origin is distinctly materialistic and anti-Christian."[25]

Because of the debate that filled the columns of the *Biblical Recorder*, Poteat decided to clarify his position. He defined evolution as "the doctrine that the animals and plants at any moment on the earth are the offspring of earlier animals and plants.'' He explained that the higher animal body is developed or evolved from a single cell, the egg-cell, by a long series of easy transitional stages. ''Such an individual evolution,'' he said, ''is an epitome and illustration of the genetic relationship of all animal forms affirmed by evolution. And the evolution of the individual is just as wonderful and hard to explain as the evolution of the race.''[26]

After defining evolution, the Wake Forest biologist wrote a second article on the topic, ''May a Christian Be an Evolutionist?'' He made two preliminary observations before answering the question. First, he explained that he spoke of evolution, a subject about which scientists were in agreement, not any particular method of evolution such as natural selection, mutation, or use and disuse. Secondly, he remarked that many men thought that the term ''theory'' was synonymous with fancy or guess. ''They forget that we properly speak of the Copernican theory of the heavens, the theory of gravitation, the atomic theory without the slightest detraction from their validity.... A tested hypothesis is usually called a theory, or law, or principle of doctrine.''

Poteat declared that the Christian experience was man's most precious possession. To show that evolution did not affect this experience, he cited various scientists who understood evolution and who saw no conflict with religion. He said, ''Evolution does not touch the fundamentals of our faith, much less antagonize them. The inspiration of the Scriptures sanely interpreted, the Deity of Christ, His incarnation, atonement, and resurrection are ours, evolution or no evolution.'' Poteat declared that it was unjust for men who had no opportunity of training in the biological sciences to seek to discredit Christian men who held evolution as God's method of creation. ''It is not fair,'' he protested. ''It is not Christian. It ought to stop.''[27]

The attacks did not stop. In fact, after Poteat stated

his position clearly, the debating in the columns of the *Biblical Recorder* increased. Livingston Johnson, the editor, was a trustee of Wake Forest College. He gave Dr. Poteat every opportunity to defend his position. On at least one occasion, Johnson sent the biologist a copy of an article before it reached the press, with a suggestion that Poteat prepare a summary of his teachings comparing evolution and the account of creation in the book of Genesis.[28] In all fairness, however, Johnson could not refuse the anti-evolutionists a place in the columns of the *Biblical Recorder*, and the articles that he printed ranged from scholarly discussions of theological minutiae to simply worded letters to the editor from alumni in support of "Dr. Billy."

Robert H. Spiro, a Baptist minister from Asheville, and J. J. Taylor wrote two of the more scholarly articles. Spiro said that evolution could not be acceptable to the Christian because evolution taught an upward journey for man while the Bible taught the fall of man from a higher state to a lower one. Also, to Spiro, the resurrection of Christ contradicted evolution which indicated that life only arose from life. Taylor analyzed Dr. Poteat's articles in detail. He said, "President Poteat has cited the Britannica as an authority on his pet theme; it says: 'The doctrine of evolution is directly antagonistic to that of creation.' Certainly the Bible, sanely interpreted, teaches the doctrine of creation as an immediate act of God." Taylor warned that the North Carolina Baptists were responsible for what was taught at Wake Forest College. He said, "The case is before them. God is the judge, and to him they must all report after a while."[29]

A number of North Carolinians, however, were satisfied with the situation at Wake Forest. One supporter of President Poteat protested that it seemed fashionable for the clergy, when digestion was bad or when they had nothing better to do, to hurl verbal brickbats at him and to lament the corruption of innocent youth by the teaching

of evolution. "As imaginary portraits of imaginary
perils, many of these effusions are not without merit. As
valid arguments against the theory of evolution they leave
something to be desired."[30] Certainly, many people were
not convinced by the accusations hurled at Poteat by his
critics. Bernard W. Spilman, a minister from Kinston and
President of the North Carolina Baptist Convention, wrote
an account of Poteat's sincere Christianity and good influence. Spilman knew "Dr. Billy" quite well, as he had
lived in the Poteat cottage, a small house near the president's home, while attending Wake Forest. He said, "If
there is a devout, humble servant of Jesus Christ who believes in the Bible from lid to lid ... if there is a man who
lives the religion of Jesus day by day, that man is W. L.
Poteat."[31] An article by D. B. Humphrey of Lumberton,
North Carolina, was even more complimentary than that
of Spilman. Humphrey was an advocate of an anti-evolution state law, and, in addition, he objected to the teaching
of evolution in denominational schools. Nevertheless, he
commented, "I never saw a more beautiful Christian character than that portrayed in the life of Dr. Poteat and in
my four years at Wake Forest it never entered my mind
one time that he was not a Christian."[32]

The discussion of evolution filled to overflowing the
columns of the *Biblical Recorder* in the spring of 1922.
To some subscribers, the debates were confusing and,
eventually, tiresome. One reader protested, "Please,
please let the discussion on evolution cease, or I very much
fear some of us simple country folk will have lost our
reason entirely. We get so bewildered in trying to think
it over that we can't decided [sic] who, or what we are, or
where we came from."[33] Livingston Johnson realized that
the continual debate would never solve the controversy.
He said, "We have reason to believe that this agitation
has shaken the faith of many who have read it, and if the
faith of any has been strengthened, we have not heard of

it.'' He therefore decided to ban further discussion of evolution in the *Biblical Recorder* after May 31, 1922.

The last word on the question came from Johnson himself on behalf of the Wake Forest trustees. He reported that they had sent out scores of letters interviewing hundreds of alumni and had found that all who came in close personal contact with Poteat, including the pastors of the Wake Forest Church, would ''bear glad testimony to his Christian character.'' In addition, members of the faculty of the Southern Baptist Theological Seminary reported that ''they had never heard from a Wake Forest man an unsound doctrine.''

The trustees also appointed a committee to interview Poteat and to ascertain his views on the fundamental doctrines. The committee reported that they found him ''in hearty accord with the great Baptist brotherhood'' in regard to God as the creator, Jesus as His Son, redemption through His atoning death, His resurrection, regeneration through the Holy Spirit, and the divine inspiration of the Bible in matters of faith and practice. After carefully presenting all the facts, the trustees expressed confidence in President Poteat by unanimous vote. Livingston Johnson felt that this action was an additional reason for discontinuing discussion of the evolution question. If the thorough study of the trustees could not convince people that Dr. Poteat was not dangerous as a teacher, there was no hope of convincing them.[34]

Other editors, however, continued to discuss the controversy. Archibald Johnson, editor of *Charity and Children*, warned concerned churchmen to go slowly because the temptations to debate and to appeal to prejudice were indeed great. He remarked that nothing could be gained but by the utmost sincerity.[35] Throughout the evolution agitation, the editorial policy of *Charity and Children* remained both intelligent and tolerant.

The editors of other publications were not so broadminded. James Larkin Pearson, later poet laureate of

North Carolina, edited a paper called *The Fool Killer*,
which he described as "A Monthly Mustard-Plaster for the
Blood Boils of Society, Church, and State." Pearson attacked Poteat's views on evolution and exclaimed that he
had once wanted to attend Wake Forest College, but it
would certainly have ruined him.[36] Thomas T. Martin
continued his attacks on Poteat in the *Searchlight*. Martin
advised Southern Baptists to purge their colleges of professors who believed in evolution before the Seventy-Five
Million Campaign was completed, because when the colleges received the money, they might then turn to liberalism. Martin reported that as soon as Wake Forest had
inherited $1,250,000, President Poteat declared himself an
evolutionist and stated that evolution had been taught at
Wake Forest for years.[37]

Dr. Poteat had never made any secret of the fact that
he taught evolution, and in spite of much opposition, he
refused to equivocate. He stated, "I frankly believe that
God created all things ... by the method of evolution. I
find myself unable to resist the considerations in support
of that method. There I stand and I cannot help it."[38]
Poteat did not, however, try to censor those who disagreed
with him. In fact, he invited Dr. Amzi Clarence Dixon,
one of the nation's leading Fundamentalists, to speak at
Wake Forest. This invitation was perhaps a wiser move
than Dr. Poteat realized at the time. "Dr. Dixon accepted,
shelled the woods, blazed away at evolution, converted no-
body, made everybody a better friend of Dr. Poteat, and
gave that institution its opportunity to show its catho-
licity."[39]

The students of Wake Forest heartily supported "Dr.
Billy." The campus newspaper, the *Old Gold and Black*,
contained articles in stanch defense of the college president. Both the *Durham Morning Herald* and the *Raleigh
Times* commended the students. An editorial writer for
the *Times* remarked, "The stand of the Wake Forest *Old
Gold and Black* against the bigots in the denomination . . .

is not a defense of President William Louis Poteat alone; it is a stand for the spiritual and intellectual freedom of every sentient person in North Carolina.'' The editorialist further stated that Dr. Poteat could take care of himself. ''He isn't going to join this excursion back into the Dark Ages, nor are we.'' According to the *Times*, making a martyr of Dr. Poteat would only move him on to a field of larger endeavor at an increase in salary, but the damage done to the spirit of the people of North Carolina would be incalculable.

A *Times* editorial described the fight against Dr. Poteat as but a part of a general campaign of intolerance in the South. It warned that this intolerance had been felt in the legislatures of South Carolina and Kentucky and would eventually break out in North Carolina. In closing, the editorial stated that Dr. Poteat had been called an atheist because he had brains and faith enough to square his scientific inquiry with his religion, but, ''If that's atheism, then it's time to enlarge hell and chunk up the fire for everybody worth knowing is headed in that direction.''[40]

Nevertheless, as North Carolina Baptists prepared for their annual state convention, agitation again increased. Many people felt that the state convention should take some action on the evolution question as had the Southern Baptist Convention. That body, which met at Jacksonville, Florida, in May, laid the foundations for further conflict in North Carolina by adopting the report of its education board. The report offered ''Some Words of Caution,'' stating that if a member of a Baptist college faculty were accused of heresy, he should be questioned and the matter settled because ''Indiscriminate criticism is not the best way to correct an error in an individual or school.''[41] Edgar Young Mullins, president of the convention, was generally considered a moderate. He said that Baptists would not tolerate in their denominational schools any departure from the great fundamentals of the faith, but neither would they be unjust to teachers nor curtail unduly their right to investigate truth. The convention, however, recommended that because of the difficulty of finding science textbooks free from erroneous statements with reference to evolution, the Education Board should seek Christian scientists to prepare texts "which will rightly relate science to the Bible and who will set forth the fact that the majority of the greatest men of science have repudiated Darwinism except as an unproven working hypothesis."[42]

When the North Carolina Baptist Associations met in the late summer or fall of 1922, evolution was often a topic for debate. The Cape Fear–Columbus Association endorsed the action of the Southern Baptist Convention and urged the Baptist State Convention to direct the trustees of denominational institutions to eliminate all teachers, texts, or discussions that encouraged evolution.[43] The Alexander Baptist Association adopted a resolution stating that "we feel that we have a God-given right to determine what shall be or what shall not be taught in these schools" and requesting the elimination of evolution from the curriculum.[44] Other associations, such as the Elkin and the Pilot Mountain organizations, discussed the question of evolution in Baptist schools but did not pass resolutions on the subject. The Tar River Association reaffirmed loyalty to Wake Forest, its faculty, and trustees.

Richard T. Vann, chairman of the education board of the Baptist State Convention, realized that the associations were concerned about the matter of evolution, so he addressed several of the associations and asked Dr. Poteat to speak to others. Poteat commented to his brother that he had been away from the college often in the fall of 1922 under the direction of Dr. Vann. He supposed that Vann thought his presence in the associations might lessen criticism because "brethren might discover that I was just a plain man without horns and cloven feet." He was cordially received wherever he went, but he understood that propaganda against evolution was determined and energetic, particularly in the western part of the state, and would probably reach the floor of the State Convention at Winston-Salem in December. Poteat knew that some resolutions passed by various associations had mentioned him by name, but he declared, "I shall not allow myself to be made an issue. The real issue is whether a man can accept scientific truth as he sees it and yet be a Christian."[45]

Because of his stand on that very issue, Poteat could not escape being the center of attention at the Winston-Salem convention. At their annual luncheon on December 13, the alumni of Wake Forest endorsed the position of Dr. Poteat. Surely this was encouraging to him as he prepared for his speech to the convention that night.

A large audience assembled to hear the report on Wake Forest. Every available seat was filled, and many stood in the rear of the auditorium. When the hour for the discussion of education arrived, an air of hushed expectancy spread over the entire congregation.[46] Benjamin W. Parham, an attorney from Oxford, presented the report of the education committee, and President Bernard W. Spilman then called for the Wake Forest report. Richard T. Vann stepped to the platform and called on T. Jerome Taylor, minister at Warrenton, who made a beautiful and touching prayer for divine guidance. Vann then spoke briefly on the history of Wake Forest College, established more than eighty-eight years previously. Having spoken of the men who nursed and cradled the institution through the long years of struggle that followed its organization, he remarked that Wake Forest had become one of the leading denominational colleges in the entire country. Vann then presented Dr. Poteat.[47]

"The tense and expectant atmosphere was punctuated with the deep breathing of a thousand delegates"[48] as the president of Wake Forest rose. Short in stature, Poteat was heavy-set. His partially bald head was outlined by a half-circle of gray hair. Impeccably dressed, he gave the impression of great dignity. He calmly spoke in a deliberate yet forceful voice as he took a small worn book from his pocket. "I want to read to you a few passages from a little Book I hold in my hand," he said. "I love this little Book, and I commend it to you." Poteat told his audience that if any of them ever heard someone flouting the Bible or trying to destroy it to "Blow your trumpet and turn the bell toward Wake Forest College, and our little band, though small, will come to your assistance."[49]

Poteat spoke for an hour, never mentioning the word "evolution." He defined Christian education as "Christianity operating in the field of enlightenment" and declared, "The Bible is the final authority for faith and practice." Poteat gave a deeply moving account of his own conversion and stated, "Our deepest need is to be good; after that, to be intelligent. . . . What the world needs now as always is the completer marriage of goodness and intelligence. Now, thank God, there is no law against this marriage. Science can say nothing against it." This was true because science could not explain the central mysteries of nature and life. "Manifestly science cannot discredit faith. Its symbols, according to Clerk Maxwell, are the balance, the footrule, and the clock. The deeper things of life are beyond their reach." Therefore, Poteat said, men should not fear the truths of science. One thing which might be unforgivable was "the fear lest the truth be bad; the fear that the Spirit of truth will not guide us into all the truth, will not glorify Christ as the theme, origin, and end of all truth. . . . Welcome Truth. . . . And do not stop to calculate the adjustment and revision her fresh coming will necessitate." Dr. Poteat concluded his speech with the challenge, "Let us have done with our questionings, and follow where He leads. We shall be together, if we follow Him. Yonder gleams His banner above the battle line. Have done with these debates in the rear. Up and after Him through blood and tears, after Him to victory!"[50]

It was the consensus that Poteat's masterly speech swept away any objections that might have been forthcoming. *Charity and Children* reported, "The victory was won.... That masterly speech swept everything before it."[51] The *Baptist Messenger* stated that not a single protest was brought, not a question asked from any point, which proved that the people were fully satisfied with the discussion made by the speaker.[52] "What opposition there had been had melted before the eloquence and convincing sincerity of the professor," declared *The News and Observer*.[53]

The following morning the convention adopted a resolution commending Wake Forest College in its present policy as expressed in the address of President Poteat and stated, "We are glad to be assured by the Board of Trustees that this policy will be continued."[54] The *Biblical Recorder* reported that many Baptists considered the Winston-Salem meeting the greatest convention ever held, and the highlight was Poteat's speech. "The only word we can think of which describes the speech was that it was overwhelming," declared Livingston Johnson.[55] With the help of friends such as Richard T. Vann, Archibald Johnson and Livingston Johnson, Dr. Poteat had met his first inquisition successfully. A Shelby editorialist expressed the sentiments of most of those who heard him speak at Winston-Salem when he said, "Let us be thankful for such brave and noble men as Dr. W. L. Poteat, who are sincere exponents of the noblest and best Christianity and yet bear aloft the sacred torch of science whose beams are destined to enlighten the world."[56]

For the moment, the victory was won, but the war for freedom of teaching was not over. It would not be over until education could reach the ignorance of thousands of well-meaning people who feared evolution as an assailant of their faith. However, Dr. Poteat had made his position clear, and, as long as he was president of Wake Forest College, he would remain a bulwark for freedom and enlightment.

Adam or Ape?

D r. Poteat's strong affirmation of faith at the Winston-Salem convention evidently satisfied the majority of North Carolina Baptists who heard him, but his speech fell far short of stopping all opposition to his ideas. Criticism from out of state increased after 1922. The deep-rooted concern of people all over the country was evident in the fact that between 1921 and 1929, thirty-seven anti-evolution bills were introduced into twenty state legislatures.[1] These attempts to secure anti-evolution laws were but one example of the many efforts to secure legislation against new forms of thought or against practices considered undesirable by conservatives. The passage of the eighteenth amendment was the outstanding example, but other such actions included attempts to curtail academic freedom on the grounds of patriotism or moral law. Shortly after World War I, the legislatures of New York, Wisconsin, Oregon, Texas, and Mississippi enacted laws to prohibit the use in public schools of textbooks found to be seditious, critical of the Founding Fathers, or in any other way disloyal to the nation and to its heritage. Americans of the 1920's had great faith in the powers of legislation. They believed that correct ideas and good morals could be imposed upon mankind by law. The fact that such legislation met with more success in the South[2] than elsewhere was probably because of the system of legislative apportionment in that section. The southern states were more heavily gerrymandered in favor of the rural districts than states in any other region in the United States. As late as 1940, Mississippi and Kentucky, respectively, had not been reapportioned since 1890 and 1893. Alabama and Tennessee had not revised their apportionments since 1901. Even in states with more recent reapportionment the cities had only a fraction of the representation they deserved.

The rural South, which thus held control of the state legislatures, was predominantly Fundamentalist in religious belief. In 1925 in North Carolina, the Baptists formed the largest denomination, with 327,600 members and 2,291 churches. The next largest denomination, the Methodist Episcopal Church, South, could claim only 112,-000 members with 776 churches. Any statement, therefore, by Poteat as a leading Southern Baptist, as well as a leader of the evolutionists, would be of particular interest to people in North Carolina and the South. J. J. Taylor, a well-known Southern Baptist who had previously criticized Poteat, affirmed that the Wake Forest biologist had been publicly lauded as the chief evolutionist teaching in a Baptist school at that time. Taylor further stated, "It has been hinted that the little fellows who talk evolution in Richmond, Mars Hill, Mercer and elsewhere, are mere imitators, children, so to speak, toddling after the giant of Wake Forest, whose voice shakes some of the saints with something like the rigors of a buck ague." In Taylor's opinion, Poteat was the man to justify the evolution creed and lift it above the slough of ignorance. "If he fails, none else need try."[3]

J. Frank Norris also recognized Poteat's leadership, but in terms quite different from Taylor's praise. Referring to Poteat as "the rankest evolutionist among Southern Baptists," Norris criticized his Winston-Salem speech and insinuated that Poteat could not possibly believe in both the words of his sermon and the doctrine of evolution. Norris went even further in his ridicule. He printed a picture of an amoeba on the front page of the *Searchlight* with the following caption:

> The following is a description of Dr. Poteat's ancestors:
> In the beginning amoeba begat sack-worms.
> Sack-worms begat skull-less worms.
> Skull-less animals begat single-nostrilled animals....
> Primeval fish begat mud fish.
> Mud fish begat gilled amphibians.
> Gilled amphibians begat primary mammals.
> Primary mammals begat pouched animals.
> Pouched animals begat semi-apes.
> And semi-apes begat evolution professors.[4]

The Texas editor waxed even more vituperative when he called Poteat "this modern ecclesiastical institutionalist that puts the lash on every brother who refuses to bow to modern Baalism," and he questioned, "Shall those who do not believe in evolution be compelled to support this Bible-denying and deity-of-Christ destroying infidelity?"[5]

Fundamentalist antagonism to Poteat flared up again in 1924 when the members of the Wake Forest Baptist Church selected him to represent them at the Southern Baptist Convention of that year. Shortly before the convention was to meet, Norris proclaimed in flaming red headlines, "Dr. W. L. Poteat's Seat in Convention to Be Challenged." Norris reported having received a letter from certain Baptists in Oklahoma who said of Poteat, "He is not a Baptist; he has denied the fundamentals of the faith; he has repudiated the Genesis account of creation; he has denied the Virgin Birth; he advocated a pagan religion ... as orthodox Baptists, we can not sit in convention with him!"[6] In reply, the *Greensboro Daily News* and the *Biblical Recorder* pointed out that in the Baptist denomination the individual congregation was sovereign, so neither Norris nor the Oklahoma Baptists had the right to challenge Poteat's seat in the convention. The only way for even North Carolina Baptists to prevent his admission was to declare that the Wake Forest church was not a true Baptist church and consequently was not entitled to send delegates to the convention. Actually, no one at the convention challenged the seating of the Wake Forest representative, and Norris was absent from the convention. Dr. Poteat commented to his brother Edwin M. Poteat that Norris did not appear. "He was doing a great work in San Antonio, preaching, according to his own statement, to fifteen thousand people in a revival meeting and could not come down, and no public allusion was made to the matter in the remotest way."[7]

After the convention was over, Poteat received applause from a variety of sources. In commenting on Norris' inconsistent behavior, the *Durham Morning Herald* said, "Norris, down in Texas where the K K K flourishes; where the cactus grows; where the greaser thrives ... where coyotes howl, jackasses bray, and jack-rabbits run, is in good company for propagating such stuff as he hurls at the head of a man who is his superior in every respect."[8] Edgar Young Mullins, president of Southern Baptist Theological Seminary at Louisville and president of the Southern Baptist Convention in 1923, expressed the position of the moderates. Mullins asserted that Christians could believe in a process of development without denying God's creation of the world. He felt, however, that evolution in its strictest sense was opposed to creation. Since evolution was a hypothesis, it should not be taught as a fact. No teacher should conceal facts discovered by scientific

research, Mullins said, but Baptists believed in the supernatural elements of Christianity, and no teacher in Baptist
schools should try to disprove these elements.[9]

In February of 1925, the Wake Forest student newspaper declared support of Poteat's belief in the Bible.
According to the *Old Gold and Black*, there were entirely
too many people in the state, especially Baptists, who knew
nothing about evolution except the hearsay that the term
meant that man came from a monkey. These people, the
paper continued, were anxious to start another argument
on the subject in spite of the fact that Dr. Poteat had expressed his views on evolution clearly and emphatically,
and he had stated his belief in the Genesis account of
creation. "Ask any Wake Forest student whether or not
he thinks Dr. Poteat believes the whole Bible and the student will tell you that there is no doubt about Dr. Poteat's
belief in the whole Bible."[10]

In the evolution controversy in North Carolina, the
attention of the public was temporarily withdrawn from
Dr. Poteat and focused upon the public schools. In 1924
a subcommittee of the Text Book Commission of the State
Board of Education drew up a list of about seven hundred
books for use in North Carolina schools. Governor
Cameron Morrison objected to two of the suggested biology
texts on these grounds: "I don't want my daughter or anybody's daughter to have to study a book that prints pictures of a monkey and a man on the same page." Morrison declared that he believed in evolution as progress from
a lower form of human life to a higher, but he stated
further, "One of those books teaches that man is descended
from a monkey and the other that he is a cousin to the
monkey. I don't believe either one of them."[11] Morrison's
strong stand against evolution, as well as Dr. Poteat's
stand for it, were contributing factors that led to the interest in anti-evolution legislation in 1925.

In February of 1925, D. Scott Poole, publisher of the
Hoke County Journal and former mayor of Raeford, intro-

duced a bill in the North Carolina House of Representatives stating that "it is injurious to the welfare of the people of North Carolina for any official or teacher paid wholly or in part by taxation to teach or permit to be taught as a fact either Darwinism or any other evolutionary hypothesis. . . ."[12] The House referred the bill to a committee which held an open hearing on the matter. It was necessary to hold the hearing in the House chamber because of the large crowd that had assembled to listen to the proceedings. Pretty female students from Raleigh colleges, State College men, representatives of practically all the state institutions of higher learning, and numerous other citizens of prominence crowded into the Capitol. The committee limited debate to one hour for each side.

Poole told the audience that their religion was on trial. As no one had asked the state to teach theology, he did not think that state-supported schools should teach that the Bible was a myth. When the floor was opened for discussion, President Harry W. Chase of the University of North Carolina declared, "I am not here to discuss evolution, but to speak in behalf of human liberty." In his appeal for freedom of speech, Chase demanded eternal vigilance for liberty and truth and ended his speech by stating, "Mr. Chairman: If that be treason and if it be treason to oppose the bill offered in the name of tyranny over mind for the purpose of abridging the liberty of one class of our people, I wish to stand here in the name of progress and make my protest." Bertram W. Wells, a professor of botany at State College, supported Chase by saying, "I stand here to deny that a man cannot believe in evolution and be a Christian. I am here as a living exponent of the Christian religion in all its essentials and also in evolution as a fact."

Miss Julia Alexander, representative from Mecklenburg County, was in favor of the bill. She said that the Bible was a supernatural book, and that she believed in it from cover to cover. Miss Alexander declared that she would be afraid to return to Mecklenburg if she voted against the bill. James R. Pentuff, a Concord clergyman, also favored the bill. Pentuff said that evolution was based on imagination. According to the Concord minister, publishers and teachers who were not willing to "dig up and to keep up with the newer sciences" were the chief expositors of the theory of evolution. Pentuff called Darwin an agnostic and insisted that his theory was based on incorrect geological information. He also discussed "missing links" that Darwin had been unable to find and insisted that the evolution theory had been exploded. A State College professor had ready answers for this bold statement. Zeno P. Metcalf, a professor of zoology and entomology, replied to Pentuff that the evolution theory was definitely accepted in scientific circles. After Metcalf had spoken, Robert L. Madison, a member of the Education Committee, queried, "May I ask the gentleman from State College at what stage of transformation of man from an amoeba that he parted with his tail and acquired a conscience?" Dr. Chase retorted, "Does the gentleman mean that necessarily both occurred at the same time?" Tradition has it that Dr. Poteat, who was sitting in the audience, said of Madison's question, "Biologically he has never lost his tail and here is some evidence that he has never acquired a conscience."[13]

Twice the audience called on Poteat to speak. Each time that his name was mentioned it was greeted by much cheering and clapping, but like Richard T. Vann, he declined to speak. Perhaps he felt that he had made his position clear; since Chase had ably stated the liberal position, anything he could say would add little and would probably stir up trouble for Wake Forest. On the other hand, perhaps Poteat had confidence that the Wake Forest men who sat in the legislature would vote according to what they had learned under his tutelage. Nevertheless, many people were undoubtedly disappointed at Poteat's refusal to speak, and this refusal seemed somehow inconsistent with his usual fearless support for freedom of teaching. However, he had talked individually with members of the Education Committee, and he felt that it might be possible to guide the debate with suggestions beforehand. As much as he enjoyed speaking, it must have been difficult for him to keep silent, but he remained in the background for he felt that the responsibility was mainly on the gentlemen who represented the institutions directly involved. He said, "I had had my say in another relationship." Harry W. Chase agreed with him as he declared, "It was exceedingly wise and proper I felt, and everybody feels here, for you to refuse to be drawn into the state end of the discussion the other day." Chase said that if the Poole Bill were defeated it would be in no small part because of the groundwork laid by Poteat "in all these years of manful struggle."[14]

The outcome of the Education Committee's voting was a tie, seventeen to seventeen. The final decision was thus left to the chairman, Henry Groves Connor, Jr., a young lawyer educated at the University of North Carolina. He broke the tie by voting against the bill. The majority report was thus unfavorable, but the minority also drafted a report.

Before these reports reached the floor of the House, the North Carolina press exhibited a marked interest in the progress of the bill. The *Greensboro Daily News* printed a searing invective against Poole and his followers which declared that politics and bigotry gave impetus to their movement. According to the *Daily News*, the same thing was happening to university men of breadth that had been happening to the Baptist liberals. All over the state there had been an outcry against Poteat because he believed "in the amoeba." Many Baptists declared that the Seventy-five Million Campaign for the support of Baptist colleges had dragged because of him. "The Wake Forest President knows he is constantly in jeopardy. His mastership over Wake Forest imperils the denominational appropriations. But he is one of those idealists, such as

Chase and Ed Graham, who foolishly declare that colleges are more than millions set into equipment and lecture rooms.''[15]

An editor of *The News and Observer* was also against the Poole Bill, but he took a more moderate stand than that of the *Daily News*. In an article called ''Liberty to Think,'' he said, ''The issue is: 'Shall teachers in State-supported institutions of learning be forbidden to state to their classes the conclusions they have reached?' '' The editor said that evolution should not be taught to children, and it should not be taught dogmatically anywhere, but teachers and students in colleges should be able to examine the arguments both for and against the theory. He concluded, ''With every feeling of respect for the convictions of those who favor the Poole Bill, *The News and Observer* urges the General Assembly not to enter upon the realm of direction of religious, or semi-religious, instruction in institutions established for the education of the youth of the commonwealth.''[16]

Nell Battle Lewis, a contributor to the same newspaper, expressed confidence in the outcome of the voting. She stated, ''It's an old, old show that the anti-evolutionists are putting on now on the legislative stage at the Capital Theater in Raleigh. . . . We now have a return engagement of Bigotry and Ignorance, the Great Barn Stormers, in the World-Famous Morality Play Entitled, 'Thou Shalt Not Think.' '' According to Miss Lewis, this play was as old as ancient Greece, but all ages had found it impossible to legislate morality.[17]

Livingston Johnson, editor of the *Biblical Recorder*, announced his support of a substitute bill suggested by Richard T. Vann which would prohibit a teacher from making an official statement disrespectful to the religious views of any citizen. Johnson questioned, ''If it does not interfere with the freedom of a teacher to say that the constitution forbids him to teach religion, how can it be an interference to say that he shall not teach anything that would destroy religion?"[18]

On February 17 at 8:00 P.M., the House of Representatives met to consider the Poole Bill. The huge crowd that had gathered made debate very difficult. Connor remarked, "If we continue, we shall be compelled to call on the mayor of Raleigh for police protection, so long as the people of North Carolina insist in overrunning the hall of the House."[19] The House then resolved to discuss the bill at a later date and adjourned.

On February 19 the Poole Bill again came before the legislature. Harrison Yelverton, a young attorney from Wayne County, and Henry Groves Connor, chairman of the Education Committee, led the opposition to the bill; D. Scott Poole, Robert L. Madison, and Julia Alexander supported the bill. The House first considered the compromise bill that would simply prohibit any teacher from making an official statement disrespectful to the religious views of any citizen or any book of religious authority. This compromise might have passed, but the proponents of the Poole Bill voted it down in hopes of passing the stronger measure. The discussion proceeded without bitterness, although there were strong feelings on both sides. Many North Carolina lawmakers felt a hesitancy to legislate on what could and could not be taught; others understood the theory of evolution and had no objection to it. According to tradition, North Carolina liberals were confident of the outcome of the voting. "Just wait until Billy Poteat's boys get a chance to vote!"[20] The outcome of the voting was indeed satisfactory to the liberal element. The House voted sixty-seven to forty-six against the Poole Bill.[21]

Freedom of teaching had triumphed in North Carolina, for underlying the evolution dispute was the question of whether a teacher's higher loyalty was to the will of the taxpayer or to the truth as his training led him to see it. The legislators decided in favor of the latter. What were the influences that led to this decision? Several historians have given credit for the defeat of anti-evolution legislation in North Carolina to Harry W. Chase and William Louis Poteat.[22]

Chase had raised the standards of scholarship at the University and had attracted a fine faculty among whom Howard W. Odum was outstanding. A sociologist, Odum launched the *Journal of Social Forces* in 1922. The periodical became a forum for liberal ideas and a target for attacks by the Fundamentalists. Odum, with the full support of Chase, continued to publish controversial material, including some written by Poteat. The stand taken by Chase and Odum was important in promoting freedom of teaching.[23]

Throughout the years, Poteat's open testimony that science and religion were not contradictory, as well as the fact that this biologist could believe in evolution and still live an exemplary Christian life, could not have failed to make a significant impression in the state. His greatest influence, however, was at Wake Forest College. As its graduates sat in the legislature and listened to the debates on evolution, perhaps they recalled their biology classes under Dr. Poteat. If they had not studied biology, they undoubtedly at some time during their college careers had come in contact with the liberal ideas of the Wake Forest president. Of the twenty-one representatives who had attended Wake Forest at some time, only three voted in favor of the Poole Bill.[24]

Although Poteat refused to speak before the legislature and did not seek publicity for his ideas on evolution and education during the agitation for the Poole Bill, his beliefs were well known because of the many years he had fought for the cause of academic and intellectual freedom. The *Greensboro Daily News* gave Poteat the credit for such leadership: "So staunchly has he stood by truth when truth had few to tell her teachings that his career has been one long triumph over bigotry and falseness and honest ignorance.'' According to the same writer, North Carolina had never appreciated the courage of William Louis Poteat, who could lead without driving and fight without leaving poisoned wounds. ''So closely do we live to the routine of our daily lives that we cannot always perceive the greatest movements that are astir about us. But someday the state will come to itself and when it does it will trace much of its intellectual freedom from Dr. Poteat.''[25]

Can a Man Be a Christian?

The Reverend Mr. John Calvin McNair, a University of North Carolina alumnus of 1849, bequeathed a sum of money to the university to be used "to employ some able scientific gentleman to deliver ... a course of lectures, the object of which lectures shall be to show the mutual bearing of science and theology upon each other, and to prove the existence of attributes (as far as may be) of God from nature." McNair further provided that the lectures should be published.[1] Although the bequest became available to the university in 1906, William Louis Poteat was the first native North Carolinian to present the lectures. He spoke in May of 1925 on the subject, "Can a Man Be a Christian To-day?" In introducing Poteat, Harry W. Chase, president of the university, asserted that Poteat offered living proof that science and religion could be reconciled. Chase stated, "We are in no position to debate the philosophical subtleties involved in the current dispute ... but a character that stands the test of half a century in a hard position is founded on something more solid than shifting scientific hypotheses.''[2]

The debate in the legislature over an anti-evolution law had increased interest in the controversy over science and religion, and many people were interested in the issue. Always a popular speaker, Poteat drew increasingly larger crowds each of the three nights he spoke. *The Chapel Hill Weekly* remarked, ''Probably no visitor to Chapel Hill—and many distinguished men have appeared on the platform here—has ever made a more profound impression upon his hearers.''[3] Poteat called upon his long experience at Wake Forest as he discussed the intellectual and spiritual problems of students. He expressed concern that what the young people learned at the university might seem inconsistent with what they had learned in their ''poor proud Christian homes'' of a ''simple sturdy democracy.'' Poteat asked, ''This adventure of the growing day,—it is likely to intoxicate a spirited youth and absorb his enthusiasm. Will it dim and then put out the candle of the spiritual life?'' Poteat questioned the general situation outside university life, the spirit and atmosphere of the time. ''Is it favorable and friendly,'' he asked, ''or chilling and hostile to the faith of our fathers? Is religion still possible? Can a man be a Christian to-day?''[4] Poteat proceeded to answer this question by first discussing the main features of the society of the day, disentangling the essential substance of Christianity from its accumulations through the centuries and finally considering what serious-minded, intelligent young people should do in order to secure and maintain peace between their education and their religion.

The first lecture entitled ''To-day'' was a rapid and comprehensive survey of the progress of physical science and of intellectual and international conditions in the world. Poteat asked whether or not scientific education should bar a man from participation in religious life. Some men, he said, had tried to use scientific truth to insult

God and offend His people; some scientists attempted to
stretch the truth and explain everything in terms of
science. Even though this outlook was erroneous, it offered
no excuse for the actions of opposing extremists, who
identified a divine religion with a man-made theology and
branded every critic of their beliefs as an enemy of Christ.
It was time, Poteat continued, for educated Christians to
oppose the extremists, not with bitter words, but firmly,
without compromise.[5]

"Baggage," the title of the second lecture, referred to
the accretions that in the course of the centuries had become associated with Christianity. To Poteat, the problem
was that religion had accumulated a huge amount of im-
pedimenta. First, Paul commented upon the basic teaching
of Christ, then others commented on Paul's commentaries,
and so on. The task of intelligent Christians was to disen-
tangle the traveler from his "baggage," because most of
that "baggage" was not entirely true. Poteat declared
that nothing that was unquestionably divine in Christianity
would be damaged in the least by subjection to the severest
tests of modern science. The discoveries that science had
made served only more emphatically to declare the glory
of God. Poteat did not defend science. He defended religion against men who persistently confused the traveler
with the "baggage" and who consequently held that Christianity must stand or fall, not with the words of Christ,
but with the words of some bishop, or pope, or council of
prelates. "The characteristic and essential thing in any
religion," he said, "is the soul's apprehension of the spirit
world and response to it. In Christianity, God and the
enveloping spirit world are mediated to our apprehension
by Christ, and to be Christian is to respond in love and
loyalty to the appeal of Christ."

Poteat went on to explain that the Bible was not intended to be interpreted literally, and when interpreted in
the light it was intended, it in no way contradicted true
science. He launched a vigorous counteroffensive against

extreme Fundamentalists because he believed that they were doing all they could to make it impossible for intelligent, educated men to be Christians. He said that religious teachers should "recognize the authority of science in its proper sphere, just as scientific teachers ought to recognize the authority of religion in its proper sphere." He warned the students to discriminate between Christ and some of His interpreters. Lack of discrimination, or perhaps lack of the knowledge to discriminate between the truth and the "baggage," was the cause of the "noisy, wholesale, denunciation of Christianity" prevalent in some contemporary literature.[6]

In the last lecture, "Peace," Poteat expressed the conviction that man was free to accommodate, with honesty and satisfaction, all authenticated progress of science and an unwavering faith in God and Christ. Poteat advised men of intelligence to "Consider Jesus," by pressing through professional interpreters to hear His original unamended word. "He has the words of eternal life, words possessing as well as imparting eternal life. They have the gift of perpetual contemporaneousness. No matter how wide-ranging and deep-running your culture, it can never get beyond them. Nor will they ever suffer discredit in the widening horizon of modern science."[7] In conclusion, Poteat explained that men could find peace if they would discriminate between Christ and some of his interpreters, between the apparatus of science and the spiritual realities of faith.[8]

Here was an answer to all those sincerely troubled by the age-old differences in science and religion. Poteat understood the problems of the sophisticated youth of Chapel Hill. He offered them the fundamentals of Christianity, expressed in modern terms and applied to the problems of modern life. Because he dealt in basic truths, Poteat presented to the youth of 1925 and to posterity an answer to the question "Can a man be a Christian today?" The lectures were a summary of Poteat's theology and philosophy of education. The statement of faith made his contribution complete, for had he merely condemned bigotry, he would have been no different from other critics. He was different because he offered to his fellow man an answer to the conflict of science and religion, and in his own life, he proved that his suggestions were applicable.

The McNair Lectures of 1925 evoked widespread interest. Published in book form, Poteat's lectures received favorable comment from both the religious and the secular press all over the nation. Papers as far away as Baltimore, Boston, New York, Chicago, St. Louis, and even Sacramento reviewed Poteat's book. The *Greensboro Daily News* praised it: "Here is the most significant volume that has come out of North Carolina in years." The purpose of these lectures, the occasion of their deliverance, the platform from which they were spoken, the moment in the life of the state, and the life, works, and faith of the speaker combined to make the event memorable. "There has been no moment in this decade ... when the interest of the state was so centered on the expression of any North Carolinian upon a scientific, philosophical, or religious subject. The moment and the man had met, and this message was the answer."[9] George W. Gilmore, editor of *The Homiletic Review*, remarked, "I would also congratulate the South since such deliverances will go far to rescue the South from the suspicion that it is a region of darkness in the thought-world."[10] Poteat's book moved one admiring lady to declare that it was the greatest book written since 1800 and that, along with the Bible, it should be placed in the hands of every man, woman, and child in America.[11] In answer to a great many letters of congratulation and praise, Poteat replied by expressing his hope that recognition denoted a usefulness for the book and that it might meet some need.[12]

Although there was much favorable criticism of *Can a Man Be a Christian To-day?* all of the critics were not complimentary. Some even attempted a refutation of the book. John W. Kurfees of Winston-Salem stated that, although his opportunities for an education had been limited to the inadequate advantages of a log cabin with slab benches for seats, he would not sit by and see the words of Jesus repudiated. Kurfees felt that Poteat was not true to the teachings of the Bible. He said, "If Dr. Poteat's brethren or any others had any misgivings beforehand as to whether he believed the Bible, all doubt should be buried now." As for Poteat's references to the Fundamentalists, Kurfees exclaimed, "Shades of Peter and Paul! Is it possible that we spread havoc by refusing to be 'tossed to and fro by every wind of doctrine?' "[13] Another critic sent Poteat an advertisement of *Can a Man Be a Christian To-day?* with this inscription: "It is hard to be one in Wake Forest under present conditions. I am surprised that a man who has lost faith in the Bible as God's inspired word has the brazen effrontery to try to stay at the head of a Christian college and undermine the faith of Christian students. I have no earthly use for your book."[14] S. J. Betts, a minister of Raleigh, North Carolina, went so far as to write a twelve-page pamphlet of criticism and refutation.

Of all criticism, the most painful was probably the accusation that Dr. Poteat's stand prevented several interested parties from donating the much-needed money to Wake Forest. At a joint meeting of the mission and education boards of the Baptist churches of North Carolina in Raleigh on May 29, 1925, opposition to Poteat was the reason given for the diminishing collections. There was a rumor that for this reason the Wake Forest president might retire. To express their loyalty, the college faculty met and composed a letter asking Poteat to remain. The board of trustees unofficially expressed undivided loyalty and complete confidence in the president's teachings. Poteat made no public statement, but his friends reported him unwilling to take any step that would appear as a surrender

of any part of the traditions that had been built up at the
college or the standards that had been maintained.

Excellent reason for the confidence of the trustees could
be seen in the progress report given at the 1925 commencement by Dr. Poteat. During his twenty years as president
of Wake Forest, the number of students had more than
doubled, as had the number of the faculty. The number
of volumes in the library had increased from sixteen thousand in 1905 to thirty thousand in 1925, while the endowment had risen from $286,932 to $2,931,060. At the age of
sixty-eight, Poteat said, "The achievements of the latter
years of our history are the harvest of the seed sown in
tears by our predecessors.... Its advances are largely the
issue of the progress and policies of the preceding administration." However, while recognizing that Wake
Forest had made considerable progress, Poteat demanded
more. "While such a record of progress is gratifying, it
has brought us to the point where we are under the necessity of taking a bolder and broader step forward."[15]

Poteat's actions in favor of freedom of teaching stood
in sharp contrast to the action of the Tennessee court that
had convicted John T. Scopes on the charge of teaching
evolution in the public schools. In speaking to the Raleigh
Rotarians on the subject of the Scopes trial, Poteat said,
"I look on this thing happening in Dayton with the deepest
humiliation.... The idea that any group of men should
undertake to settle a scientific fact by majority vote in any
assembly is a travesty on the intelligence of our race." He
felt that the excitement that had been generated was arti-
ficial because the leaders of the prosecution were misguided. "They have felt that the most precious thing in
life has been threatened." He said that William Jennings
Bryan, prosecutor in the Scopes case, and others like him
would have to take the responsibility for the injury that
might come to the young people of the country if they
should reject religion when given the choice between the
anti-evolutionists' interpretation of Christianity and the

facts of science. Poteat said that people accepted the words
of Bryan because men of science had been remiss in not
educating the common man. He felt that Christian ministers had not been as alert as they might have been in preparing the ground for the evolution controversy because
they had allowed the average member of their congregations to hold unwarranted conceptions and theories about
the purpose of the Bible. The difficulty arose because of
the "dictation theory"—that God spoke and told men what
to write. Poteat said that according to this theory the
world was created in 144 hours and the date of completion
was October 15, 4004 B.C., at 9 A.M. He warned that when
young people were offered the choice between the facts of
science and this interpretation of the Bible, hundreds of
boys and girls would say, "Take your religion! Away
with you! Begone! I'll have none of it." Because of this
possibility, Poteat exhorted, "The time has come for men
who have vision and responsibility of religious guidance
to say that this interpretation is false and these are false
issues and, so help me God, I'll not allow them to stand."[16]

In the last days of July and early August, 1925, Poteat
repeated "Today," "Baggage," and "Peace," along with
three other lectures at Northfield, Massachusetts. The
Northfield General Conference of Christian Works began
in 1880 when Dwight L. Moody called the first meeting.
In 1925, speakers at the forty-third session included John
A. Hutton of Westminster Chapel, London; W. Pearson
Halliday of Selly Oak Colleges, Birmingham, England;
Harry Emerson Fosdick of New York City; and William
Louis Poteat of North Carolina.[17] A Presbyterian periodical reported a new note at Northfield: "Old timers had
good reason to open their eyes in wonder, and question the
accuracy of their ears as speaker after speaker at the
recent conference gave forth a barrage of Modernism."
According to this article, Dr. Poteat was one of the "chief
offenders against orthodox Christian truth."[18] Poteat had
been doubtful as to how the audience (estimated at about

one thousand) would receive his lectures. He confided to his brother, "I was a little dubious about the hospitality of that atmosphere to such a discussion. I was delighted with the reception it received, a vote of thanks, etc., when it was concluded."[19]

After the Northfield conference, more people became familiar with Dr. Poteat's "little book," as he called *Can a Man Be a Christian To-day?* The *Christian Leader* commented, "What he says rings true, as something which has been wrought out of personal experience."[20] A Missouri publication remarked, "It is emphatically a book for such a time as this, if religion and science are to learn how to work together in such a world as this."[21] Henry L. Mencken praised Poteat as "a writer of singular grace and charm, well-informed, full of plausibility, and not without eloquence."[22] Further praise came from W. H. P. Faunce, president of Brown University, who declared, "That such an utterance should come out of the Southland must fill all thoughtful New England people with gladness and that the utterance should be so calm and yet so fearless, so broad and yet so pungent, gives me personally very great satisfaction."[23] Dr. Poteat replied that the impression that the South was backward could be attributed to the fact that ultraconservatives had held the center of the stage and men with different attitudes had not cared to compete for publicity. Poteat illustrated, "I have heard of a farmer who had engaged to deliver a wagon load of bullfrogs to the cafe steward ... actually presenting only two frogs, with the explanation that he did not know two bullfrogs could make so much noise."[24]

The criticism by the ultraconservatives seemed to increase as North Carolina Baptists prepared for the state convention in November. Lawrence Stallings, playwright and son-in-law of Dr. Poteat, warned, "There hasn't been a theological or denominational paper in the South that hasn't been afire with this book [*Can a Man Be a Christian To-day?*]. It will be the rock upon which the fires will be lighted when the Legislatures and convocations rally in the fall hunts and the open season on intelligence begins.''[25] Poteat recognized the criticism but had no objection to it. He commented to his publisher, ''While I have never been hopeful of pleasing everybody and accordingly am not greatly disappointed that some criticisms are antagonistic, criticisms favorable and unfavorable alike will probably help the book to get abroad.''[26]

However, more than literary criticism was involved. Some stanch Baptists were determined to oust the ''evolutionist'' from the presidency of Wake Forest. The first open fight occurred in the August, 1925, meeting of the Buncombe County Baptist Association. R. J. Bateman, a minister in Asheville, was chairman of a committee that proposed a resolution calling for the resignation of Poteat. When he arrived at the meeting, Bateman was surprised to see a group of Wake Forest graduates waiting for him. He inquired, ''What are you boys doing here?'' They replied that they had come to fight him. Bateman protested, ''We must not have a fight,'' and they asked him who brought it on.[27] The debate lasted about five hours. The Wake Forest alumni submitted the argument that during Poteat's service of about forty-two years, Wake Forest had rendered conspicuous service to the cause of religion. One alumnus reminded the association that 75 per cent of the Wake Forest graduates actively supported their home churches and argued, ''Ye shall know them by their fruits,'' not by their theories. The outcome of the argument was a compromise resolution that omitted all personalities and asked for a general investigation of the teaching in all Baptist schools in the state. Even the compromise measure, however, was positive on the matter of evolution. It requested that the North Carolina Baptist State Convention should ''secure and accept the resignation of any and all in these colleges ... who believe and teach the doctrine of evolution as a fact contrary to the faith and historic position of at least ninety-eight per cent of the Baptists of

North Carolina." In the event that the convention refused to accede to this petition, the Buncombe association reserved the right in the future to contribute to specific institutions rather than to the general fund.[28]

George Pennell, a young lawyer who led the opposition to the Bateman resolution, commented that the fight demonstrated that graduates of Wake Forest were willing to stand by Dr. Poteat regardless of where or from whom an attack might come; and, secondly, that the Wake Forest literary societies had produced men who were able to take care of themselves in a rough and tumble fight. Pennell told Dr. Poteat, "I learned one thing, that a fight in a political affair is a tame one compared to one in the Baptist Association, and that you will probably not get hit under the belt as much in a knock-out, drag-out political fight as you will in a fight with the brethren."[29] Poteat replied that the resolution raised was not a personal issue, nor was it a Wake Forest issue. He said, "The issue is rather whether our Christian faith is to be identified with the interpretation which sets it in opposition to the assured results of the science of the time." He expressed the hope that something could be done to keep the Baptist State Convention from going on record in approval of the position taken by the Buncombe association.[30]

Soon after the Buncombe meeting, the secretary of the Tennessee River Baptist Association sent Dr. Poteat a copy of a resolution "Respectfully Submitted and Indorsed by the Association." The resolution stated: "Resolved that we the Tennessee River Baptist Association in session request Dr. W. L. Poteat of Wakeforest to Rezine [sic] as our Baptist Folks will not support Christian Education and him at the head of one of our colleges."[31] The Mecklenburg-Cabarrus association passed a more elaborate "Resolution on Evolution," reaffirming faith in creation by God and urging trustees of Baptist colleges to employ only teachers who believed implicitly in the "Word of God as God's revelation of Himself to the world, and His revelation to us of the beginning of the material universe."[32] The only other local association to adopt a resolution in 1925 directly opposed to evolution was the Gaston County Baptist Association which declared that "all officers and teachers who believe and teach the theory of evolution in reference to the creation of man, or who give lectures or write books endorsing this theory ... should not be allowed to hold positions in our Baptist schools." The resolution further specified that all trustees of Baptist schools should be elected by the Baptist State Convention. The Gaston association selected W. C. Barrett to go to the Charlotte meeting and to attempt similar state-wide action by the Baptist State Convention in November.[33]

The growing agitation over evolution among the members of the Baptist denomination was a matter of concern for the friends of Wake Forest. The dispute had reputedly resulted in a marked decrease in denominational funds for education, missions, and charities although some Baptist leaders attributed the drop in contributions to bad crop conditions in the state. Under the budget plan, any deficiency in one fund was made up from the others, so the only way to refrain from contributing to the college was not to contribute to the purposes of the denomination. On several occasions, Poteat had offered to resign in order to eliminate friction, but the board of trustees had consistently refused his resignation. On August 24, 1925, members of the executive committees of the board of trustees and the alumni of the college, members of the executive committee of the Baptist Board of Missions, Poteat, Livingston Johnson, and several leading ministers met at Raleigh to discuss the matter of evolution. The special meeting in Raleigh lasted more than five hours, but Poteat's supporters reached no conclusion except that they were heartily against his retirement.[34]

The alumni association was the first to take a positive step. At their meeting on September 15, 1925, the alumni issued a statement affirming to the public that Wake Forest was loyal to the fundamentals of the Christian faith. Livingston Johnson published the statement in the *Biblical Recorder* along with a letter from Poteat endorsing the statement.[35] A representative of the New York City alumni expressed the support of Poteat by that group.[36] One ardent advocate even told Poteat, ''Speaking of torches, let me know when the boys propose to burn you. I will gladly get ready to step into the fire with you.''[37] The Baptist association that included the Wake Forest Baptist Church heartily endorsed the college president.[38] When S. J. Betts, a Raleigh minister, blamed Poteat and evolution for $693,525.83 in uncollected funds,[39] V. O. Parker, chairman of the executive committee of the Wake Forest trustees, replied that North Carolina stood among the leading states of the South in contributions to the support of the Baptist denomination. Parker said plainly that it was a known fact that some who made the greatest noise against education made the least contribution and did the least work. He continued, ''In fact, some of us often wonder if some of our brethren are not trying to justify themselves in doing nothing by making criticism against the churches or against our other institutions.''[40]

Poteat himself expected that an anti-evolution resolution would be presented at the Baptist State Convention in November.[41] He wrote to a friend, ''That pressure is, as I understand, likely to come to a head at the Baptist State Convention in Charlotte, where your humble servant will likely be asked to step down and out in one form or another. My present feeling is that, while I may be beaten, I am not disposed to surrender.''[42] In an address before the Mecklenburg Wake Forest College Alumni Association in late October, he said that he planned to be a bystander at the convention, but he would abide by whatever the convention decided. He declared, ''I am willing to serve in any place, but I will wear no chain except such as He puts on me. Eliminate me, stand by the college.'' The Mecklenburg alumni highly endorsed Poteat, the administration, and faculty.[43]

Thus the lines had been drawn by convention time. Poteat had stated his ideas boldly on the teaching of evolution in his controversial book *Can a Man Be a Christian To-day?* Surely the Fundamentalists now had the best opportunity to oust Poteat from the presidency of Wake Forest, and they would undoubtedly seize this opportunity at the November meeting of the Baptist State Convention. The Gaston and Buncombe associations had directed their representatives to attempt to get convention action on the evolution question. Barrett and Bateman, along with other Fundamentalists, went to Charlotte eager to seize the opportunity to act against evolution and Poteat while interest was high. These Fundamentalists felt strongly on the subject of heresy, and the first day of the convention they had a powerful majority. However, that night Wake Forest alumni from all over the state converged on Charlotte. Poteat had said, "I decline to be whipped out on an issue that involves the respectability and opportunity of my *alma mater*."[44] Other alumni of Wake Forest came to the rescue of their alma mater, and a thousand new delegates appeared at the convention prepared to fight.

There was a hasty consultation among the Fundamentalists, who revised their position. When R. J. Bateman introduced his resolution, it stated first a belief in the divine nature of Jesus Christ, and secondly, belief in creation by God as a fact. The third provision pledged an attempt to refrain from using terminology that might "commit us to forms of thought at variance with God's word; but with no intention to bar investigation of all discoverable facts...." The fourth provision advised against the expression of immature conclusions that conflicted with Baptist beliefs. The fifth and last part of the resolution declared opposition to worldly philosophies that "seek to revolutionize the interpretation and undermine the character of God and Christ.''[45] The Bateman resolution was so mild that even Poteat voted for it.[46]

A number of ardent Fundamentalists regarded Bateman's resolution as innocuous because it contained no direct attack on the theory of evolution and no demands for the resignation of teachers who taught the theory, but they realized that trustees sympathetic to the Fundamentalist cause could easily accomplish this in individual schools. At that time, boards of trustees of Baptist institutions were self-perpetuating; they elected persons to fill any vacancies that might occur, and these elections were subject only to the approval of the state convention. Under this system, trustees of Wake Forest who favored Poteat would be likely to elect men of similar feelings to fill vacancies on the board. At the Charlotte meeting, W. C. Barrett moved that the trustees of all Baptist institutions be elected directly by the state convention. Surely many members of the convention must have been surprised when Poteat's friend Bernard W. Spilman rose to second the motion. They understood Spilman's motive, however, when he further moved that the resolution be referred to a committee and that under the new system the trustees be allowed to nominate persons to fill vacancies in their ranks. Thus the only real change was that rather than merely approving a slate of trustees, the convention would elect trustees with the possibility of nominations from the floor. In seconding Barrett's resolution, Spilman really took the sting out of it. Consideration by the committee would take at least a year, and in two years, Poteat would probably retire.[47]

This Charlotte convention put Wake Forest in a new light; a Baptist college dared to acknowledge the teaching of evolution, and the alumni were willing to fight to protect this right. Faced with such strong alumni support, the Fundamentalists reconsidered their stand. Throughout the remainder of the convention, there was no official mention of the word "evolution," and the only reference to Poteat occurred when the chairman called on him to read a letter from Benjamin N. Duke of Durham and New York donating $100,000 to Wake Forest College. Fundamentalist leaders in the South were usually able to intimidate college presidents, especially when endowments were low, but Poteat had stood his ground, and when his position was in danger, the alumni had appeared to support him. Gerald W. Johnson, an outstanding alumnus of the college, said, "He merely stood his ground and whistled, and instantly around him sprang up a thousand alumni, grim alumni, with red eyes and no scruples about flying at a Fundamentalist throat." Why did they go to Charlotte, those "thousand men who whetted their knives as they came and fervently hoped that somebody would start something?"[48] Few of those men cared much about the theory of evolution. Some did not even understand it thoroughly, and certainly most of them were devout churchmen. But they remembered that Wake Forest had opened for them the wonderful door to the world of the mind, and they did not intend to have that door closed in the faces of their sons. They saved Wake Forest for freedom of teaching and for their beloved Dr. Billy. Gerald W. Johnson paraphrased Daniel Webster as he said of his alma mater, "She is small, but there are those who hate her, and her enemies have made her great."[49] The Charlotte convention marked the final battle with Poteat. There were other small skirmishes from time to time, but there was no organized movement against him personally. He had won his fight. He had stood firm, and the Fundamentalists began to realize that he would never be moved. The *Greensboro Daily News* saw the Charlotte convention as reassuring from a political point of view: "It would seem that if the Baptists will not fight in their own convention over their own faith, the political fundamentalists ... will have mighty little encouragement." Nearly all the militant churches, the *Daily News* continued, had ceased quarreling over evolution because the liberals and conservatives learned to work together. "The Charlotte convention has done a great deal to dispirit the politi-

cal fundamentalists. . . .'"[50]   Poteat had thus helped to enable liberals and conservatives to meet on the common
ground of a conservative, albeit an intelligent and well-
informed, Christianity. Christian people had confidence in
Poteat because they could see his living faith. He helped
to make the new science acceptable when he explained it as
God's way of creation. Poteat was the living example that
science and Christianity were in no way contradictory.

In the spring of 1926, there was one last anti-evolution
demonstration in North Carolina. A great many sincere
people among North Carolina Baptists and the interested
public in general were thoroughly disappointed at the lack
of action against evolution in the Charlotte convention.
The Fundamentalists proceeded to organize the Committee
of One Hundred for the purpose of stopping the teaching
of evolution in state-supported schools. Certain Baptists,
such as J. R. Pentuff, W. C. Barrett, and S. J. Betts, and
legislative leader Zebulon Vance Turlington were active in
the organization. Both Judge Walter H. Neal, president
of the committee, and Zebulon Vance Turlington declared
that the organization was not against Poteat.[51] Anti-evolution societies rushed representatives to the scene to aid
in the movement. V. T. Jeffreys of New Jersey came to
represent the Anti-Evolution League and immediately stig-
matized himself by declaring his intention to persecute
Poteat. "Ye gods and little fishes!" the Durham *Herald*
exclaimed. "Is North Carolina going to permit a meddler
from New Jersey to come into this State and work for the
destruction of our educational institutions?"[52]   J. T.
Maples, an evangelist known as the "Texas Cyclone,"
came to Charlotte to help, and Thomas Theodore Martin
arrived to represent the Bible Crusaders of America.
Martin challenged T. G. Pownall of Cumberland, Maryland, field secretary for an association of atheists, to a debate on the subject, "Should the Teaching of Evolution
That Man Evolved from Lower Orders of Animals Be
Excluded from Tax-Supported Schools?" After the Ku

Klux Klan issued a public warning to any atheist who dared come to Charlotte, Pownall declined to make an appearance, saying that his daughter from Texas was visiting him. Numerous freethinkers volunteered to debate with Martin, but he would accept only a declared atheist; as the Ku Klux Klan had made it risky for any atheist to visit Charlotte, Martin did not have to follow through.[53]

At the first meeting of the Committee of One Hundred on May 4, 1925, *The News and Observer* reported, "Scorching epithets and heated discussions which twice looked as if they would end in physical encounter marked a stormy all day session of the committee of 100, the State organization of Fundamentalists held here today." Proponents of anti-evolution action proposed to make a "treaty" with state-supported educational institutions not to teach evolution and to dismiss all teachers who held to the theory. If the "treaty" proved unsuccessful, then the committee would work for suppressive legislation. One speaker at the morning session referred to evolution as "the blackest lie ever blasted out of Hell." The climax came in the afternoon when E. D. Broadhurst, a member of the Greensboro School Board, described some of the ministers who spoke at the morning session as "bitter tongued," intimating that they were afraid to speak again. Broadhurst declared that "such conduct is discouraging to laymen." Walker West, a minister from Lincolnton, immediately jumped to his feet at the rear of the auditorium and rushed down the aisle shouting, "I resent such an insult and I am not going to let it go unchallenged." Some more peaceable delegates forcibly restrained West while Broadhurst continued his speech. Another commotion arose when someone objected to allowing Frank R. McNinch, former mayor of Charlotte, to speak because of his liberal ideas. Tom M. Glasgow, another Charlotte liberal, demanded that McNinch be heard. As Glasgow became more insistent, scores of Fundamentalists jumped to their feet, voiced heated remarks, and threw the meeting into pandemonium. Finally Judge Walter H. Neal restored order.[54]

This type of conduct won the committee a poor reputation in North Carolina. In speaking of the May 4 meeting of the committee, the *Charlotte Observer* announced, "For bitterness of expression, and vindictiveness of purpose, it exceeded any meeting, of any description... and if anything, certain of the ministers were even more rabid than the laymen."[55]   The general atmosphere of the meeting alienated many who had previously supported the committee.   A. A. McGeachy, pastor of the Second Presbyterian Church that housed the meeting, apologized to reporters for the scene they had witnessed.   He personally decided to sever connections with the committee.   Other prominent personalities objected to the Charlotte exhibition.   The *Charlotte News* had at first strongly endorsed the committee, but after the meeting, the paper withdrew its support.   Many people also objected to the interference of the anti-evolution representatives from out of state. Thomas Theodore Martin even had trouble finding an auditorium in which to speak because proprietors were afraid of disastrous results and destruction of property.   He remarked, "In all my years of experience in this work, I've never met up with as much antagonism as I have encountered here.   They talk about 'freedom of thought,' but they don't seem anxious to extend that right or courtesy to me."   The *Greensboro Daily News* reported Martin's statement and answered, "How much 'freedom of thought' is involved in the demand of a self-invited savior and some atheists he has imported to be allowed the use of a church or a city auditorium to stage a vaudeville exhibition in which the state thus far has exhibited a profound indifference might be a pretty question itself for debate."[56]

The Fundamentalists had been their own worst enemy, for they had injured their cause by their misguided zeal. North Carolina had long been a moderate state, her climate neither very hot nor very cold, her people neither rich nor poor. She had been cautious about joining the Union and cautious about attempting to leave it in 1861. North Carolina found her place in history under the leadership of moderate men. In the 1920's the weakness of the Fundamentalists was the strength of Poteat, for though a stanch defender of truth, he was a moderate man. According to *Charity and Children*, when a Fundamentalist declared that everyone who believed in evolution was an atheist, he did not establish his position as a leader among men, he was simply put down as another crank. Archibald Johnson, editor of *Charity and Children*, heartily supported Poteat throughout the evolution controversy and explained his influence thus: "The strength of W. L. Poteat that so puzzles visitors from outside the state is due to the fact that, although he leans toward modernism, he is a moderate man."[57] Poteat's ideas about evolution did not seem moderate to some people at that time. In fact, they seemed somewhat revolutionary to many. But in his personality, in his way of presenting his ideas, Poteat was a moderate man. He was a quiet, easygoing person who spoke slowly and deliberately and seldom raised his voice. He never resorted to the attention-seeking actions of some of his opponents, nor would he exchange epithets with them. One of his favorite sayings was, "Profanity shows a small vocabulary." To a letter criticizing him in vicious language, he might simply reply, "Dear Sir: It is always interesting to get the opinion of a good man. W. L. Poteat."[58]

It is apparent that publication of *Can a Man Be a Christian To-day?* was a significant event in the history of education in North Carolina. The lectures provoked the Presbyterian Synod of North Carolina to adopt a memorial suggesting that a liaison be established between the Synod and the University of North Carolina to insure that the McNair lectures would be carried on according to the will of John Calvin McNair. Members of the Synod felt that McNair was a conservative and that the university had made his lectures a forum for liberal thought. The Presbyterian clergyman who introduced the resolution called Poteat's lectures "a controversial assault on fundamentalism rather than a defense of the Christian faith."[59] Dr. Poteat's "little book" had roused conservative Baptists to attempt to oust the biologist from the presidency of Wake Forest, but the alumni had intervened to save him. Gradually, both the praise and the criticism faded, but *Can a Man Be a Christian To-Day?* remained as a vital question and an inspiring answer for all generations.

Apostle Emeritus

A lthough by 1926 the evolution controversy was beginning to decline in some parts of the South,[1] to many
Southern Baptists evolution was still a vital issue. In
the spring of 1926, A. L. Pickens, a professor of biology
at Furman University, was forced to resign because he
taught Darwin's theory. Later the Southern Baptist Convention met at Houston, Texas, and adopted on May 15,
1926, a resolution stating that it "accepts Genesis as teaching that man was the special creation of God, and rejects
every theory, evolution or other which teaches that man
originated in or came by way of lower animal ancestry."
The convention further recommended that such a statement be required of teachers and officers of Baptist
schools.[2]

No doubt the action of the convention pleased some
Baptists, but it displeased many others. Josiah W. Bailey,
a prominent North Carolina layman and former editor of
the *Biblical Recorder*, wrote to Edgar Young Mullins, presi-

dent of the Southern Baptist Convention, that the organization did not have the authority to order teachers formally to subscribe to such a statement and that the Baptist institutions should ignore the resolution.[3] The *Biblical Recorder* saw the resolution as a result of politics instigated by S. E. Tull of Arkansas, a persistent agitator. Livingston Johnson said that "those agitators who profess to be so much concerned for the unity of the convention are doing more to create division than any other class." Johnson also indicated that the majority of those who voted for the Tull resolution did so to settle the matter once and for all so that the convention could go on to other and more important business. Another obstruction to the business of the convention had been the activities of J. Frank Norris. Johnson referred to him as "the brakeman on the great Baptist train" and questioned, "How long will some good people continue to be deceived by this Baptist(?) Bolshevick [sic], who has been repudiated by his own association...?"[4]

In the final analysis, Norris' efforts undoubtedly injured the Fundamentalist cause by identifying it with fanaticism. The very persecution of the evolutionists stimulated interest in their ideas, with the result that the fear of evolution gradually abated. The radio played an increasingly important part, for when people could hear evolutionists, they were better able to formulate their own independent opinions as to whether or not the evolutionists were "heretics." Educational opportunities broadened in the 1920's, and this increased public receptiveness to new ideas. Even the Tennessee legislature that passed the anti-evolution bill provided a longer school term and the largest appropriation ever made to the state university. Laws to bar evolution did little good, for people discussed it in spite of the law. As more people learned to understand evolution, they lost interest in Fundamentalist agitation. The Fundamentalists found themselves on the defensive, and they lost confidence in their ability to convince others to repudiate the evolution theory.

By 1926 several Fundamentalist societies had lost their effectiveness as a result of the growing public coolness toward their work. The widespread endeavor of the World's Christian Fundamentals Association narrowed perceptibly with the loss of enthusiasm and a disappointing attendance at the Toronto convention of 1926. The Bible Crusaders, founded by real estate tycoon George F. Washburn and then under the leadership of Thomas T. Martin, declined rapidly. Representative E. K. Wyndham of Louisiana was irritated by the lobbying of the organization. He suggested that some Crusaders were motivated less by religious convictions than by a desire for financial betterment.[5] After 1926 no representative of the Crusaders appeared where anti-evolution bills were under discussion.

Following several years of charges and resolutions, the Southern Baptist Convention seemed free of the evolution dispute, and after 1926 Southern Baptists exhibited little interest in anti-evolution agitation. Financial difficulty, especially for foreign missions, forced churchmen to turn their energies elsewhere.[6] The prohibition issue loomed large on the national scene and demanded the attention of churchmen.

In the 1926 legislative elections, North Carolinians replaced many proponents of the Poole Bill with representatives who were not in favor of anti-evolution legislation. The Bible League of North Carolina, which replaced the Committee of One Hundred, sponsored another attempt for such a law in 1927. The Education Committee defeated Poole's second anti-evolution bill by a vote of twenty-five to eleven, and the measure never reached the floor of the House.[7] North Carolinians no longer seemed vitally interested in the subject. Poteat had proved that Fundamentalist pressure could not force him to resign or to compromise his position on either science or religion. For years he had refused to resign under pressure, but in the summer of 1926, he felt that the pressure had subsided sufficiently to enable him to carry out his intention to retire. Nearing his seventieth birthday, Poteat announced in August of that year that he would retire the following June.

There had been some criticism of Wake Forest in the spring of 1926. The dissatisfaction seemed to arise from the fact that plans for expansion of the college, announced in 1923, had not materialized. One critic stated, "The campus and buildings everywhere have the appearance of being just patched up sufficiently to keep things going after a fashion." Wake Forest may have missed some financial support because of Poteat's stand on the evolution question but probably not enough to make a significant difference. However, it was true that Poteat had been more interested in the quality of scholarship than in the physical plant.

Another criticism involved an allegation that Poteat had mistreated a former dean of the college, but several alumni declared publicly that this charge had no basis of fact. It was believed by some that those with ambitions to take over his position magnified the criticism against Poteat.[8]

Although the desire to avoid such unpleasantness may have had some influence, it is probable that advancing age was the primary factor in prompting Poteat's resignation since he had previously announced his intention to relinquish the position of president at age seventy. He wrote to the Wake Forest trustees, "My seventieth birthday is scarcely four weeks behind me. On the sole consideration of my age and no other, and in conformity with a long settled purpose, I now ask you to relieve me at the end of the present session...." He declared that his devotion to the college was unabated and that his loyalty to her ideal of enlightenment in the service of Christ was uncompromised. "Such powers as are yet mine," he said, "are at your command for her use and behoof in other directions."[9]

The college student body adopted resolutions pledging love and confidence and deplored Poteat's intention to resign. When student body president Cloyce R. Tew presented the resolutions, the students gave a rousing cheer. The resolutions stated that during the same period there had been no more successful administration in the South. "It is equally safe to say that it would be difficult to find ...a college president anywhere in the United States who has commanded a wider hearing, attracted more widespread attention from thoughtful people or wielded a larger influence."[10]

Despite many protests, Poteat had definitely decided to resign, and he refused to heed the insistence of the trustees that he await the naming of a successor. The remarkable record of the college's growth and achievement under Poteat helped to explain the reluctance of the trustees to accept his resignation. When he became president, he found an enrollment of 313 students, a faculty of 17 members, a plant appraised at $194,500, a library of 16,000 volumes, and an endowment of $210,176.93 par value. The enrollment for the 1927 session was 748, the faculty numbered 42, the appraised value of the physical equipment and plant was $576,086.34, while the library contained 50,000 volumes, and the endowment had reached nearly $3,000,000. In expressing appreciation for Poteat's services, a committee of the Board of Trustees stated, "The breadth and accuracy of Dr. Poteat's learning, his superb platform ability and his impressive personality have won for him the respect and admiration of the thinking men of America...." They noted that this respect extended to the college which he represented. "It is pleasant to add," the committee continued, "that Dr. Poteat's beautiful and brotherly spirit, devout piety and reverent regard for all things holy have won for him the love of all who know him well."[11]

In his final baccalaureate address as president, Poteat struck once more the keynote of his contribution. He explained that Wake Forest had come to be known for an attitude of faith in the truth. "And those men of science who pushed out the sphere of light on any radius,—what have we to fear from them?" he asked. "Whether they explore over seas or underground, on wings of light probe the stellar deeps, reconnoiter on the obscurer pathways of the soul, or, in the hallowed isolation of the laboratory, watch Nature at her secret handiwork, they are the children of the dawn and heralds of the light of the world." He added that fear of their revelations made people ignorant. Poteat reported that there was evidence that Wake Forest was the first southern institution to introduce the laboratory method of teaching biology. "Forty years ago, she was not afraid to learn," he said. "She is not afraid today. For a laboratory worker with the light of Christ shining in his heart is like a miner with a lamp on his cap, illumination keeping pace with his penetration." Poteat declared that a Christian college must insist upon freedom of inquiry and freedom of report, and it is apparent that he had been able to maintain this kind of freedom at Wake Forest because of his rare talent in dealing with the Baptist State Convention. That august body might easily have intimidated a lesser man, but Poteat could rise above petty controversies of personality and deep-seated antagonism toward science because of his unusual combination of intellect, culture, and Christian character. He had thrilled liberals with his fight for freedom of thought and reassured conservatives by his inspiring sermons to Baptist associations, churches, and sometimes to the convention itself. He fully understood and believed, "Deal frankly with youth, or not at all. Dodge no problem, religious, historical, social, or scientific."[12]

When William Louis Poteat left the presidency of Wake Forest College, he accepted the title of President Emeritus and continued to teach biology. He also retained his position as the outstanding figure in the evolution controversy in the South. William Jennings Bryan had been

more famous, but he had won recognition mainly in other
fields. Poteat's unique position as a college president, a
scientist, and a leader in the Baptist denomination had
given him the opportunity to lead the people of the South
to understand that the truths of science and religion were
in no way contradictory. In spite of concentrated Fundamentalist efforts, the North Carolina legislature had refused to pass an anti-evolution bill. As long as Poteat
maintained his stand, agitators could not force any teacher
of science in the state to resign. At his retirement, Poteat
could see the fruits of his work, not only in the material
growth of Wake Forest College, but in the existing freedom
of thought in North Carolina. The *Greensboro Daily News*
reported, ''Because the Poteat of another day stood with
a faith no man might question and demanded all that the
searchers after truth might find, the Poteat of this day can
enunciate his doctrine of freedom under the benediction of
a people who themselves have seen the light.''[13] Angus W.
McLean, governor of North Carolina, declared that the
greatest era in the growth and usefulness of Wake Forest
was the period during which Poteat directed its destinies.
''He gave it not only national but international standing.
... The benign influence and quickening power of his
unselfish life will be felt here as long as the cardinal virtues
of truth and devotion to duty are revered of men.''[14]

The *New York Times* recognized his contribution in the
evolution controversy as follows: ''His own life as student,
teacher and head of a college in North Carolina for more
than half a century has given ample evidence that it is
possible for one to be a man of deep religious faith and yet
of profound scientific scholarship.'' Although the controversy might never be over, higher freedom had been
assured to the spirit of man.[15] The *Durham Morning
Herald* declared that North Carolina Baptists would do
well to elect Poteat ''Apostle Emeritus'' for their denomination in the state and for the entire South and that they
should endow him so that he could devote full time to

proclamation of the gospel. "Few thinkers have as
thorough and inspiring comprehension of the Gospel of
Jesus Christ as has Dr. Poteat." The newspaper continued, "Although a layman, he has given the most careful
thought to the meaning of the life and person of Christ.
He has espoused with enthusiasm the appeal to youth
that Christ was continually making during his ministry on
earth."[16]

Although the title was never officially his, "Apostle
Emeritus" seemed to fit William Louis Poteat. He continued a full career of lecture engagements in addition to
his duties at the college. He spoke in churches, to Baptist
associations, at Armistice Day celebrations, and prohibition
rallies. He was probably the most sought-after speaker in
the state for baccalaureate addresses. In discussions of the
gospel, disarmament, modern morals, Christian education,
and prohibition, he usually had a special message for youth.
Science and religion was a topic much less frequently, for
that controversy was evidently settled.

However, in 1931, a situation arose which proved that
appearances could be misleading. Poteat had agreed to
give the report of the Education Commission of the Southern Baptist Convention when that body met in Birmingham. Much to his surprise, there seemed to be some objection to his appearing because of his scientific views. He
informed his brother Edwin, "One member of the Commission, Dr. Wiley of Illinois, writes Cullom that if it is announced in the papers that an evolutionist is to appear on
the Convention platform, there will be public protest, which
I understand to mean that he himself will make the protest." Other members of the commission warned that an
embarrassing situation might develop on the floor of the
Convention. Therefore, Poteat withdrew his acceptance
to speak in order that he might save the commission from
any possible embarrassment. He said, "My first reaction
was to speak, protest or no protest; it might do the pro-
testers good, and I have a deep seated resentment against

Paul's weaker brother determining policy for the whole bunch.'' Nevertheless, he was greatly relieved that he need not attend the convention and labor several weeks in the preparation of the speech. ''I am chagrined,'' he declared, ''that the old silly controversy, which I had thought dead and deeply buried, has arisen to say the report was greatly exaggerated.''[17]

In his younger days, Dr. Billy would probably have become even more determined to attend the convention when opposition seemed imminent, for he was not above baiting the Fundamentalists occasionally. But nearing his seventy-fifth birthday, he was more interested in a quiet trip to Europe than in a fight at the convention, so he made reservations for Emma and himself to join a tour group. What better way could there be to celebrate a Golden Wedding anniversary than with a second honeymoon?

As they celebrated their fiftieth wedding anniversary, Emma and Louis Poteat must have been very pleased with the records of half a century. In 1901, when he was only fourteen years old, Hubert had remarked to his father that he would like to become a professor of Latin at Wake Forest. After earning his doctorate from Columbia University, he realized this ambition. His achievements included many excellent translations of Latin works as well as leadership in fraternal orders. He had two sons, William and Hubert. William became an attorney while Hubert chose the medical profession.

Louie married Wheeler Martin, a successful businessman. Her parents often visited them and their son Wheeler, Jr., at their home in Williamston, North Carolina. Louie was active in civic work and in the church, where she directed the choir for many years.

Helen, voted the prettiest and most stylish girl in the senior class at Meredith College, married Lawrence Stallings, a graduate of Wake Forest who became a famous playwright and author. Helen wrote poetry and book reviews that appeared in *Bookman*, *Scribners'*, and the

American Mercury. Their daughters, Sylvia and Diana,
also chose journalistic careers as literary critics on the
staffs of large newspapers. The Stallings restored Forest
Home to its former beauty and added a wing on each side.
In addition to the pleasure of having the Stallings branch
of the family within the state after several years of living
in New York and Hollywood, the opportunity to return to
his boyhood home gave Dr. Billy much happiness. Forest
Home was a wonderful place for family gatherings. "We
live in and for our children at my time of life," the grandfather said, "indeed from the beginning of that happy
relation. And you hardly know the difference between
children and grandchildren."[18]

The Poteat's marriage was a happy one. In many ways
husband and wife were alike; in other ways, they comple-
mented each other. Both had good cultural backgrounds
and appreciated the finer things of life. Both enjoyed
music and played the guitar, an instrument that was very
popular in their youth. Louis Poteat was a heavy-set man
of tremendous energy and stamina, deliberate, painstaking,
and self-controlled in manner. He always looked for the
best in people and was able to inject a touch of humor into
most situations. Emma, an only child of devoted parents,
was beautiful, highly sensitive, and talented, with aspira-
tions that sometimes exceeded her physical strength. During her frequent illnesses she received the devoted attention of her husband. The life of the Poteats was a busy one.
Their family circle was often enlivened in the evening by
groups of friends who gathered for musical entertainment,
discussions of literature, or conversations on current affairs. When it was necessary for Poteat to be away from
home, his letters to Emma and hers to him were always
love letters. While en route from Venice to Milan, in
celebration of their fiftieth wedding anniversary, Poteat
wrote a poem to Emma reminiscent of those written during
their courtship.

An Itinerary
(To E.P.P.)

In quiet academic paths
In the mirk and jam of the cañoned city,
On the curved blue breast of the sea,
Under the streaming mane of plunging iron-horses,
On forest-columned cathedral aisles,
On the heights where Beauty walks arm-in-arm with
    Raphael and Michaelangelo,
In ghostly silences of Pompeii,
On Anacapri's precipice, in the blue wonder below,
In a gondola spiriting away to the young moon above
    Salute,
By blue-green Reuss breaking anger-white in his
    wild gorge,
Impatient for his tryst with fair Lucerne,
Down the liquid lane of legend and romance to the
    twin glories of Cologne,—
I have loved you
These fifty golden days of thirty-one,
These fifty golden years since eighty-one,
And, please God, at length we'll take together
The same street in the golden city of our dreams.[19]

Poteat thoroughly enjoyed the trip, which included
Paris, Naples, Geneva, Rome, Venice, Lucerne, Cologne,
and London. He said that in his estimation a conducted
tour was the best way for the average man to travel in
Europe although a tour had certain drawbacks. "One is
haste with slight opportunity for study and observation,"
he declared. "What can you learn about politics or industries from a car window or in an art gallery?" He
noticed that Europe was severely hit by the drop in tourist
trade brought about by the depression. Nevertheless, the
fine wheat harvest suggested that Europe would be feeding
itself the next year. He was especially impressed with
agricultural prosperity in Italy but found France better

off financially because people had employment repairing war damage while Germany paid the bill. In spite of hopeful aspects in some places, Poteat apprehended the future when he warned, "I was told that the laboring people of Germany are in a very bad way, so bad that they are trembling on the edge of violence."[20] Poteat would not live to see this violence involve the United States, but his grandson, Wheeler Martin, Jr., would give his life while serving his country against Germany.

The European trip was a pleasant vacation from college duties and lecture engagements. Soon after his return, prohibition became a major issue that claimed much of his time. Franklin D. Roosevelt, elected president in 1932, pledged repeal of national prohibition. When North Carolinians began a crusade to keep liquor out of the state, they turned again to Poteat for leadership.

The years since his retirement in 1927 had been rather peaceful ones, unhampered by dedication to any particular cause, but Poteat was a crusader, and he could not remain on the sidelines when an issue of principle arose. Soon the "Apostle Emeritus" would again be an active worker in the field.

Beat John Barleycorn!

In the 1930's many patrons of John Barleycorn were determined not to "see America thirst" any longer. They blamed the Eighteenth Amendment for bootlegging and its related crimes. To the advocates of legalized liquor, speakeasies and bathtub gin seemed proof that the noble experiment had failed. On the other hand, prohibitionists maintained that consumption of alcohol had decreased considerably under the Eighteenth Amendment and declared that the fact that some people disobeyed the law was not a valid reason for its repeal.

William Louis Poteat and many other intelligent citizens, especially in the South, supported the dry cause. Although Poteat realized that bootleggers swelled the ranks of the prohibitionists and enforcement of the law was difficult, he believed that such enforcement was possible and that its achievement would be a major step in the right direction. Far from being fanatical on the subject, he had no objection to alcohol in moderation, but he felt that the

serious social problems related to alcoholism were sufficient
reason to eliminate the legal sale of all intoxicating
beverages.

In North Carolina where the Democratic party leadership and the churches favored the dry cause, prohibition
had been in effect since 1908. Poteat as a leader of the
drys had served as president of the Anti-Saloon League.
Annual or semiannual rounds of temperance field days,
during which churches in a certain area were used as a
public forum for prohibition, kept the issue alive. This
form of grass-roots campaigning gave the movement its
sustained political power in North Carolina, and no decidedly wet candidate attained high office in the state from
1908 to 1932.[1]

There was a rift in this co-operative atmosphere in
1928 when the Anti-Saloon League broke with the Democratic party to support Herbert Hoover for the presidency
over the wet candidate, Al Smith. While party leaders
Furnifold M. Simmons and Frank R. McNinch helped campaign for Hoover, those who remained loyal to the Democratic candidate included Josephus Daniels, Cameron Morrison, and Clyde Hoey.[2] Because of this split and the financial pinch of the depression, the Anti-Saloon League was in
desperate straits. The Reverend Mr. Charles A. Upchurch,
superintendent of the League, decided on a bold effort to
heal the ranks. He called a convention for January 21 and
22 to meet in Greensboro. This group elected William L.
Poteat president and formed a new board of directors that
promptly proceeded to oust Upchurch. The latter claimed
he was a political scapegoat, tainted by the 1928 election,
but the board claimed he had failed to finance the League
properly. It is also possible that Democratic leaders feared
they would be unable to control such a militant leader.
Some believed that the League had served its usefulness
and a new organization was needed.[3]

The North Carolina senatorial election of 1932 provided
evidence of such a need. Robert R. Reynolds, "in favor of

repeal and real temperance," entered the Democratic primary against the incumbent, Cameron Morrison, a dry.[4] Poteat signed a statement appealing to the voters of the state to choose Morrison. The statement said in part, "Moral forces in their support of Cameron Morrison for the United States Senate ... will never feel the humiliation of being dominated and ruled by the liquor lovers of the nation, who, selfishly seeking their own desires, are demanding the repeal of the 18th Amendment in the name of good government."[5] In spite of the stand taken by prohibitionists, Reynolds won the election, and the wets interpreted this as evidence that the state was ready to repudiate prohibition.[6] The dry forces mobilized to prevent such a move.

As a part of the dry campaign, Poteat wrote a series of articles for the *Biblical Recorder,* attempting to refute certain ideas about alcohol which he felt to be erroneous. He said that the propaganda advanced by the potential manufacturers of alcohol had misled many people. He stated, "It may be useful to specify and correct some popular errors about alcohol, ignored when not positively promoted by many of the enemies of prohibition." Contrary to popular belief, Poteat declared, alcohol was neither a food nor a medicine. It could not be a food because it supplied only energy, not material with which to rebuild cells. Although alcohol could be medically useful in a few instances to relax tension or modify distribution of blood, it could not cure a disease. One of the most popular fallacies, Poteat continued, was that alcohol was a stimulant. It was a depressant, he continued, for it acted to dull nerve sensation.[7]

Poteat declared that the federal constitution should define the control of alcohol, for the constitution was the only medium of legislation for all the states which was secure against politics. Thirty-three states had attempted to enforce prohibition, Poteat stated, but they had been unable to do so successfully because of the possibility of obtaining alcohol from other states that did not prohibit the sale. To the accusation that the Eighteenth Amendment was ineffective, Poteat replied, "Name me a law which prevents its own violation. The Ten Commandments do not prevent their violation. Better repeal them!... To say that there has been no enforcement of the Prohibition law and no decline of liquor drinking is an outrageous misrepresentation of manifest fact.... In North Carolina it is the judgment of judges and solicitors that the Prohibition law is better enforced than any other law of the criminal code."[8]

Josiah W. Bailey, United States senator for North Carolina, noticed one of Poteat's articles and wrote to him for advice about the national Democratic platform for 1932. Bailey said, "I am to be on the Platform Committee and would appreciate a letter from you discussing this matter in your own intelligent and considerate way. The question in my mind is not political; it is personal and social. I do not intend to pursue a vote-getting course in a matter so serious."[9] Poteat replied, "Flat repeal, as well as wine and beer, means the saloon again. On state determination and control we have accumulated a decisive mass of experimental data. Constitutional prohibition honestly administered appears to be our only hope." Poteat's suggestion was bold defiance of the wet propaganda and commitment to law enforcement. Bailey may have accepted Poteat's suggestion at that time, but he later favored repeal. Despite some prohibitionist sentiment among Democrats, the party platform of 1932 demanded repeal of the Eighteenth Amendment. After Franklin Delano Roosevelt's success in the November presidential election, it was evident that there would be an attempt to end the prohibition era.[10]

At the 1932 meeting of the North Carolina Baptist State Convention, Poteat continued his attempts to insure the protection of the Eighteenth Amendment. He introduced resolutions stating that the convention, representing more than 400,000 Baptists, reaffirmed devotion to the Eighteenth

Amendment and protested against any and all efforts to repeal or modify it. The resolutions also authorized a committee to transmit an account of the protest to the President of the United States, the President-elect, and to the Senators and Representatives from North Carolina.[11]

Santford Martin, editor of the *Winston-Salem Journal*, was an outstanding advocate of prohibition in North Carolina, and he summarized some of Poteat's *Biblical Recorder* articles in his editorials. Martin recognized Poteat's leadership when he said, "Dr. Poteat is rendering a singular service to our people, and I have already given editorial expression to that opinion. He is laying the foundation for a campaign that ought to save North Carolina from the clutches of the legalized liquor traffic in days to come."[12]

In the early months of 1933, the North Carolina General Assembly became a battleground for the prohibition issue. On January 10, 1933, Representative Giles W. Cover of Cherokee County introduced a bill to repeal the Turlington Act that provided for prohibition enforcement in North Carolina, but the House voted sixty-five to thirty-three against the Cover bill.[13] On January 25, Walter Murphy of Rowan County and Thomas C. Bowie of Ashe County introduced a joint bill to permit the sale of light wines and beer in the event of national repeal. Murphy proposed another bill to permit the sale of whiskey in drugstores by prescription. Both bills were referred to Judiciary Committee Number One.

The North Carolina Anti-Saloon League made an effort to influence public opinion against the proposed bills to legalize the sale of intoxicating beverages. Poteat spoke at an Anti-Saloon League Field Day in Raleigh on January 15 and at another in Winston-Salem on January 29. Sixty churches in the Winston-Salem area participated, and Poteat spoke at the Brown Memorial Baptist Church. He declared the evils of the saloon, explained that the federal enforcement bureau had announced that the national consumption of beverage alcohol had been reduced 60 per cent

since 1920, and pointed out that enforcement of the prohibition law had reached a higher efficiency than that of any
other federal law. He observed that the election of Roosevelt over Hoover as a mandate for the repeal of the Eighteenth Amendment was questionable. "The primary factor
in the popular vote," Poteat said, "was . . . an angry revolt
against a diseased economic system and the stupid and
wicked policy of maintaining the privileges of the few
against the rights of the many." Poteat challenged
Christian men and women to halt the forces in favor of
legalized liquor. He concluded, "We must triumph in the
end. A cause so just, so loaded with present blessing, so
charged with happy destiny for the children of the future,
must not fail. That would look like insurrection in the
Kingdom of God. I have faith in the God of righteousness
and in you His loyal representatives, and bells keep saying
victory from the steeples of my soul."[14]

George J. Burnett, superintendent of the North Carolina Anti-Saloon League, thanked Poteat for speaking on
behalf of the organization. He said, "You are gracious to
do the speaking on so many occasions. You do it so well
you are in great demand. You are the first person asked
for in my efforts to fill the speaking engagements since
June 1st when I began here in Greensboro."[15]

In spite of the efforts of the League, the legislature continued consideration of the enabling measures. On February 14, the Judiciary Committee Number One unexpected-
ly reported favorably on the Bowie-Murphy bill to legalize
the sale of wine and beer in North Carolina, contingent
upon like action by Congress. The House, however, sent
the bill back to the committee for a public hearing.[16] On
February 16, the United States Senate approved repeal of
the Eighteenth Amendment, thus bringing the nation one
step closer to the legal sale of alcoholic beverages. The
following Tuesday, February 21, the Judiciary Committee
Number One held an open hearing on the Bowie-Murphy
bill. Dry leaders appearing before the committee de-

manded that a referendum be held before adoption of that or any other measure materially changing the existing state of prohibition. Their argument was that the state had adopted prohibition by referendum; therefore, the people should have a right to vote on any basic change in the prohibition law. Poteat, the leader of the dry forces at the committee hearing, said, ''I do not believe the mind of North Carolina has changed on this question—especially upon the disgrace of the saloon.'' The crowd of about 150 persons at the hearing applauded Poteat's declaration that the dry forces intended to fight the return of the saloon.[17]

On March 2, Poteat again led the dry forces at the open hearing on the Murphy bill that would permit the sale of liquor by drug stores if prescribed by a doctor. Despite efforts of the prohibitionists, the committee reported the bill favorably. The House, however, on March 6, defeated the measure by a vote of seventy-five to nineteen.[18]

After the national Congress authorized the sale of beer and wine on March 22, 1933, the North Carolina Senate discussed an enabling measure for the state. Poteat once more spoke at the committee hearing. *The News and Observer* reported, ''Drys who stand unequivocably for retention of the law as now written exhorted the committee to kill the bill, introduced by Senator W. Roy Francis of Haywood, and their supporters vigorously applauded sentiments presenting the case against beer.'' Advocates of the bill condemned prohibition as unworkable and obnoxious. They cited the provisions of the Francis bill as pathways to temperance and sources of revenue. Some proponents of the measure flaunted gaudy red and black pennants proclaiming, ''We want Beer!'' Once when Poteat was engaged in introducing a witness for prohibition, a voice from the gallery called, ''We want a wet speaker.'' Poteat replied, ''Well you'll have an hour of that later. I hope it'll drown you.''[19]

This time the prohibitionists were defeated. The Senate voted thirty-three to eleven in favor of the bill, and on

April 4 the House confirmed this verdict by a vote of
seventy-two to twenty-five.[20]   After 12:01 A.M. on May 1,
sale of beer, lager beer, ale, porter, fruit juices, and light
wines containing not more than 3.2 per cent of alcohol by
weight would be legal in North Carolina.[21]

The next task before the North Carolina General Assembly concerning the prohibition question was the setting
up of a convention to vote on the Twenty-first Amendment,
repealing the Eighteenth, which Congress had submitted to
the states. The Constitution of North Carolina provided
that if an amendment were submitted, the electorate would
vote at the next general election on whether or not to call
a convention. If a majority opposed the amendment, they
could vote against calling a convention and thus eliminate
the expense of such a meeting. If, however, the electorate
desired a convention, delegates would be elected on the
basis of representation in the General Assembly. Candidates would be nominated by petitions signed by 2 per
cent of the total vote cast for governor in the county. The
rules of regular elections would apply, but there would be
neither markers nor absentee ballots.[22]

The next general election was to take place in November of 1934, and some North Carolina legislators felt that
this date was too far away. November 7, 1933, seemed
preferable. Since the question involved the North Carolina Constitution, the General Assembly referred it to the
Supreme Court, which ruled that November 7, 1933, would
be an acceptable date. Judge Heriot Clarkson cast the
only dissenting vote in the Supreme Court decision. Clarkson, in favor of prohibition, felt that there was a need for
some direction of the dry movement. The drys in the state
were still divided over the Al Smith campaign, and Clarkson saw the need for unity. He called a meeting of leaders
of the Anti-Saloon League, the Woman's Christian Temperance Union, and various other organizations interested
in prohibition to form an organization for combating the
wet measures in the General Assembly. At a meeting on

February 16 at the Raleigh Y.M.C.A., the name "United Dry Council" was suggested,[23] but it was later changed to "United Dry Forces of North Carolina." The organization did not take permanent form until May 25 when, at the written invitation of Poteat, temporary chairman of the dry forces, the state's leading prohibitionists met at Raleigh. There was some disagreement among the various organizations represented there, and Zebulon Vance Turlington, author of the state prohibition enforcement act, stressed the need for unification. He said that the drys "are not fighting for the life of the Anti-Saloon League or the life of the Woman's Christian Temperance Union, but for the moral life of the State of North Carolina." The drys applauded Turlington's remark and succeeded in overcoming dissension. The group formed a steering committee for the United Dry Forces and gave the committee instructions to lay plans for calling a state-wide meeting larger than the existing one. The steering committee was also to choose a permanent executive committee of forty members. The United Dry Forces of North Carolina unanimously elected Poteat president of the organization and chose Charles L. Ruffin, operator of a Raleigh printing plant, as secretary.[24]

Poteat did not wish to serve as president of the organization and told Ruffin, "You will, I think, understand my embarrassment in the position of President of the United Dry Forces, when I am unable to do the work of the position." He explained that he did not like figureheads and asked Ruffin to present his resignation to the steering committee.[25]

At this time Poteat was seventy-six years old. In addition to writing articles and lecturing throughout the state, he continued to teach biology and hygiene at Wake Forest. Despite his advancing years, his mind was sharp and his sense of humor was as quick as ever. Occasionally the students thought their mischief went undetected, but with all his years of experience with young men, Dr. Billy

did not miss much. On the day before Christmas holidays
were to begin, several students decided to leave early and
asked classmates to answer the roll for them. As Dr.
Billy called the roll, the few students present grew more
and more elated as he seemed not to notice the incongruity
of the sparsely populated classroom and the number marked
present on the roll. Finally, he came to a name for which
there was no response. He looked up from the roll book,
licked his lips in his own peculiar way, and with deliberate
emphasis said, "What? No answer? Very well, *I'll*
answer for Mr. Jones.... Present." Then amid gasps of
surprise, he calmly began the day's lesson.[26]

With his busy schedule of teaching, writing, and lecturing, Poteat really did not have the time to supply active
leadership to the United Dry Forces. However, the steering committee of that organization ignored his protests and
refused to accept his resignation. They placed Cale K.
Burgess, a Raleigh attorney, in charge of the campaign
with Frances R. Doak, vice-president of the North Carolina
Federation of Social and Civil Agencies, as his assistant.
Experienced Anti-Saloon League men C. A. Upchurch and
George J. Burnett were two of the four field organizers
elected by the committee. The United Dry Forces obtained
office equipment from the Anti-Saloon League and began
a campaign of advertising. The declared objectives of the
organization were to use every legitimate means to educate
the voters of the state to sustain the prohibition laws, to
promote temperance by aiding school authorities in teaching the danger of alcohol, to co-operate with other prohibition agencies, and to remain non-partisan, non-political,
and non-denominational.

On June 28, the United Dry Forces published an appeal
to the voters of North Carolina, signed by Poteat and the
other officers, in the *Biblical Recorder*. The statement declared, "We would regard the repeal of the Eighteenth
Amendment as a calamity to our Nation. We believe that

prohibition at its worst is better than the legalized sale of intoxicating liquor for beverage purposes at its best.''[27]

While the North Carolina drys were organizing and working hard for their cause, the wets did nothing. Many felt that a wet victory was assured at the November election, but *The State* magazine warned, ''Something has got to be done about co-ordinating the anti-prohibition forces in North Carolina; otherwise they're all going to be pulling in different directions, and their boat won't get anywhere.''[28] In July, Walter Murphy set up wet headquarters in Raleigh and proceeded to lead the work for repeal.

At the same time, the United Dry Forces intensified its campaign. The steering committee, renamed the Central Committee, divided the state into two sections. The eastern division with headquarters at Raleigh was under the direction of Cale Burgess as chairman and Paul J. Garringer, a prohibitionist from Sanford, as vice-chairman. Former Secretary of State James A. Hartness was chairman of the western division at Statesville with Zebulon Vance Turlington as vice-chairman. The divisional chairmen opened their offices immediately for laying the groundwork of the statewide campaign.[29]

On July 20 *The News and Observer* reported that Arkansas and Alabama had voted wet. Walter Murphy declared, ''What Arkansas and Alabama have done in July, North Carolina should do in greater measure in November.'' Burgess and Hartness in unison replied, ''Regardless of what other States might do, North Carolina will stand against repeal as fixed as the Rock of Gibraltar.''[30] Poteat also believed that the dry cause would triumph, that the people of North Carolina were much too sensible to pave the way for a return of the saloon. Carl Goerch, editor of *The State*, reported Poteat's sentiments and called him ''quite a man.'' Goerch praised, ''Recognized as one of the outstanding educators in the state, he has won for himself the respect of everyone who knows him. Even

the most ardent anti-prohibitionist in the state admits that
the Doctor is sincere.'' Goerch quoted Poteat as saying,
''There will be no convention if we can help it, and we are
going to do all we can to prevent it from being held.''[31]

James M. Northington, editor of *Southern Medicine
and Surgery*, wrote to Poteat that this statement in opposition to the convention did not seem consistent with his
stand for individual freedom in the evolution controversy
of the 1920's. Northington declared, ''Whatever may be
your opinion as to the wisdom of repealing the 18th Amendment, I would have thought that you would have exerted
all your strength against any movement which would refuse to allow the people to express themselves on any
subject.''[32] Poteat replied, ''I am very pleased to reply to
the suggestion of inconsistency in my general attitude of
democracy and my present opposition to a convention on
the 18th Amendment.'' Poteat explained that he felt that
the people of North Carolina had already expressed themselves on the question and added, ''The people, instead of
clamoring to express themselves anew on the issue, in reality don't want to.'' Poteat continued, ''As one of the
people I object to being dragged about by a small number
who are financially interested in the restoration of the
liquor traffic.''[33]

The United Dry Forces emphasized the fact that the
November election would have several effects on the future
status of liquor in North Carolina. On August 11, Cale
Burgess issued a statement to the members of the Central
Committee saying that something more than the Eighteenth
Amendment was at stake. If the wets won, they would
insist that the next North Carolina legislature accept the
vote as a mandate for the repeal of the state prohibition
statutes. Burgess warned, ''I heard one Wet leader say
that they must roll up a majority of 75,000 in order that
they might force the Governor to call a Special Session of
the General Assembly to repeal the Turlington Act.

Whether we prefer it or not, the real issue is whether North Carolina will legalize the liquor traffic."[34]

In August the United Dry Forces set up a speakers' bureau to supply lecturers upon request. "Throughout the campaign the bureau functioned like a well-oiled machine."[35] The first concerted action was on September 3. In a hundred or more churches, courthouses, and halls, dry speakers launched the campaign of speaking that lasted until election day. Poteat spoke in one of the Greensboro churches. He began, "I make no apology for bringing forward in these holy precincts the important moral issue of curtailing and destroying the traffic in beverage alcohol. This is the precise place to attack all the enemies of the life of man and of the progress of the Kingdom of Christ." Poteat declared that alcohol was a universal narcotic poison whether its vehicle was wine, beer, or whisky. He warned that "those who traffic in it...will entice our sons and daughters within reach of their net, then debauch them for gain, then kick them into the gutter, and send you and me to pick up the pitiful soiled remnants of beauty and promise." Defeat of repeal in the November election was necessary, he felt, to insure the effectiveness of the North Carolina prohibition laws. If North Carolina could maintain prohibition, Poteat said, with "safe roads and decent streets" she would soon be "a fair and prosperous island in a waste of turbulent sea."[36]

Poteat repeated his views on prohibition in *The State* on September 23. He wrote a rebuttal to an article, "How Shall We Handle the Liquor Question?" by Harris Newman, representative from New Hanover in the General Assembly. Newman, favoring the repeal of prohibition, said, "With repeal of the 18th Amendment, we may yet become a sober nation." Poteat replied, "Not quite so simple, Mr. Newman. As seen above, Prohibition did not make us drunk, and lifting that restriction will not make us sober." Newman asserted, "We did not stop the use of whiskey." Poteat countered, "Who said we would? The law against larceny has not stopped either petty or grand."[37]

Poteat's main contributions to the dry campaign were speaking and writing on behalf of the prohibition cause although his value as a figurehead should not be underestimated, much as he disliked the connotation. His reputation in North Carolina was instrumental in inspiring respect for the United Dry Forces from the very beginning, but Poteat did not direct the movement. Cale Burgess was the principal figure in the actual organization of the work. He directed the four field men who covered the state to set up county organizations. The county workers selected candidates, completed nomination petitions, and then obtained thousands of signatures on cards that stated that the signers would vote dry, against the convention. The cards were to be used on election day to make sure that all who were contacted got to the polls. The county workers made engagements for local speakers, kept the county papers supplied with news, sent reports to headquarters, and raised funds locally. Mrs. Frances Renfrow Doak, secretary of the United Dry Forces, reported that "the whole campaign was 'run on a shoe string.'" Of the $8,000 spent, perhaps not more than one hundred contributions were for more than one dollar.[38] Cale Burgess said, "It is astonishing how so much has been accomplished with so little money. There is but one explanation: The people of North Carolina do not want the curse of the liquor traffic to come back."[39]

The young people of North Carolina formed their own organization, the Junior Phalanx, under the auspices of the United Dry Forces. Poteat, especially interested in North Carolina youth, spoke at a meeting of the Negro Baptist Young People's Union and the Negro Baptist Ministers on August 10, the Wake County Junior Phalanx on August 31, and the Durham Junior Phalanx on October 3.

By October 7, the last day for filing petitions, the United Dry Forces had succeeded in obtaining a candidate for each of the 120 positions. When Burgess reported the dry candidates on October 8, Murphy could not present the wet slate, because there was some doubt as to whether the wets had nominated the maximum number of candidates. *The News and Observer* reported a change in sentiment in North Carolina. Just after the state legalized beer, many people expected an overwhelming majority for repeal, but in October the predicted majorities were much smaller than had been expected earlier. One reason for the trend was that the dry campaign was much more vigorous than that of the wet forces. In addition, the mounting list of wet states had a more adverse effect on the wets than on the drys because, when it became evident that North Carolina's vote was not necessary for national repeal, wets tended to lose interest. The mounting tide of wet states served to stimulate the dry leaders, however, because they wanted a public expression on the question to insure continuance of state-wide prohibition.[40]

As the election date neared, the United Dry Forces intensified the campaign. On October 22 Clyde Hoey, North Carolina congressman, spoke in Raleigh. Poteat introduced Hoey, who told his audience that it was not the business of the Democratic party to undertake to tell anybody how to vote on the repeal question. Hoey said, "When others stack arms, let the pure white banner of temperance float triumphantly in at least one part of the dominion of these United States, and let that part be North Carolina." Senator Robert R. Reynolds was the outstanding wet speaker. In a speech at Mount Airy on October 24, Reynolds declared that if hypocrisy were eliminated and the people voted as they drank, North Carolina "would join the parade of repealists with the largest majority ever recorded in an election." Burgess replied, "The United Dry Forces are ready to go to the polls on this issue he has laid down, namely: That all drinking patrons and bootleggers vote 'wet' and all law-abiding voters who do not drink vote 'dry.'[41] Reynolds visited about half the counties in the state and made more than twenty speeches. Surely some wets approved and appreciated Reynolds' speeches, but one of the dry county managers told Burgess, "Reynolds' influence nil. More help to drys than hindrance.... Scarcely 80 people to hear him, a large percentage of whom were dry."

The so-called "big-gun" of the repeal drive was the visit of Postmaster General James A. Farley to North Carolina. The drys believed that Farley's appearance would work to their benefit, simply because North Carolinians did not like outside dictation about their voting. Drys changed the old cry of "Beat John Barleycorn" to "Beat Jim Farleycorn."[42] A friend wrote to Poteat, "I boil at the contemplated visit of Mr. Farley, to flaunt his insult into our faces.... As I heard you say the other day, it is the tradition of North Carolina, not to follow tamely but to lead. And here is a needed chance for moral leadership. All drys look to you to lead in this matter."[43]

In a speech on October 31 at Henderson, Poteat made the assertion that he had an intimate friend whose brother was a rural mail carrier in Polk County and was the chairman of the dry campaign for Polk. Poteat said that Farley advised the mail carrier either to resign the chairmanship of the dry campaign or to find employment outside the postal service.[44] A Farley supporter told Poteat that he was surprised that Poteat would quote "hearsay" evidence.[45] Poteat replied, "The gentleman who told me about the Farley letter is himself a minister.... He said to me that he saw the letter in question and that it contained the statement which I quoted at Henderson. Now I must say that this does not look exactly like hearsay testimony."[46]

About three thousand persons gathered to hear Farley on November 3 at Raleigh's Memorial Auditorium. His speech had a decidedly political tone. He appealed to the Democrats to support the president. Farley said, "The President has indicated to me his personal interest in the early accomplishment of repeal. I feel not the slightest hesitancy in saying that he would suffer a personal disappointment should repeal fail next Tuesday.''[47]

On November 4, Cameron Morrison, former governor and senator, replied to Farley on behalf of the dry forces. He declared that he admired Roosevelt more than any other living man as a statesman but that, in ordinary relations of life, humble citizens knew as much as political leaders. Morrison said, ''I do not need a President or a chairman of a political party to instruct me on the evils of liquor.''[48]

The anti-repealists continued to present speakers in practically every county, while the repealists depended largely on Farley's speech. The United Dry Forces sent out about 100,000 copies of an appeal to women voters composed by Mrs. Doak[49] and also had it published in the *Biblical Recorder*. Mrs. Doak warned, ''There is grave danger that a majority vote in this State for repeal of the Eighteenth Amendment might be interpreted by the Legislature and the world at large as meaning that North Carolina wants legalized liquor; whereas a vote against repeal can be interpreted in no other way than as a mandate against repeal of our State laws.''[50]

On November 5, two days before the election, Poteat spoke at the First Baptist Church in Raleigh. He declared, ''I would no more think of voting for repeal of the Eighteenth Amendment than I would think of laying a trap in the highway and covering it over for my neighbor to fall in.'' He appealed to the large congregation to remember that the future of North Carolina prohibition was at stake in the Tuesday election.[51] Both Burgess and Murphy spoke on radio the night before the voting was to take place. On election eve, the wets were still confident. *The State* predicted a wet victory with seventy wet candidates to fifty dry candidates.[52]

November 7 dawned cloudy, and by noon it was raining throughout the state. The rain continued all day, but nothing kept the drys at home. Dry workers used the pledge cards to recall names of drys whom they could contact; they organized transportation to the polls and encouraged all prohibitionists to vote. Old women who had never voted before, young boys and girls who were casting their first vote—hundreds went to the polls in the rain and voted against repeal.[53] The trend was unmistakable from the earliest returns in both rural and urban counties. Mecklenburg, regarded as doubtful, and Wake, considered sure for repeal, were the first large counties to land in the dry column. Rowan, home county of Walter Murphy and reportedly one of the wettest counties in the state, soon joined them. Counties with a large Republican percentage voted overwhelmingly dry.[54] The total vote was 262,314 in favor of no convention to 111,812 for a convention.[55]

The News and Observer said that the principal reason for the dry victory was that "North Carolina has never been as wet as was indicated by the majority of 113,000 Senator Robert R. Reynolds received over former Senator Cameron Morrison last year and the enthusiastic manner in which the Legislature legalized beer last spring." Another reason for the success of the prohibitionists was the dynamic organization of the drys, while the wets had no such organization. The drys had the advantage of church support in every county—local leadership already crystalized—while the wets had no such basis upon which to build.[56] "When the preachers and the church folks git together," remarked a wet at the polls, "tis mighty hard to go agin' them."[57]

Mrs. Doak reported that the drys were fortunate in their leader, Dr. Poteat. She said, "His intelligent championship of prohibition, for which he had stood all of his life, guaranteed its respectability and freed supporters from the fear of ridicule and belittlement. No one dared attempt ridicule of Dr. Poteat." The campaign of satire and caricature resorted to by the wets in other states never succeeded in North Carolina, a state in which being a prohibitionist was nothing to be ashamed of.[58]

Many people wrote to Poteat congratulating him personally for the dry victory.[59] One admirer acknowledged that many aided in the campaign but he felt it was Poteat's leadership that made possible the victory. He continued, "I had a feeling that your noble stand, through the years, backed by your scientific knowledge, would result in keeping the Old North State in the dry column."[60] John D. Langston, a field worker for the United Dry Forces said, "I want to express my appreciation of and admiration for the great work you did as the leader of the Dry Forces in the State in the late campaign."[61] Poteat replied, "I am happy to have had a small part in the remarkable victory of November 7, but really it was men like Mr. Burgess and you and other field workers who are entitled to the credit of it."[62]

There is no doubt that the actual work of organizing the campaign was very important, but why was such a competent organization possible in such a short time? Probably few people in the state had ever heard of Cale Burgess or John Langston, but William Louis Poteat was familiar to them and highly respected. With Poteat as president of the United Dry Forces, some of this respect accrued to the organization. Poteat had prepared the way for the United Dry Forces by his articles and speeches throughout his career. In the 1933 campaign, he delivered about twenty addresses, including one on the radio, a remarkable record for a seventy-seven-year-old man. The dry victory in the 1933 election was the result of the interaction of many forces, not the least of which was the contribution of Poteat.

In retrospect, Poteat's activities in promoting prohibition might seem futile and small in comparison with his work for social progress in other directions. North Carolina drys had exerted considerable pressure on Poteat to join their cause, and it is probable that to the old man the opportunity for leadership was very flattering. However, William Louis Poteat was not the kind of person who would champion a cause merely because it was popular. He was deeply concerned about all problems of society, including alcoholism, and he believed that prohibition would deter if not eliminate this disease. His stand on the prohibition issue was consistent with his usual role of interpreting progress for, to Poteat, a working, enforced prohibition law would have been a giant step in the progress and improvement of society. He continued to work for it throughout his life.

Preceptor of a Generation

Even though all of the states except North and South Carolina had voted for the Twenty-first Amendment and the era of national control was gone, the prohibition issue was far from dead. In January, 1934, Poteat spoke to the Maryland Anti-Saloon League meeting in Baltimore. He told his audience, "We have lost an important battle, but we have not lost the war." He urged them to use all organs of public opinion—the press, the platform, the pulpit, radio, home, school, college—for new education on the liquor problem.[1] As his own contribution toward this education he wrote a book, *Stop-Light*, describing the history of alcohol, its chemical content, physiological effects, and methods of control. He explained that the highway of gaiety and indulgence was often thronged with youthful feet, and it was his purpose to set up a "Stop-Light" to arrest attention and direct it upon the facts of beverage alcohol. This was intensely important to him because he believed, "Beverage alcohol is the greatest single enemy of mankind, and some means of limiting its devastation mankind must discover, or suffer a progressive deterioration which will land us once again in the gulf of barbarism.''[2]

The professor used a portion of the information from *Stop-Light* in his hygiene lectures at the college and emphasized the physical effects of alcohol. He also discussed smoking, recommending that if a young man decided to smoke, he should limit himself to ten cigarettes or fewer a day. One of Poteat's special concerns was ''ladies' toothpick heels.'' He entertained the students by drawing pictures on the blackboard of what high heels could do to the spine.

In studying the human body, the hygiene classes spent some time on the reproductive system. Each year at examination time some young man who was a better scientist than speller would report, ''The sperm cells are transported in the mail.'' In going over the papers with the class, Poteat licked his lips and in mock seriousness asked, ''By parcel post, I presume?''

Dr. Billy especially enjoyed botany, and he did not limit his teaching to the classroom. As he walked across the campus he watched for interesting specimens or unusual phenomena of nature. Students, seeing him carefully studying a wild flower or a cocoon, would stop and Poteat would explain what had caught his attention. Once when there was a train wreck between Raleigh and Wake Forest, the passengers became excited and somewhat unruly until someone noticed that Dr. Billy had calmly left the train and was studying the flora and fauna nearby. Soon the crowd gathered around him, and he kept them enthralled with the wonders of nature until the train could be repaired.[3]

The biologist was extremely active for someone who had supposedly retired. With a twinkle in his eye, he said, ''You can't go by a calendar to determine a man's age.'' In explanation of his youthfulness he penned a limerick:

> There is an old man, Dr. Billy,
> Resolved to stay young, willy nilly:
> So he drinks buttermilk,
> Plays with boys of his ilk,
> And prances on the campus like a filly.[4]

In addition to boys and buttermilk, exercise helped him to keep fit. Dr. Billy played nine holes of golf almost every afternoon. Although he could not hit the ball an extremely long distance, he managed to keep it in the middle of the fairway, and accuracy made up for lack of distance. His score was excellent for a man more than seventy years old. A friend remarked that playing golf with Dr. Billy was something like a spiritual experience because he could not be out of doors without communing with nature.[5]

Dr. Billy maintained his good health and continued most of his activities, but after fifty-two years' service, he finally retired from the church choir. Baxter Durham, state auditor at that time, told him, "The cadence of your voice may be denied the choir, but your song will still thrill and throb through the hearts and souls of thousands of your friends." Nevertheless, such long service seemed almost beyond the call of duty. Durham continued, "Fifty-two years a member of a choir! How on earth have you kept your religion?"[6]

Although he no longer sang in public, Poteat continued to lecture on both religious and secular subjects. One of his favorite lecture topics during this period was international peace. He suggested abolishing the high protective tariff and insisted on making military training in state schools voluntary. He recommended United States entry into the League of Nations and adherence to the World Court. He also lectured on education and, of course, temperance.[7]

In June of 1936, on the way to Winston-Salem to deliver a temperance address at the First Baptist Church, Dr. Poteat survived an automobile wreck. At an intersection another car struck the Poteat auto driven by William Poteat, Dr. Billy's grandson. Although their car turned over, the two Poteats suffered only bruises. Dr. Billy chartered another car, proceeded to Winston-Salem, and made his speech. In contemplating his narrow escape, he wrote a poem called "The Rendezvous."

> I had a rendezvous with Death;
>   But he appeared and then withdrew.
> Did he forbear, or just forget.—
>   So resolute, so prompt, so true?
>
> Thought he of tasks but just begun
>   Of services still incomplete,
> Of clinging friends disconsolate,
>   Of up-stretched hands my hand to meet?
>
> Of five and fifty years' close-linked
>   Dependence all the happy way,
> Of a dark and lonely path ahead
>   For her, my crown, my joy, my stay?
>
> Or did a gracious Heavenly call
>   Arrest the ill-concerted plan,
> Announce to sly insurgent Death,
>   "It's there, not here, I want my man."[8]

Poteat evidently felt no lasting ill effects from the accident, for he continued, and even increased, his activities. In November of 1936, at the meeting of the North Carolina Baptist State Convention the Reverend Mr. Eugene Olive, a friend and former student of Dr. Billy, nominated him for president of the convention. Following several long speeches nominating others, Olive simply said, "I would like to place in nomination a man so well known and widely loved by all of us that any remarks about him would be superfluous and would not do him justice." Poteat won on the first ballot. His friend, Senator Josiah W. Bailey told him, "I think the Convention honored itself in honor-

ing you and the occasion gives me the utmost satisfaction.''⁹ For Poteat, who had held such a controversial
position in former years, this was indeed a distinction.
For his presidential address to be given the following year,
he could have chosen a safe, familiar subject about which
most people were in agreement, but Poteat, the instrument
of progress, again chose a controversial issue. His topic
was ''Christ and Race.'' Although he was no longer active
in the Commission for Interracial Co-operation, he remained an honorary member, and his nephew, E. McNeill
Poteat, Jr., pastor of the Pullen Memorial Baptist Church
in Raleigh, was president of the commission. Along with
the depression had come an aggravation of racial tensions,
and Poteat felt that this was the issue of most importance
to the convention at that time. Again he was ahead of his
day, an eighty-year-old man, paving the way for future
progress.

Unfortunately he was unable to deliver his speech
personally because of illness. J. Allen Easley, pastor of the
Wake Forest Baptist Church, presented it for him, and
later the convention published the address in pamphlet
form. In the address Poteat stated that the real problem
of living together was universal, and racial prejudice was
not always a question of color. But there could be no
doubt about the Christian attitude and standard for human
behavior; no matter what the barriers, the religion of Jesus
is love—translated into practical life, the brotherhood of
man under one Father. He said, ''I wonder if we do not
come here into the valley of decision, the spot and point of
testing where hesitation shadows loyalty and denial reacts
Calvary.'' Poteat pointed out that the gifts of God to
mankind are widely distributed and that any person would
be poor without the contributions of all. He suggested
that racial brotherhood would open the door of opportunity
in education, industry, and public service and would
guarantee justice in court, equal public accommodations
for equal money, and a decent wage North and South. ''If

to racial brotherhood," he declared, "the obligations of
Christian brotherhood are added ... it becomes possible
for peoples who are so diverse as whites and Negroes to
live together successfully ... mutually respectful, mutually
helpful, and cooperant in advancing the common well
being."[10]

This was the last major speech of a long career. The
previous June, Dr. Billy had visited his brother Edwin in
Duke Hospital. Ed said, "Bud Loulie, I'm about to shed
my chrysalis." His brother replied, "Well Ed, you always would get ahead of me." Ed asked him to speak at
his service and Dr. Billy agreed. As he took his leave, he
turned at the door, waved his hand, and said, "So long,
Ed, I'll be along soon." In October, 1937, Dr. Billy suffered a slight stroke that prevented him from speaking at
the convention, and on March 12, while awaiting a visit
from his son after supper he joined his brother.[11]

More than a thousand friends, including Governor and
Mrs. Clyde Hoey, attended the funeral. Dr. John Allen
Easley declared that Poteat's life answered affirmatively
the question, "Can a man be a Christian today?" Easley
said, "After the pattern of his Master, Dr. Poteat was a
teacher ... a seeker after truth.... He was the champion
of world peace, the friend of the under-privileged race, and
the inveterate foe of all who would exploit the appetites
of their fellows."[12] Numerous messages from former students, friends, and admirers in various parts of the country
paid tribute to William Louis Poteat. He was undoubtedly
one of the most outstanding North Carolinians of his generation. His work for quality education, mental health
facilities, better prison conditions, child labor reforms, and
interracial co-operation had helped to improve social conditions in North Carolina. Near the close of his life he
had said, "If you should ask me about the secret of my
happy experience ... I believe it would be ... that I took
an early interest in public affairs." Explaining that he
had been interested in social uplift in all directions, he

said, "All this takes time, of course, but what's time for... ?"[13]

He did spend a great deal of time in the service of others and in promoting the social uplift that he sought. He was indeed a prophet of progress as he guided his fellow man to accept new ideas and better ways of life. He could interpret change so that it lost many terrors. He knew that when people could understand the meaning of progress, they could accept it more readily. The greatest area of this kind of contribution was, of course, in reconciling science and religion, and there have been several attempts to explain the leadership of Dr. Poteat in the evolution controversy. The New York *World* said, "Your Fundamentalist would rather be burned at the stake than approach creative evolution from any laboratory angle giving him understanding of the matter, but he will read Dr. Poteat. He reads him either to heckle or dismay."[14] The Fundamentalists did read Poteat's book, *Can a Man Be a Christian To-day?* and in reply determined to oust him from the presidency of Wake Forest College. But they had been unable to defeat or refute him. They disputed his Christianity, but he reaffirmed it with his words and with his exemplary life. Henry L. Mencken interpreted Poteat as "a sort of liaison officer between the Baptist revelation and human progress in his native State of North Carolina." Mencken expressed the paradox of Dr. Poteat in the following way: "On the one hand he has stuck valiantly to such curiosities of the Baptist sorcery as total immersion and Prohibition; on the other hand he has served his State magnificently as a public critic of the Bryan bibliolatry." Mencken believed that because of Dr. Poteat North Carolina was "the most intelligent" of all southern states. "They are still Christians down there, but they no longer believe that the earth is flat, that man is not a mammal, or that Jonah swallowed the whale."[15]

Poteat was the only man in history to serve as president

of both the North Carolina Baptist State Convention and the North Carolina Academy of Science. It was certainly unusual for one man to be called a heretic and an evolutionist and at the same time "an old-fashioned, Bible-reading, family-altar, Sunday-school, mid-week prayer meeting Christian."[16] But these words fit.

To Poteat, his stand was not at all paradoxical. It was an integral part of all that he thought and did, and it found excellent expression in the field of education. His view of education was idealistic as opposed to the strictly materialistic view. His concept of education was not based on the number of students at a college, nor the wealth of its buildings, nor the enthusiasm of its alumni, but rather on the development of an attitude of mind that regarded the search for truth as the holiest duty and the highest adventure.[17] To Poteat the most serious danger to students was "the peril of being content in our own little cabbage garden, while the illimitable universe challenges us in vain."[18] Poteat presented the challenge and, in his own life, gave an excellent example of how it might be met. He brought to Wake Forest material growth, enterprise, exalted ideals of scholarship and of Christian service, but his most important contribution was the vision to look beyond textbooks, buildings, and athletic events in a search for, and devotion to, truth, not only scientific truth but the basic truths of everyday living. At his retirement, the Richmond *News Leader* declared, "The high faith that has marked the life of Dr. Poteat, the courage of his devotion to the principle of soul-liberty, and his influence upon the youth of the South have made him more than the president of a college; he has been the preceptor of a generation."[19]

Poteat's influence did indeed reach beyond the Wake Forest College campus. As a leading Baptist in favor of the teaching of evolution, Poteat provided the focal point for the start of the anti-evolution controversy of the 1920's, and Thomas T. Martin's articles criticizing Poteat stimulated interest in the possible conflicts between evolution and religion. The entire controversy reached mammoth proportions, filling the columns of both the religious and the secular press and even invading the state legislatures. Throughout the controversy, Poteat remained the most outstanding religious leader for the liberal side. Because of his moderate, intelligent stand, he became a significant factor in the controversy, not only in the South but in the nation as a whole. He was the outstanding example of the position of many intelligent southerners who wished to assure freedom of teaching within the strongholds of Fundamentalism.

Poteat's position as a leader in the Baptist denomination and as president of one of North Carolina's foremost colleges gave him a great responsibility. North Carolina Baptists looked to the president of Wake Forest, not only to uphold academic standards, but to hold the college true to the fundamentals of the Baptist faith. Poteat met the challenge by explaining in lectures, articles, and his book, *Can a Man Be a Christian To-day?* that science and religion were not contradictory. People who knew Poteat could accept his explanation because of his exemplary Christian life. To them, the conciliation of evolution and religion was less painful and disillusioning. Poteat led the people of the South to a more enlightened religion, and in so doing, he helped to insure freedom of teaching and a reverence for truth that would last far beyond his lifetime. A former pupil stated, "He dared to face truth and ask of her all that she had in store and having won some of her precious treasures, he had the superb courage to declare it to the world. What a rich legacy!"[20]

North Carolina today is one of the most progressive of the southern states, having made significant improvement in areas of education, mental health, welfare, and race relations. Many of the ideals in which Poteat believed have at last reached partial fulfillment if not maturity. In

interpreting progress for his generation, surely he helped
to prepare the way for present-day achievements.

In spite of the fact that advancement has been made in
many fields, there is one area of particular interest to
Poteat in which improvement is slow. The search for truth
convinced him that man's greatest satisfactions come from
the wealth of his inner resources. He believed that America was far richer in materials and scientific knowledge than
in culture. "Boredom is said to be the American malady,"
he declared, "which is to say that we are destitute within,
having scant inward resources and a narrow range of
interests." To the Wake Forest students, he challenged,
"I charge you, build yourself up on the inside. In whatever calling you spend your days, you will be a man first
and a preacher, lawyer, doctor, teacher, banker after-
wards...." To obtain culture, Poteat advised, "Sweep
the universe with telescope and microscope. Range backward through all the corridors of history.... Walk with
Phidias and Angelo and Rembrandt.... Attend when
Beethoven and Wagner strike all the singing chords in the
soul of man." Even so, Poteat said that without Christ
culture would lack consistency and elevation; it would be
empty, cold, and aimless. "He will transform and ennoble
...if you give yourself to Him without evasion or reserve,
and in all coming days, bright days and dark days, you
will find His joy to be your joy and your strength."[21]

In the philosophy of William Louis Poteat there was
the constant intermingling of the religious, the scientific,
and the cultural. With science he associated the gift of
"seeing things straight and telling them truly" while ex-
ercising caution, independence, and tolerance. With liberal arts he associated "the philosophic temper, the gentle
judgment, the interest in knowledge and beauty for their
own sake."[22] In his life and work these ideals of Christianity, science, and culture merged until at last they
found a final blending evident in his description of science

which might be a description of his life—"walking to and fro in God's garden, busying itself with its forms of beauty, its fruits and flowers, the crystals shut in its stones and the gold grains of its sands, and coming now at length in the cool of the long day upon God Himself walking in His garden."[23]

Notes

CHAPTER I

1. W. L. Poteat, ''Memories,'' 1928, p. 3, William Louis Poteat Papers (MSS in the Wake Forest College Library, Winston-Salem, N.C.). Hereinafter cited as Poteat Papers.

2. *Ibid.*

3. Marriage records, Caswell County Courthouse, Miles Poteet and Susanah Topley, May 12, 1796. See also W. L. Poteat to John W. Poteet, Jr., n.d., Poteat Papers.

4. Ella Graves Thompson, personal interview with author, January 12, 1963, Leasburg, N.C. Miss Thompson is a cousin of W. L. Poteat. She has volumes of family records.

5. ''History of Caswell County, North Carolina,'' in the *Catalogue of the Caswell County Fair Association*, 1941, p. 2. A copy is preserved in the Caswell County Courthouse.

6. Poteat, ''Memories,'' p. 3.

7. *Ibid.*, p. 14.

8. *Ibid.*, p. 4.

9. *Ibid.*

10. Caswell County Census Records for 1860, Schedule 2, p. 84, and Schedule 4, p. 29, North Carolina Department of Archives and History, Raleigh, N.C.; see also Poteat, ''Memories,'' p. 12.

11. Caswell County Census Records for 1860, Schedule 4, p. 29; see also *Greensboro Daily News*, March 27, 1938; *Durham Morning-Herald*, March 28, 1948.

12. Poteat, ''Memories,'' pp. 5-6.

13. *Ibid.*, pp. 9-10.

14. *Ibid.*, p. 9.
15. *Ibid.*, p. 11.
16. *Ibid.*, p. 10.
17. *Ibid.*, pp. 10-11.
18. *Ibid.*, p. 9; see also W. L. Poteat, Journal, 1897-98, p. 117, Family Collection (MSS and scrapbooks in possession of Mrs. Helen Poteat Marshall, Forest Home, Blanch, N.C.). Hereinafter cited as Family Collection.
19. Poteat, ''Memories,'' pp. 8-9.
20. *Ibid.*, p. 18.
21. *Ibid.*, p. 16; see also the *Religious Herald* (Richmond), February 5, 1931.
22. Poteat, ''Memories,'' p. 19.
23. *Ibid.*, pp. 15-16.
24. *Ibid.*, p. 12.
25. *Ibid.*, p. 13.
26. *Ibid.*, pp. 13-14; see also *Greensboro Daily News*, March 27, 1938.
27. Edwin Anderson Alderman to W. L. Poteat, November 8, 1898, Poteat Papers; see also *The War of the Rebellion, A Compilation of the Official Records of the Union and Confederate Armies* (Washington: Government Printing Office, 1880), II, Ser. I, 96; IX, Ser. I, 260; W. L. Poteat, Journal, 1896-97, p. 13, Poteat Papers.
28. Joseph Gregoire de Roulhac Hamilton, *Reconstruction in North Carolina* (''Columbia University Studies in History, Economics, and Public Law,'' Vol. LVIII [New York: Columbia University Press, 1914]), pp. 473-75, 496-520, *passim*. For a description of Klan activities, see John G. Lea, MS, July 2, 1919, North Carolina Department of Archives and History. This manuscript, left by Lea to be opened after his death, describes his part in Klan activities and gives other memories of Reconstruction in Caswell County.
29. W. L. Poteat to Josephus Daniels, April 11, 1896, as recorded in Journal, 1895-96, pp. 81-82, Family Collection.

CHAPTER II

1. *Greensboro Daily News*, March 27, 1938.
2. Minutes of Euzelian Society, October 11-12, 1872, Wake Forest College Library, Winston-Salem, N.C.; see also George Washington Paschal, *History of Wake Forest College* (Wake Forest: The Wake Forest College Press, 1943), II, 58, 132.
3. *Greensboro Daily News*, March 27, 1938.
4. Minutes of Euzelian Society, April 5, 1873.
5. *Ibid.*, January 31, 1873.
6. *Greensboro Daily News*, March 27, 1938; see also Paschal, *History of Wake Forest College*, II, 136.
7. Caswell County Census Records for 1860, Schedule 1, p. 98, and 1870, Schedule 1, p. 271, North Carolina Department of Archives and History, Raleigh, N.C.
8. *Biblical Recorder* (Raleigh), August 14, 1866; July 31, 1872.
9. Records of the Registrar, Wake Forest College, Winston-Salem, N.C.
10. Minutes of Euzelian Society, December 19, 1874; March 20, 1875; September 18, 1875.
11. *Wake Forest Student*, I (June, 1882), 269; see also Paschal, *History of Wake Forest College*, II, 373, 374, 378.
12. Paschal, *History of Wake Forest College*, II, 140.
13. *Greensboro Daily News*, March 27, 1938.

14. W. L. Poteat, ''Gleanings,'' I, 1879-81, January 1, 1879, n.p., Poteat Papers.

15. *Ibid.*, March 14, 1879, n.p.

16. *Ibid.*, n.d., n.p.

17. *Ibid.*, November 27, 1879, n.p.

18. *Ibid.*, November, 1879, n.d., n.p.

19. *Biblical Recorder* (Raleigh), January 7, 1880.

20. *Ibid.*, February 18, 1880.

21. Poteat, ''Gleanings,'' I, February 20, 1880, n.p.

22. *Biblical Recorder* (Raleigh), January 7, 1880.

23. *Wake Forest Student*, II (April, 1883), 8.

24. *Biblical Recorder* (Raleigh), June 16, 1880.

25. Paschal, *History of Wake Forest College*, II, 172.

26. Poteat, ''Gleanings,'' II, October 20, 1881, n.p., Poteat Papers.

CHAPTER III

1. *Durham Morning Herald*, March 21, 1938.

2. *Biblical Recorder* (Raleigh), March 31, 1880; see also Virginius Dabney, *Liberalism in the South* (Chapel Hill: The University of North Carolina Press, 1932), p. 193.

3. *News and Courier* (Charleston), August 19, 1886; May 28, 1886.

4. *Biblical Recorder* (Raleigh), September 23, 1885.

5. George W. Paschal, *History of Wake Forest College* (Wake Forest: Wake Forest College Press, 1943), II, 366.

6. W. L. Poteat, ''Gleanings,'' II, 73, 46-47, n.d., Poteat Papers.

7. *Wake Forest Student*, IV (September, 1884), 20.

8. *Greensboro Daily News*, March 27, 1938.

9. *Wake Forest Student*, III (November, 1883), 118, 120; III (December, 1883), 169; III (January, 1884), 213; IV (April, 1885), 360.

10. *Ibid.*, II (October, 1882), 85; III (December, 1883), 172; II (January, 1883), 5, 227.

11. *Ibid.*, II (April, 1883), 336.

12. Dr. J. Allen Easley, Professor Emeritus of Religion, Wake Forest College, interview with author, July 25, 1963, Winston-Salem, N.C.; Jasper Memory, professor of education, Wake Forest College, interview with author, March 20, 1963, Winston-Salem, N.C.; see also *Wake Forest Student*, V (October, 1885), 16-17; VII (October, 1887), 39; VII (November, 1887), 77.

13. Paschal, *History of Wake Forest College*, II, 397.

14. *Ibid.*, p. 172.

15. *Ibid.*, pp. 172, 208, 229.

16. *Wake Forest Student*, VI (January, 1887), 160-61, 165.

17. *Ibid.*, III (September, 1883), 33; VI (May, 1887), 378; III (November, 1883), 123.

18. *Ibid.*, IV (June, 1885), 459; IV (December, 1884), 170; VI (May, 1887), 388; VI (July, 1887), 463; see also *Biblical Recorder* (Raleigh), April 2, 1884.

19. *Wake Forest Student*, VIII (October, 1888), 35.

20. *Ibid.*, VI (November, 1886), 83; IX (June, 1890), 388.

21. *Ibid.*, III (April, 1884), 351.

22. W. L. Poteat, Journal, 1898-1902, pp. 174-75, Family Collection; see also Rufus Weaver to W. L. Poteat, August 12, 1895, Poteat Papers.

23. Poteat, ''Gleanings,'' II, 65-69, n.d., Poteat Papers.

24. *Wake Forest Student*, IV (October, 1884), 35-37, 40-41.

25. *Biblical Recorder* (Raleigh), May 9, 1888; May 16, 1888; June 6, 1888.

26. Charles E. Taylor to "To Whom It May Concern," May 25, 1888, Poteat Papers; see also W. L. Poteat to Edwin Poteat, September 7, 1888, Family Collection.

27. *Greensboro Daily News*, March 27, 1938; see also W. L. Poteat, Biology Notebook, June 23, 1888, p. 1, Poteat Papers.

28. Poteat, Biology Notebook, July 3, 1888, p. 4, Poteat Papers; see also W. L. Poteat, *Laboratory and Pulpit: The Relation of Biology to the Preacher and His Message* (Philadelphia: The Griffith and Rowland Press, 1901), p. 66.

29. Albert Guttstadt, "The National Scientific Institutions at the University of Berlin," *Annual Report of the Board of Regents of the Smithsonian Institution Showing the Operations, Expenditures, and Conditions of the Institution to July 1889* (Washington: Government Printing Office, 1890), p. 125.

30. W. L. Poteat to James Poteat, October 14, 1888, Poteat Papers.

31. *Wake Forest Student*, IX (April, 1890), 305; see also W. L. Poteat, "Notes on the Fertility of Physa Heterostropha Say," *Science*, XIX (June 10, 1892), 323.

32. Certificate, August 19, 1891; W. L. Poteat, Biology Notebook, n.d., pp. 9-61, *passim*, Poteat Papers; see also W. L. Poteat to Emma Poteat, August 9, 1893, Poteat Papers.

33. Poteat, Journal, 1896-97, June 13, 1896, pp. 12-13, Poteat Papers.

34. John S. Hardaway to Columbus Durham, June 10, 1895; J. A. Stradley to Columbus Durham, June 7, 1895, copies in Poteat Papers.

35. Poteat, Journal, 1896-97, May 6, 1896, p. 1, Poteat Papers; J. L. Kesler to W. L. Poteat, February 24, 1896; H. M. Evans to W. L. Poteat, November 6, 1898, Poteat Papers.

36. Poteat, Journal, 1896-97, November 21, 1896, p. 110, Poteat Papers.

37. Poteat Journal, 1897-98, January 15, 1897, p. 133, Family Collection.

38. *Ibid.*, 1895-96, February 2, 1896, p. 47; see also *Wake Forest Student*, III (May, 1885), 414; III (March, 1884), 309.

39. Poteat, Journal, 1896-97, August 21, 1896, p. 48, Poteat Papers.

40. Poteat, Journal, 1898-1902, November 3, 1898, p. 80; 1895-96, April 17, 1896, p. 85, Family Collection.

41. Poteat, Journal, 1896-97, n.d., p. 14, Poteat Papers.

42. Emma Purefoy Poteat to W. L. Poteat, June 24, 1896, Poteat Papers.

43. Emma Purefoy Poteat to W. L. Poteat, August 6, 1896, Poteat Papers; see also Poteat, Journal, 1896-1897, n.d., pp. 31-32, Poteat Papers.

44. Poteat, Journal, 1896-1897, August 7, 9, 10, 16, 1896, pp. 35, 37-40, Poteat Papers; see also George Pennell to author, December 16, 1965.

45. Poteat, Journal, 1895-96, March 4, 1896, pp. 63-64, April 6, 1896, p. 78, and *passim*, Family Collection; Poteat, Journal, 1896-97, *passim*, Poteat Papers; Poteat, Journal, 1897-98, *passim*, and 1898-1902, *passim*, Family Collection.

46. Poteat, Journal, 1896-97, August 24, 1896, p. 53, Poteat Papers; Poteat, Journal, 1898-1902, September 6, 1898, p. 81, Family Collection.

47. *Ibid.*, 1896-97, October 20, 1896, pp. 86-87, Poteat Papers; see also Julia McNeill Poteat to W. L. Poteat, October 20, 1896, Poteat Papers.

CHAPTER IV

1. Henry Steele Commager, *The American Mind: An Interpretation of American Thought and Character Since the 1880's* (New Haven: Yale University Press, 1950), pp. 83-85, 200-4.

2. *Wake Forest Student*, I (January, 1882), 3-4, 6, 7-10; see also Walter Rauschenbusch to W. L. Poteat, February 21, 1895, Poteat Papers.

3. Poteat, Journal, 1895-96, October 5, 1895, pp. 2-4, Family Collection.

4. *Ibid.*, October 6, 1895, pp. 4-5.

5. *Ibid.*, October 8, 1895, p. 10, and November 6, 1895, p. 17; see also "Physiological Basis of Morality" notebook, p. 13, Poteat Papers.

6. Poteat, Journal, 1895-96, October 4, 1895, p. 10, Family Collection.

7. "Physiological Basis of Morality" notebook, pp. 3-4, 6, 20-23, Poteat Papers.

8. Edwin Poteat to W. L. Poteat, December 17, 1895, Poteat Papers; see also Poteat, Journal, 1895-96, November 26, 1895, p. 24, Family Collection.

9. Poteat, Journal, 1895-96, December 4, 1895, p. 31, Family Collection.

10. *Ibid.*, p. 30.

11. Poteat, Journal, 1896-97, July 6, 1896, p. 15, Poteat Papers.

12. Poteat, Journal, 1897-98, June 3, 1897, pp. 46-47, and 1898-1902, February 25, 1898, p. 6, Family Collection.

13. Mary Lynch Johnson, *A History of Meredith College* (Raleigh: Meredith College, 1956), 37.

14. See notes on the life of Jesus, "Stilling the Tempest," "Jairus' Daughter," "John's Gospel," and "Nicodemus," in the Poteat Papers.

15. *Wake Forest Student*, VIII (June, 1889), 392.

16. "Christian Education and Civic Righteousness" notebook, pp. 69-70, 74-76, 83-87, Poteat Papers.

17. Poteat, Journal, 1898-1902, n.d., p. 158, and September 18, 1901, pp. 170-71, Family Collection.

18. W. L. Poteat, *Laboratory and Pulpit: The Relation of Biology to the Preacher and His Message* (Philadelphia: The Griffith and Rowland Press, 1901), pp. 11-12.

19. *Ibid.*, pp. 55, 93, 95.

20. *Biblical Recorder* (Raleigh), May 15, 1901; *Baptist Argus* (Louisville, Ky.), May 30, 1901, *The Baptist Commonwealth* (Philadelphia), June 13, 1901.

21. *The Watchman-Examiner* (New York), March 16, 1916.

22. *Biblical Recorder* (Raleigh), June 14, 1905; November 5, 1902.

23. George W. Light to W. L. Poteat, June 19, 1905, Poteat Papers; see also other letters from Mercer alumni to Poteat in the Poteat Papers.

24. *Biblical Recorder* (Raleigh), July 26, 1905.

25. *News and Observer* (Raleigh), December 8, 1905.

26. *Ibid.*

27. *Ibid.*

28. *Ibid.*

29. Clipping in scrapbook, Family Collection.

30. W. L. Poteat, *Youth and Culture* (Wake Forest: The Wake Forest College Press, 1938), pp. 11-12, 14, 22.

CHAPTER V

1. W. L. Poteat, *Youth and Culture* (Wake Forest: The Wake Forest College Press, 1938), pp. 30-31.

2. Norman F. Furniss, *The Fundamentalist Controversy, 1918-1931* (New Haven: Yale University Press, 1954), p. 11.

3. George McCready Price, *Outlines of Modern Christianity and Modern Science* (San Francisco, 1902), cited in Furniss, *Fundamentalist Controversy*, p. 11; and W. L. Poteat to J. J. Taylor, August 21, 1925, Poteat Papers.

4. *Bible Student and Teacher*, IX (1904), p. 347; *Cosmopolitan*, XLVI (1909), p. 665.

5. George McCready Price, *Back to the Bible, or the New Protestantism* (Washington: Review and Herald Publishing Company, 1920), p. 217.

6. Kirsopp Lake, *The Religion of Yesterday and Tomorrow* (London: Christophers, 1925), 161. See also Robert Moats Miller, *American Protestantism and Social Issues, 1919-1939* (Chapel Hill: The University of North Carolina Press, 1958), p. 18.

7. Furniss, *The Fundamentalist Controversy*, p. 27.

8. *Ibid.*, p. 12.

9. W. L. Poteat, "The Effect on the College Curriculum of the Introduction of the Natural Sciences," *Science*, XXI (March 31, 1893), pp. 170-72.

10. W. L. Poteat, "Lucretius and the Evolution Idea," *Popular Science Monthly*, LX (December, 1901), pp. 166-72, *passim*.

11. Poteat, *Youth and Culture*, pp. 24-25.

12. George Washington Paschal, *History of Wake Forest College* (Wake Forest: Wake Forest College Press, 1943), III, 146, 163.

13. *Ibid.*, pp. 35, 135-38, 17-18.

14. *Ibid.*, pp. 121, 71-74.

15. *Wake Forest Student*, XXX (December, 1910), p. 282.

16. *Ibid.*, XXIX (May, 1910), p. 802.

17. *Ibid.*, XXXIII (November, 1913), p. 132; (December, 1913), p. 203.

18. Bill McIlwain and Walt Friedenberg, *Legends of Baptist Hollow* (Wake Forest: Delta Publishing Company, 1949), pp. 59-61; and Paschal, *History of Wake Forest College*, III, 222-24.

19. Constitution of the North Carolina Conference for Social Service and report by Ann Jane Barbrey and Margaret McArthur, December 17, 1953, Papers of the North Carolina Conference for Social Service, North Carolina Department of Archives and History, Raleigh, N.C.; and *Biblical Recorder* (Raleigh), February 19, 1913.

20. *Biblical Recorder* (Raleigh), January 29, 1913; and *State Journal* (Raleigh), May 16, 1913.

21. North Carolina *Legislative Documents* (1909), III, No. 15, 10-13.

22. Committee of the Board of Missions on Destitution in Prisons, MS, 1913, Poteat Papers.

23. *Biblical Recorder* (Raleigh), February 4, 18, 1914.

24. Elizabeth Huey Davidson, "Child Labor Reforms in North Carolina Since 1903," *The North Carolina Historical Review*, XIV (April, 1937), p. 128; see also W. L. Poteat, "Guiding Principles in Child Labor Legislation," MS, February 3, 1915, Poteat Papers; *News and Observer* (Raleigh), February 20, 1919.

25. Minutes of the North Carolina Society for Mental Hygiene, December 4, 1913; February 14, 1914; January 8, 1915. Papers of the North Carolina Society for Mental Hygiene, North Carolina Department of Archives and History, Raleigh, N.C.

26. *News and Observer* (Raleigh), January 10, 1915.

27. Minutes of the North Carolina Society for Mental Hygiene, January 29, 1916, and January 12, 1917; and *News and Observer* (Raleigh), January 14, 1917.

28. W. L. Poteat, "The Social Significance of Heredity," Presidential Address to the Southern Baptist Education Association, February 21, 1923, clipping in the Poteat Papers; "Would Deny Marriage to Ten Per Cent of the Population," 1928; "Dr. Poteat Urges Uniform Marriage and Divorce Laws," 1932; "Improve Human Stock By Eliminating Unfits in Mating, Says Poteat," 1928; clippings in Family Collection. See also *Raleigh Times*, February 16, 1928.

29. *Public Laws and Resolutions of the State of North Carolina Passed*

by the General Assembly at Its Session of 1919 (Raleigh: Commercial Printing Company, State Printers and Binders, 1919), p. 504.

30. Hugh T. Lefler and Albert R. Newsome, *North Carolina: The History of a Southern State* (Chapel Hill: The University of North Carolina Press, 1963), 496, 509; see also Joseph Flake Steelman, ''The Progressive Era in North Carolina, 1884-1917'' (Doctoral dissertation, University of North Carolina, 1955), pp. 548-49, 556.

31. May F. Jones, ed., *Public Letters and Papers of Locke Craig, Governor of North Carolina 1913-1917* (Raleigh: Edwards and Broughton Printing Company, State Printers, 1916), pp. 103-4; see also *Wake Forest Student*, XXXIII (January, 1914), p. 278.

32. May F. Jones, ed., *Public Letters and Papers of Locke Craig*, pp. 103-5; see also Poteat, Journal, July 7, 1914, pp. 1-2, Poteat Papers.

33. Lefler and Newsome, *North Carolina*, p. 568; and *Biblical Recorder* (Raleigh), February 17, 1915; February 24, 1915.

34. *News and Observer* (Raleigh), January 20, 1915, and January 16, 1917.

35. Poteat, Journal, ''International Peace and the Roots of Honor,'' pp. 1, 36, 39, 55, 91, Poteat Papers.

36. Paschal, *History of Wake Forest College*, III, pp. 90, 86-95, *passim*.

37. Robert Burton House, ed., *Public Letters and Papers of Thomas Walter Bickett, Governor of North Carolina, 1917-1921* (Raleigh: Edwards and Broughton Printing Company, State Printers, 1923), pp. 294-95.

38. Maurice N. Corbett to Ida B. Poteat, May 22, 1908, Family Collection.

39. Miller, *American Protestantism and Social Issues*, pp. 298, 309.

40. Paul E. Baker, *Negro-White Adjustment: An Investigation and Analysis of Methods in the Interracial Movement in the United States* (New York: Association Press, 1934), p. 17; see also Jerome Dowd, *The Negro in American Life* (New York: The Century Company, 1926), pp. 555-58.

41. Dowd, *The Negro in American Life*, 558.

42. Baker, *Negro-White Adjustment*, pp. 18-19.

43. R. W. Miles, ''The North Carolina Inter-Racial Committee,'' *The Journal of Social Forces*, I (January, 1923), 154-55.

44. W. L. Poteat to Edwin M. Poteat, December 6, 1920, and March 22, 1921, and George E. Haynes to W. L. Poteat, March 8, 1929, Poteat Papers.

45. *New York Times*, March 16, 1930.

CHAPTER VI

1. Kenneth K. Bailey, *Southern White Protestantism in the Twentieth Century* (New York: Harper and Row, 1964), pp. 44-45.

2. Guy B. Johnson, ''A Sociological Interpretation of the New Ku Klux Movement,'' *Journal of Social Forces*, I (1923), 442-43.

3. *Biblical Recorder* (Raleigh), April 19, 1922.

4. For a discussion of the influence of World War I, see Norman F. Furniss, *The Fundamentalist Controversy, 1918-1931* (New Haven: Yale University Press, 1954), pp. 10-25; Gaius Glen Atkins, *Religion in Our Times* (New York: Round Table Press, 1932), pp. 233-34.

5. Charles F. Bluske to W. L. Poteat, September 17, 1925, Poteat Papers.

6. William Bell Riley, ''The Faith of the Fundamentalists,'' *Current History*, XXVI (June, 1927), 434-40.

7. Furniss, *The Fundamentalist Controversy*, pp. 49-51. Henceforth in the text, Fundamentalist with a capital letter will refer to those who subscribed to the general beliefs and objectives of the World's Christian Fundamentals Association.

8. *Enquirer-Sun* (Columbus, Georgia), July 3, 1927; see also *World* (New York), September 24, 1925.

9. Dr. Cronje B. Earp, Chairman of the Department of Classical Languages, Wake Forest College, interview with author, February 4, 1962, Winston-Salem, N.C.

10. Gerald W. Johnson, "Billy with the Red Necktie," *Virginia Quarterly Review*, XXX (Autumn, 1943), 552.

11. *Ibid.*, 553.

12. See Poteat Papers. Many clippings of articles have notes in Poteat's handwriting. The notations show how some references were taken out of context, misquoted, or outdated.

13. W. L. Poteat, "In Praise of Ignorance," quoted in Homer Henkel Sherman, ed., *Education and Religion* (Nashville, Tennessee: Cokesbury Press, 1929), p. 131.

14. *Biblical Recorder* (Raleigh), April 19, 1922.

15. W. L. Poteat, "Sermon to Chapel Hill Baptist Church," clipping in the Poteat Papers, dateline: Chapel Hill, March 2, 1924.

16. *Sun* (Baltimore), May 4, 1926.

17. W. L. Poteat, "Wherein Lies the Efficacy of Jesus' Work in the Reconciliation?" *Proceedings of the Baptist Congress* (New York: Baptist Congress Publishing Company, 1900), p. 103. For clarification see George McLeod Bryan, "The Educational, Religious, and Social Thought of William Louis Poteat as Expressed in His Writings, Including Unpublished Notes and Addresses" (Master's thesis, Wake Forest College, 1944), pp. 121-23.

18. *Western Recorder* (Louisville, Ky.), January 22, 1920.

19. *Biblical Recorder* (Raleigh), February 11, 1920.

20. W. L. Poteat to Edwin M. Poteat, March 8, 1920, Poteat Papers.

21. In the *Biblical Recorder* (Raleigh), April 19, 1922, Poteat said, "Of a well-used list of twenty-one such 'really great scientists' adduced to show the present adverse state of scientific opinion, two do not appear in the biographical dictionaries, five are misrepresented, seven won recognition in other than biological fields, and six have been in their graves more than forty years, two of these having died before Darwin's great book was published."

22. *Western Recorder* (Louisville, Ky.), February 5, 1920.

23. *Baptist Advance* (Little Rock, Ark.), March 25, 1920.

24. *Biblical Recorder* (Raleigh), March 8, 1922.

25. *Ibid.*, April 5, 1922.

26. *Ibid.*, April 19, 1922.

27. *Ibid.*, April 26, 1922.

28. See Poteat Papers, galley proof of J. W. Porter's article, "Can an Evolutionist Be a Christian," comments penciled in the margin signed by Livingston Johnson, n.d.

29. *Biblical Recorder* (Raleigh), May 10, 1922.

30. *Ibid.*, May 3, 1922.

31. *Ibid.*, May 10, 1922.

32. *Ibid.*, March 22, 1922, and May 24, 1922.

33. *Ibid.*, May 10, 1922.

34. *Ibid.*, May 31, 1922.

35. *Charity and Children* (Thomasville, N.C.), May 18, 1922.

36. *The Fool Killer* (Boomer, N.C.), June, 1922.

37. *Searchlight* (Ft. Worth, Tex.), November 10, 1922. Paschal gives the endowment of Wake Forest as of June 30, 1922, as $699,149.96. In 1923, however, the college received $1,600,000 from the estate of J. A. Bostwick.

See George Washington Paschal, *History of Wake Forest College* (Wake Forest: Wake Forest College Press, 1943), III, 135.

38. *Biblical Recorder* (Raleigh), May 3, 1922.

39. "Dr. Brown Wants to Speak to Students," clipping in Poteat Papers, dateline: Raleigh, May 16, no year and no name of publication.

40. *Raleigh Times*, April 25, 1922.

41. This statement was probably the reason for the investigation of Dr. Poteat by the trustees in May, 1922.

42. *Annual of the Southern Baptist Convention*, 1922, pp. 35-36.

43. *Minutes of the One Hundred Seventeenth Annual Session of the Cape Fear–Columbus Baptist Association of North Carolina*, 1922, p. 12. Associations were groups of Baptist churches in particular areas, sometimes ascertained on the basis of counties, but not necessarily so. There were sixty-five associations in North Carolina in 1922. At that time, associations sent delegates to the Baptist State Convention.

44. *Minutes of the Thirty-fifth Annual Session of the Alexander Baptist Association of North Carolina*, 1922, p. 7.

45. W. L. Poteat to E. M. Poteat, October 28, 1922, Poteat Papers.

46. *Biblical Recorder* (Raleigh), December 20, 1922.

47. *Winston-Salem Journal*, December 14, 1922.

48. *Highlander and Shelby News*, December 21, 1922.

49. *Winston-Salem Journal*, December 14, 1922.

50. "Christianity and Enlightenment" (pamphlet published by the Baptist State Convention of North Carolina, 1922), *passim*.

51. *Charity and Children* (Thomasville, N.C.), December 21, 1922.

52. *Baptist Messenger* (Biltmore, N.C.), January, 1923.

53. *News and Observer* (Raleigh), December 16, 1922.

54. *Annual of the Baptist State Convention of North Carolina*, 1922, p. 33.

55. *Biblical Recorder* (Raleigh), December 20, 1922.

56. *Highlander and Shelby News*, December 21, 1922.

CHAPTER VII

1. Howard K. Beale, *Are American Teachers Free? An Analysis of Restraints Upon the Freedom of Teaching in American Schools* (New York: Charles Scribner's Sons, 1936), p. 227.

2. Arkansas, Oklahoma, Florida, Tennessee, Mississippi, and Louisiana had some type of restriction on the teaching of evolution. Norman F. Furniss, *The Fundamentalist Controversy, 1918-1831* (New Haven: Yale University Press, 1954), p. 95.

3. *Western Recorder* (Louisville, Ky.), February 1, 1923.

4. *Searchlight* (Ft. Worth, Tex.), January 19, 1923. Norris objected to Poteat's leadership as President of the Southern Baptist Education Association in 1922.

5. *Ibid.*, April 13, 1923.

6. *Ibid.*, February 29, 1924.

7. W. L. Poteat to Edwin M. Poteat, June 26, 1924, Poteat Papers.

8. *Durham Morning Herald*, March 13, 1924.

9. "Opening Address of President Mullins," *Southern Baptist Convention Bulletin* (Kansas City, Mo.), May 17, 1923, p. 1; see also *Baptist Courier* (Greenville, S.C.), March 15, 1923.

10. *Old Gold and Black* (Wake Forest College), February 7, 1925.

11. *News and Observer* (Raleigh), January 24, 1924.

12. *Ibid.*, February 12, 1925.

13. *Ibid.*, February 11, 1925; see also *Greensboro Daily News*, December 5, 1926.

14. W. L. Poteat to Howard W. Odum, February 16, 1925, Howard W. Odum Papers; see also H. W. Chase to W. L. Poteat, February 16, 1925, University Papers, Southern Historical Collection, University of North Carolina Library, Chapel Hill, N.C.

15. "Politics and Religious Bigotry Hand in Hand Fight on Dr. Chase." Clipping in the Poteat Papers, dateline: Daily News Bureau and Telegraph Office, Raleigh, February 15, no year.

16. *News and Observer* (Raleigh), February 12, 1925.

17. *Ibid.*, February 15, 1925.

18. *Biblical Recorder*, (Raleigh), February 25, 1925.

19. *News and Observer* (Raleigh), February 18, 1925.

20. Cronje B. Earp, personal interview with the author, February 4, 1962, Winston-Salem, N.C.

21. *Journal of the House of Representatives of the General Assembly of the State of North Carolina*, 1925, pp. 290-91.

22. For instance, see F. B. Simkins, *The South Old and New: A History, 1820-1947* (New York: Alfred A. Knopf, 1947), p. 317; Furniss, *The Fundamentalist Controversy*, p. 85; and Beale, *Are American Teachers Free?* p. 242.

23. Willard B. Gatewood, Jr., "Embattled Scholar: Howard W. Odum and the Fundamentalists, 1925-1927," *The Journal of Southern History*, XXXI (November, 1965), 375-88, *passim*.

24. *North Carolina Manual*, 1925, *passim*; see also *Journal of the House of Representatives of the General Assembly of the State of North Carolina*, 1925, pp. 290-91.

25. *Greensboro Daily News*, May, 1925, clipping in the Poteat Papers, day of the month deleted.

CHAPTER VIII

1. Excerpt from the will of John Calvin McNair, in the frontispiece of W. L. Poteat, *Can a Man Be a Christian To-day?* (Chapel Hill: The University of North Carolina Press, 1925).

2. *Greensboro Daily News*, May 26, 1925.

3. *Chapel Hill Weekly*, May 7, 1925.

4. Poteat, *Can a Man Be a Christian To-day?* pp. 1-2.

5. *Ibid.*, 9-41, *passim*.

6. *Ibid.*, 45-79, *passim*.

7. *Ibid.*, 106-7.

8. *Ibid.*, 83-110, *passim*.

9. *Greensboro Daily News*, July 12, 1925. For other reviews, see Poteat Papers.

10. George W. Gilmore to W. L. Poteat, July 31, 1925, Poteat Papers. *The Homiletic Review* was published in New York City.

11. Mrs. M. F. Godfrey to W. L. Poteat, January 27, 1933, Poteat Papers.

12. See Poteat Papers for many letters of commendation and carbon copies of Poteat's answers.

13. *Charlotte Observer*, May 16, 1925.

14. R. P. Rixey, to W. L. Poteat, n.d., Poteat Papers.

15. *News and Observer* (Raleigh), June 4, 1925.

16. *Ibid.*, July 22, 1925.

17. "Posters Open Northfield Christian Meeting To-day," clipping in

Poteat Papers, dateline: East Northfield, Mass., July 30, 1925, name of paper deleted.

18. *United Presbyterian* (Pittsburgh), September 24, 1925.

19. W. L. Poteat to Edwin M. Poteat, August 18, 1925, Poteat Papers.

20. *The Christian Leader* (Boston and Chicago), April 23, 1927.

21. *The Christian Evangelist* (St. Louis), August 12, 1925.

22. *Charlotte News*, November 8, 1925.

23. W. H. P. Faunce to W. L. Poteat, December 30, 1925, Poteat Papers.

24. W. L. Poteat to W. H. P. Faunce, January 6, 1926, Poteat Papers.

25. *World* (New York), September 25, 1925.

26. W. L. Poteat to W. T. Couch, August 20, 1925, Poteat Papers.

27. W. L. Poteat to Edwin Mims, September 5, 1925, Poteat Papers.

28. The account of the debate is taken from the *Asheville Citizen*, August 14, 1925. The resolution is quoted from the *Minutes of the Forty-fourth Annual Session of the Buncombe County Baptist Association of North Carolina*, 1925, p. 15.

29. George Pennell to W. L. Poteat, August 14, 1925, Poteat Papers.

30. W. L. Poteat to George Pennell, August 18, 1925, Poteat Papers.

31. Quoted from a penciled copy of resolutions in Poteat Papers. For clarification, see *Minutes of the Sixty-fifth Annual Session of the Tennessee River Baptist Association of North Carolina*, 1925, p. 4.

32. *Minutes of the Fortieth Annual Session of the Mecklenburg-Cabarrus Baptist Association*, 1925, pp. 18-19.

33. *Minutes of the Seventh Annual Session of the Gaston County Baptist Association of North Carolina*, 1925, p. 10.

34. *News and Observer* (Raleigh), August 26, 1925; and "Baptist Committees Meet In Raleigh and Discuss Position of Dr. Poteat," clipping in the Poteat Papers, name of paper deleted, dateline: August 25, 1925.

35. *Biblical Recorder* (Raleigh), September 23, 1925.

36. J. A. McKaughan to W. L. Poteat, September 14, 1925, Poteat Papers.

37. Henry Alford Porter to W. L. Poteat, October 9, 1925, Poteat Papers.

38. *Charlotte Observer*, October 1, 1925; see also *Minutes of the Sixty-sixth Annual Session of the Central Baptist Association of North Carolina*, 1925, p. 9.

39. *Charlotte Observer*, November 11, 1925.

40. *Ibid.*, November 15, 1925.

41. W. L. Poteat to V. P. Harris, October 12, 1925, Poteat Papers.

42. W. L. Poteat to W. W. Barnes, April 26, 1925, Poteat Papers.

43. *Charlotte Observer*, October 31, 1925.

44. *Ledger-Dispatch* (Norfolk), November 19, 1925.

45. *Annual of the Baptist State Convention of North Carolina*, 1925, pp. 28-30.

46. *News and Observer* (Raleigh), November 19, 1925.

47. *Ibid.*

48. *Greensboro Daily News*, May 16, 1926.

49. *Ibid.*, Gerald W. Johnson gives this "behind the scenes" account of the convention.

50. *Greensboro Daily News*, November 21, 1925.

51. *Ibid.*, n.d., clipping in Poteat Papers.

52. *Durham Morning Herald*, April, 1926, n.d., clipping in Poteat Papers.

53. *Sun* (Baltimore), May 4, 1926.

54. *News and Observer* (Raleigh), May 5, 1926.

55. *Charlotte Observer*, May 6, 1926.

56. *Greensboro Daily News*, May 23, 1926.

57. *Charity and Children* (Thomasville), May 13, 1926.
58. Cronje B. Earp, personal interview with the author, February 4, 1962, Winston-Salem, N.C.; William M. Poteat, personal interview with the author, February 27, 1962, Greensboro, N.C. William M. Poteat is a grandson of W. L. Poteat.
59. Clipping in the Poteat Papers, name of paper deleted, October 17, 1926.

CHAPTER IX

1. *News Leader* (Richmond), March 24, 1926.
2. *Annual of the Southern Baptist Convention*, 1926, p. 98.
3. Josiah W. Bailey to E. Y. Mullins, June 16, 1926, copy in Poteat Papers.
4. *Biblical Recorder* (Raleigh), May 26, 1926.
5. *Times-Picayune* (New Orleans), February 13, 1926, as quoted in Norman F. Furniss, *The Fundamentalist Controversy, 1918-1931* (New Haven: Yale University Press, 1954), p. 62.
6. For example see *Biblical Recorder* (Raleigh), May 26, 1926.
7. Willard B. Gatewood, Jr., "Politics and Piety in North Carolina: The Fundamentalist Crusade at High Tide, 1925-1927," *The North Carolina Historical Review*, XLII (Summer, 1965), 289-90.
8. "College Heads Hotly Criticized," clipping in Poteat Papers, n.d.; *News and Observer* (Raleigh), May 21, 26, 1926; Coy C. Carpenter, interview with the author, December 8, 1965, Winston-Salem, N.C. Dr. Carpenter is vice-president of Wake Forest College in charge of medical affairs. He was personal physician to Dr. Poteat after 1926.
9. W. L. Poteat, n.d., to the Board of Trustees of Wake Forest College, Family Collection.
10. *Asheville Citizen*, November 18, 1926.
11. *News and Observer* (Raleigh), June 2, 6, 1927.
12. *Ibid.*, June 2, 1927.
13. *Greensboro Daily News*, June 3, 1927.
14. David Leroy Corbitt, ed., *Public Papers and Letters of Angus Wilton McLean, Governor of North Carolina, 1925-1929* (Raleigh: Council of State, State of North Carolina, 1931), p. 437.
15. *New York Times*, June 6, 1927.
16. *Durham Morning Herald*, as quoted in the *Times* (Raleigh), January 24, 1928.
17. W. L. Poteat to Edwin M. Poteat, April 7, 1931, Poteat Papers. "Cullom" probably refers to Willis R. Cullom, professor of Bible at Wake Forest College.
18. W. L. Poteat, Journal, 1898-1902, p. 159, Family Collection; see also W. L. Poteat to Louie Poteat Martin, June 21, 1932, Poteat Papers.
19. Poem in Family Collection signed W. L. P., July 23, 1931.
20. "Dr. W. L. Poteat Fifty Years Wed," and "Dr. Poteat For Conducted Tours," clippings in Family Collection dated 1931.

CHAPTER X

1. Daniel Jay Whitener, *Prohibition in North Carolina, 1715-1945* ("James Sprunt Studies in History and Political Science," Vol. 27 [Chapel Hill: University of North Carolina Press, 1946]), p. 186.
2. *Ibid.*, pp. 193-94.
3. *Ibid.*, pp. 195-97.

4. Frances Renfrow Doak, *Why North Carolina Voted Dry* (Raleigh: United Dry Forces of North Carolina, 1934), p. 3.

5. "An Appeal to the Moral Forces of North Carolina to Give Their Support to Hon. Cameron Morrison [sic] in the Democratic Primary on July 2nd, 1932," handbill in Poteat Papers.

6. Doak, *Why North Carolina Voted Dry*, p. 3.

7. *Biblical Recorder* (Raleigh), August 31, 1932.

8. *Ibid.*, September 7, 1932.

9. Josiah W. Bailey to W. L. Poteat, June 22, 1932, Poteat Papers.

10. W. L. Poteat to J. W. Bailey, June 24, 1932, Poteat Papers.

11. *Annual of the Baptist State Convention of North Carolina*, 1932, pp. 42-43.

12. Santford Martin to Robert E. Royall, September 19, 1932, Poteat Papers.

13. *News and Observer* (Raleigh), March 15, 1933.

14. *Winston-Salem Journal*, January 30, 1933.

15. G. J. Burnett to W. L. Poteat, December 26, 1932, Poteat Papers.

16. *News and Observer* (Raleigh), February 15, 1933.

17. *Ibid.*, February 22, 1933.

18. *Ibid.*, March 7, 1933.

19. *Ibid.*, March, 29, 1933.

20. *Ibid.*, April 5, 1933.

21. *Public Laws of North Carolina*, 1933, Chapter 216, p. 335.

22. *Ibid.*, Chapter 403, p. 600.

23. Lex Kluttz to W. L. Poteat, February 23, 1933, Poteat Papers. Kluttz reported the February 16 meeting to Poteat and said, "The suggestion was made that other outstanding prohibition leaders be asked to cooperate. Some several who were there who are interested in the Anti-Saloon League, the W.C.T.U., the Allied Campaigners, and the Businessmen's Prohibition Foundation felt the keen need in our State for a council that would serve as a clearing house for matters of strategy, during the weeks and months which lie just ahead of us."

24. *News and Observer* (Raleigh), May 26, 1933.

25. W. L. Poteat to Charles L. Ruffin, June 10, 1933, Poteat Papers.

26. William M. Poteat, personal interview with the author, February 27, 1962, Greensboro, North Carolina.

27. Doak, *Why North Carolina Voted Dry*, pp. 5-6; see also *Biblical Recorder* (Raleigh), June 28, 1933.

28. *The State*, I, No. 4 (June 24, 1933), p. 8.

29. *News and Observer* (Raleigh), July 12, 1933.

30. *Ibid.*, July 20, 1933.

31. *The State*, I, No. 8 (July 22, 1933), p. 15.

32. J. M. Northington to W. L. Poteat, August 1, 1933, Poteat Papers.

33. W. L. Poteat to James M. Northington, August 7, 1933, Poteat Papers.

34. Cale Burgess to members of the Central Committee, August 11, 1933, Poteat Papers.

35. Doak, *Why North Carolina Voted Dry*, p. 11.

36. *Biblical Recorder* (Raleigh), September 21, 1933.

37. *The State*, I, No. 17 (September 23, 1933), p. 1.

38. Doak, *Why North Carolina Voted Dry*, pp. 9-10, 15.

39. *Biblical Recorder* (Raleigh), September 27, 1933.

40. *News and Observer* (Raleigh), October 15, 1933.

41. *Ibid.*, October 23, 28, 1933.

42. *Ibid.*, October 21, 1933.

43. S. L. Morgan to W. L. Poteat, October 13, 1933, Poteat Papers.
44. *News and Observer* (Raleigh), November 1, 1933.
45. M. S. Revell to W. L. Poteat, November 1, 1933, Poteat Papers.
46. W. L. Poteat to M. S. Revell, n.d., Poteat Papers.
47. *News and Observer* (Raleigh), November 4, 1933.
48. *Ibid.*, November 5, 1933.
49. *Ibid.*, October 31, 1933.
50. *Biblical Recorder* (Raleigh), November 1, 1933.
51. *News and Observer* (Raleigh), November 6, 1933.
52. *The State*, I, No. 23 (November 4, 1933), p. 5.
53. Doak, *Why North Carolina Voted Dry*, p. 16.
54. *News and Observer* (Raleigh), November 8, 1933.
55. *The State*, I, No. 24 (November 11, 1933), p. 2.
56. *News and Observer* (Raleigh), November 8, 1933.
57. Inez Bolin Wall, ''How North Carolina Went Dry,'' *Christian Century*, L (November 29, 1933), p. 1505.
58. Doak, *Why North Carolina Voted Dry*, p. 6.
59. See Poteat Papers for many letters of congratulations.
60. J. T. Watts to W. L. Poteat, November 16, 1933, Poteat Papers.
61. J. D. Langston to W. L. Poteat, November 29, 1933, Poteat Papers.
62. W. L. Poteat to J. D. Langston, December 3, 1933, Poteat Papers.

CHAPTER XI

1. *Sun* (Baltimore), January 22, 1934.
2. W. L. Poteat, *Stop-Light* (Nashville: Broadman Press, 1935), p. 88.
3. Robert P. Morehead, M.D., professor of pathology, Bowman Gray School of Medicine, interview with the author, December 3, 1965, Winston-Salem, N.C. Dr. Morehead was laboratory assistant to Poteat, 1931-32. Coy C. Carpenter, vice president of Wake Forest College for medical affairs, interview with the author, December 8, 1965, Winston-Salem, N.C.
4. ''Refuses to Believe He is Eighty,'' dateline Wake Forest, October 20, 1936, clipping in Family Collection; *News and Observer* (Raleigh), October 17, 1937; [W. L. Poteat], unsigned limerick in Poteat's handwriting, 1933, Family Collection.
5. Dr. Coy C. Carpenter, interview with author, December 8, 1965, Winston-Salem, N.C.
6. Baxter Durham to W. L. Poteat, September 22, 1933, Poteat Papers.
7. ''Dr. Poteat is Speaker at Woman's College,'' n.d., clipping in Family Collection.
8. ''A Brave Soldier Fights On,'' n.d., clipping in the Family Collection; see also W. L. Poteat, ''The Rendezvous,'' June 14, 1936, Family Collection.
9. Eugene Olive, personal interview with the author, December 2, 1965, Winston-Salem, N.C.; see also J. W. Bailey to W. L. Poteat, November 19, 1936, Poteat Papers.
10. W. L. Poteat, *Christ and Race* (Raleigh: North Carolina Baptist State Convention, 1938), *passim.*
11. Cronje B. Earp, personal interview with author, February 4, 1962, Winston-Salem, N.C.; see also *Meredith Bulletin*, November, 1940; *Greensboro Daily News*, March 13, 1938; *Times* (Raleigh), October 30, 1937; *News and Observer* (Raleigh), n.d., clipping in Family Collection.
12. Various clippings in Family Collection, n.d.
13. *News and Observer* (Raleigh), October 17, 1937.
14. *World* (New York), September 25, 1925.

15. *Charlotte News*, November 8, 1925.
16. *Religious Herald* (Richmond), August 19, 1926.
17. *News and Observer* (Raleigh), May 18, 1924.
18. *Biblical Recorder* (Raleigh), July 1, 1925.
19. *News Leader* (Richmond), June 10, 1927.
20. Fred H. Manning to Emma Poteat, March 16, 1938, Family Collection.
21. W. L. Poteat, *Youth and Culture* (Wake Forest: The Wake Forest College Press, 1938), pp. 149-50.
22. *Ibid.*, p. 147.
23. *Ibid.*, p. 146.

Index